THE RIVER OF GOD

A NEW HISTORY OF CHRISTIAN ORIGINS

GREGORY J. RILEY

HarperSanFrancisco
A Division of HarperCollins*Publishers*

To Susan, Mark, and Alex

⁓

HarperCollins books may be purchased for educational, business, or sales promotional use. For information please write: Special Markets Department, HarperCollins Publishers, Inc., 10 East 53rd Street, New York, NY 10022.

HarperCollins Web site: http://www.harpercollins.com
HarperCollins®, 🎬 ®, and HarperSanFrancisco™ are trademarks of HarperCollins Publishers, Inc.

FIRST EDITION

Library of Congress Cataloging-in-Publication Data
Riley, Gregory J. (Gregory John)
     The river of God : a new history of Christian origins / Gregory J. Riley.— 1st ed.
          p. cm.
     Includes index.
     ISBN 0–06–066979–9 (cloth)
     ISBN 0–06–066980–2 (pbk.)
          1. Christianity—Origin. 1. Title

  BR129 .R55 2001
  270.1—dc21

                                                                    20001016888

01 02 03 04 05 RRD(H) 10 9 8 7 6 5 4 3 2 1

CONTENTS

1

THE RIVER OF GOD

An Introduction

Where did Christianity come from? It went from no adherents in the year zero to become the world's largest religious tradition today. What were its origins? This is a different question from "Why was it so successful once it began?" It is a question about the historical process that led to its invention. "Invention" is a word rarely used in this connection, but it is an apt word. Early Christians themselves were quite conscious that what they were about was something new. The Synoptic Gospels have Jesus declaring that what he was doing was "new wine" requiring "new wineskins" (Mark 2:22). The cup of the last supper and the eucharist is called the cup of "the new covenant," from which language we get the name for the New Testament in contrast to the Old Testament. The book of Colossians describes the message of the Christians as "the mystery that has been hidden throughout the ages and generations, but has now been revealed" (1:26, NRSV). From the viewpoint of the first-century followers of Jesus, they were onto something fresh, something hidden from the past.

That genuine sense of newness, that excitement about being in the leading ranks of God's new spiritual kingdom, should itself come as some surprise, given the efforts of the early church to claim the opposite. Christians were quite sensitive to the often-voiced criticism that they were a novelty, and for ancients, nothing new was good, especially in religion. A "new man" was an upstart politician from outside the established families; a "new thing" was a political revolution, an attempt to overthrow the state. The Golden Age, like the Garden of Eden, lay in the past, and the world had long since been devolving into chaos. Any religion that had arisen just a few years earlier was clearly something suspect, defective, revolutionary.

Christianity was in fact something new, but it was drawn from and contained ideas very old. As a result of criticism about their recent rise on the one hand, and their own need for understanding and legitimation on the other, Christians traced their beginnings back to the Old Testament and cast themselves as the continuation of the history of Israel. Jesus and nearly all of his early followers were Jews, so their own traditions as Jews were their natural background. These Christians saw themselves as heirs to the promises made to the patriarchs, Moses, David, and especially the prophets. They were the new Israel, with roots that went back through old Israel to the beginning of creation itself.

But Christianity in reality had a much wider historical base and a far more complex lineage than the small nation of Israel alone. It is how best to understand that complex lineage that is the subject here. We will begin with three helpful models for interpretation: that of a genealogy, that of a great river system, and that of a relatively new and brilliantly logical view of evolution known as "punctuated equilibrium."

THE GENEALOGY OF CHRISTIANITY:
GENEALOGY VS. HISTORY

The "genealogy of Christianity" is a wonderfully productive, and potentially controversial, phrase. For most of our era, Christianity cannot be said to have had a genealogy at all. It has been classed among the "revealed" religions, and revealed religions have no genealogies; they appear for the first time when God grants the revelation to the prophet. Christianity has, however, had a history, often called "salvation history," found in the traditional reading of the biblical account of Israel, the life of Jesus, and the rise of the early church. Such a tradition of interpretation has left its mark even today. Since the church understood itself to have arisen out of the matrix of Judaism, one reads often of the Jewish background of Christianity. And further, because Christianity arose in the Roman world, one finds studies of the Greco-Roman context. Each of these concepts—the history of Christianity, the Jewish background, and the Greco-Roman context—does not necessarily, but can, carry with it considerable, though often unconscious, theological investment. Each can be a subliminal affirmation of an old method of interpreting history in the face of new and contradictory evidence.

The church's traditional interpretation of the history of salvation traces the dealings of God from Adam to Abraham, from Abraham to God's choice of the people of Israel led by Moses in Egypt. The story then moves from Moses to Joshua and the kingdom of David in Palestine, with its fall in the Exile and eventual rebirth, and, with a leap over the intertestamental period, to Jesus and the church spread throughout the Roman world. It is a wonderful story and has been for millennia both a great comfort to individuals and a part of the foundation of Western civilization.

God was there at the beginning, the same God whom we know today, creating, leading, instructing humanity all along. Humans were there pretty much at the beginning also, just as we understand ourselves today. The other religions, that is, human flirtations with polytheism and other foibles, were departures from what was right because of human failings, our sins. We lost our originally wholesome way. Since that time God has been slowly guiding us back to the purity of the Garden from which our original parents departed by disobedience. God has been unfolding little by little a developing revelation. Abraham knew the true God, as did Moses, who actually saw God on Mount Sinai. The revelation to Moses was enhanced by the promises to David, with God providing further guidance through the prophets. And finally came Jesus and the inspired early Christian biblical authors.

So goes, more or less, the history of the church from its Jewish background into its Greco-Roman context. But let us consider some of the major theological implications of this story. God revealed "true" religion to Israel, not to the Gentile nations, through a series of prophets; from Israel arose both Jesus and the church. Individual Gentiles in pre-Christian times could join themselves to the nation of Israel by accepting its Law and traditions, but the Gentiles as a whole are included in the history of salvation only after the founding of the church, and that by converting to the religion of the Judeo-Christians. In both cases Gentiles are required to reject their own religious traditions, turning "to God from idols, to serve a living and a true God," to use Paul's description (1 Thess. 1:9). In another account, the risen Jesus tells Paul that he is sending him to the Gentiles "to open their eyes so that they may turn from darkness to light and from the power of Satan to God" (Acts 26:18). Gentile religion is the false worship of dead idols; it is darkness and even demonic. Judaism and its successor Christianity constitute the one lineage of true religion.

Here is the basis for the relatively common theological loading of the concepts "Jewish background" and "Greco-Roman context" mentioned earlier. According to traditional Christian interpretation of the biblical story, Christianity arose as the final installment of the revelation of God's true religion that up to that time had been the sole possession of Israel. Jesus himself was a Jew, and his name "Jesus Christ" signals that he was the promised Jewish Messiah. The proper "background" of Christianity, therefore, is Judaism.

The results of this traditional position most visible in biblical scholarship over the last century or so are twofold: (1) the still-common efforts to derive all of the good ideas of Jesus and the early Christians from the Old Testament and pre-Christian Judaism; and (2) the reluctance to give credit for any of those ideas to non-Jewish nations or thinkers. We seldom read of "the Greco-Roman background" in the same sense as "the Jewish background," meaning the derivation of Christianity from Greece and Rome, and almost never of "the Egyptian background" or "Mesopotamian background." Yet each of these cultures, and others besides, contributed to the store of ideas and doctrines that eventuated in the church.

On the other hand, the early church arose in the historical context of the Greco-Roman world. Again according to traditional Christian interpretation, it arose "in" the Greco-Roman world but was not "of" the Greco-Roman world. Early defenders of the faith—the apologists, as they are called—fought against the criticisms of outsiders that the church had simply imitated in many of its most valuable rites (baptism and eucharist, for example) the practices of the pagan mystery cults. Christians were forced to claim that the Devil had known beforehand and inspired the cults to imitate the true faith of the Christians; these similarities in the Greco-Roman religions were demonic deceptions.[1] The reality, of course, was that the critics were right: the Christians had taken not only these but many other ideas and practices from their own Greco-Roman world.

Today the study of the Greco-Roman context of the New Testament is necessary to help us understand certain aspects of our texts or traditions that we find obscure. The study of the Jewish background and the Greco-Roman context is both defensible and safe—*defensible* because both subjects are clearly legitimate parts of the study of Christianity, and *safe* because, as commonly used, the results of such study tend to support the traditional Christian interpretation of history. Both subjects easily meld with the "salvation history" model for interpreting the role of Israel in the rise of the church. We may call this model an "Israel-alone" model, because in it the sole "background" or parent of Christianity is Israel. If one employs an Israel-alone model to interpret the rise of Christianity, both the questions asked and the answers obtained will be Israel-alone questions and answers. One's model of interpretation determines one's conclusions; one's telescope determines one's cosmology.

This section began with a contrast between the terms *genealogy* and *history*. We are quite used to reading histories of Judaism and Christianity, but the very idea of a genealogy of Christianity is rare. The terms represent two distinct methods and are based on different approaches to the way human culture should be understood. A human being, for example, has both a history and a genealogy. To write a personal history, one would look back over one's life, select and describe the major events in more or less detail, review one's choices in the face of opportunity and adversity, and perhaps add reflections on their significance. Such a personal history is not unlike what one in fact finds in the Bible as the history of Israel. A genealogy, however, would be quite different. The two are of course related, and some aspects of the genealogy would appear in the history. But contrary to the way we would like to understand our personal histories, the more important of the two, it seems to me, is the genealogy, for the genealogy determines major aspects of one's history. If one is dealt only one hand, it is better to be lucky than good.

A person is born into a family as the direct product of parents, grandparents, and so on, with specific inherited genetic characteristics. One's genealogy determines whether one is short or tall, blond or dark, and the like. In addition, however, one is born into a particular time and place, into a family and culture with a specific language, customs, resources, social strata, and many other such things. One is free to create and develop a personal history only within certain rather narrow limits. One cannot flower, for example, as an eighteenth-century Renaissance philosopher if one is a ninth-century Mayan peasant. Both the philosopher and the peasant, to be sure, will develop their individual histories uniquely; no other person of any time or culture will be exactly like either. But most human possibilities, available to others elsewhere in different cultures and at different times, will not be available to either of these two. (The Mayan, for example, will not speak Turkish or play ice hockey.) Their individual choices are so limited by their genealogies that we regularly ignore them as individuals and write histories of Mayan civilization or the Renaissance as if the individuals that made up those cultures did almost nothing distinct from their neighbors, while the few who did were still near predictable as products of their times.

If we apply this model of a genealogy to the birth and history of Christianity, we find some rather striking differences from the traditional Israel-alone model. One is now required to look for parents and grandparents, so to speak, who were not only present as the environment, but contributed the very substance of the offspring they produced. If Judaism is the mother of Christianity, then the Greco-Roman world is the father, not merely the context. By this model, half of the substance of Christianity, half of the good ideas, comes from the Greco-Roman side. This does not of itself determine what Jesus and the early Christians did with their inheritances; they had their own histories and made their own choices. But their histories, as noted above, were very narrowly circumscribed by their genealogies, by their time and place, by the possibilities available. The ancient observers and critics were right: the early Christians really did take many of their ideas and practices from the Greco-Roman world in which they lived.

The genealogical model also helps us to understand one of the more interesting aspects of early Christianity. Parents most often have more than one child, each with its own personality and traits derived from their inherited and shared genealogy. From the very beginning, there were several distinct varieties of Christianity. The reason, in fact, that we have four Gospels in our New Testament is that they arose out of four different communities of early Christians. While each differs in many ways from its neighbor, the four that we have in our Bible were chosen late in the second century because they were being used by groups that agreed more or less with one another on their picture of who Jesus was.

There were, however, more than eighty Gospels produced by the early church. Many of these other Gospels outside the New Testament had very different views of Jesus, produced in communities that held widely different understandings of Jesus and the proper Christian life. These communities often went under the name of a founding apostle to whom the community looked back as guarantor of their Christian tradition. So we hear of Pauline Christianity, Matthean Christianity, and Johannine Christianity, among others to be found in the New Testament. But there were several other brands of Christianity under the name of these and other influential apostles. Among Jews especially in the East there were Christian communities and literature under the name of Peter and James that stood in opposition to Paul and John. Among Gnostic Christians there were communities under the name of John and Thomas and many other lesser and later disciples. The picture of early Christianity is not unlike that which we find today, with our many denominations that also often go under the name of their founders, such as Lutheran or Calvinist or Mennonite.

The genealogical model also helps us to understand why modern versions of Christianity and Judaism are so vastly different in both emphasis and substance from what they once were in antiquity. The ancients knew nothing, for example, of the Big Bang, or the seeming randomness of cosmology and evolution, or the propensity for humans to engage in world wars—concepts among many others to which all modern religious traditions have had to respond. These modern versions are themselves products of younger parents in different times, drawing on and reacting to things in their own modern worlds. But for the study of ancient Israel and Christianity, there are grandparents and even great-grandparents to contend with, who contributed the substance that made up pre-Christian Judaism and the Greco-Roman world. For a better understanding of those ancestors, we turn to another model, that of a great river system.

THE RIVER OF GOD

Imagine a great river system with several large tributaries enlarging the total flow downstream. Each of the tributaries is itself a smaller version of the great river, with its own series of smaller streams, brooks, and seasonal washes flowing together into the larger and larger current of the system as a whole. As the river progresses, some of the water is lost along the way through evaporation and absorption into the soil, but the river as a whole grows and grows as it progresses, until it becomes enormous and irresistible, at flood stage overwhelming all before it. Eventually it comes to the sea, forming a delta that covers sometimes hundreds of square miles, composed of scores of separate streams all divided off from the final unified mixture of the great river.

Let us use the Mississippi river system as an illustration. One could go out into the river above the delta in Louisiana and find coal dust from the Ohio valley, a child's doll from Wisconsin, gold-bearing silt from North Dakota, a Styrofoam cup from Montana. Above the delta, there would be a mixing of all the elements that had survived the trip downstream, perhaps something from nearly every stream and rivulet in the entire system. Not everything would survive, of course, but given the fact that one can hardly see at Baton Rouge from one side of the Mississippi to the other, a huge amount does survive. Once the river enters the delta, as if in reverse, it begins to divide again into many smaller rivers and streams on their way to the sea. Some of the elements in the flow above the delta are common to all these delta rivers—the gold-bearing silt from the Dakotas, for example, or coal dust from Ohio—while some go only here or there: the Styrofoam cup and the child's doll can go into only one or another delta river.

If we apply this model of a great river system to the rise of Christianity, we again find contrast with the traditional picture of the history of salvation. The river is, of course, the totality of the historical and religious background of Christianity. This is the River of God, the flow over time of the relationship between God and humanity in the ancient Near East. The flow is composed of contributions from both sides: inspiration from the divine world on the one hand, and the formulation of religious ideas and doctrines by inspired prophets, teachers, and wise people on the other. The relationship stretches over thousands of years and travels through many cultures, from before the dawn of writing in approximately

3200 BCE to the time of the early Christians and beyond. The river has only rarely been placid, because the relationship between the human and divine is seldom without struggle. The major tributaries are the civilizations of Egypt, Mesopotamia, Canaan, Persia, Greece, and Rome, with many untold contributions from other cultures less visible that influenced each of these. These tributaries added substance to the whole; the river does not, *cannot,* exist without them. The point just above the delta is the life of Jesus and the inception of Christianity; the many divisions of the delta are the many versions of the Christian movement that arose immediately after his death.

Modern scholarship on the nation of Israel has demonstrated that Israel was but one expression among many others of the larger Canaanite culture in which it arose. That means, using this model of the great river system, that Israel was not a single stream, the lone river of living truth in the vast wasteland of human religious error. In fact, it was not originally even one of the major tributaries, but only one of the smaller streams flowing into a larger tributary of the Canaanites.

One of the values of this river model is that it illustrates the melding together of ideas from different cultures into one system of thought and shows that the melding takes place in stages as each culture joins the whole at different historical moments. Another value is the observation that once something is in the river, for no matter how long, it can find its way to the delta. Ideas from earliest times in Persia or Mesopotamia or Canaan have found their way into Christianity, although they are not found or emphasized in the major expressions of contemporary Judaism. Jesus, to choose some obvious examples, fights the Devil (from Persia) in the Synoptic Gospels, fights both the Devil and Death, the personified ruler of the underworld (from Canaan), in Paul, and fights the Devil as the great Dragon (from Mesopotamia) in the Book of Revelation.

Just as parents may produce siblings that differ widely from one another, so the River of God produced many delta rivers of widely different types of Christianity. As the early apostles and disciples went into different areas of the Greco-Roman world, they founded denominations that often differed strikingly from one another. Some early Christian communities, for example, believed that Jesus was a mere man whose father was Joseph, and that he was chosen to be the Messiah because of his personal righteousness. Others thought that he was a god from heaven, and still others that he was some combination of these two extremes. All these possibilities existed in one or another of the religious traditions that early Christians inherited.[2]

At the beginning there were no rules; there was no central authority to dictate what was true doctrine and what was heretical teaching. That authority developed slowly in the competition between denominations, but especially between Jewish Christians, Gnostic Christians, and the self-styled orthodox, beginning in the mid and late second century and lasting for nearly three hundred years. The orthodoxy that resulted was itself again a product of the River of God, but this time drawing not only on pre-Christian traditions but also on the several types of Christianity that had developed up to the time of Constantine and the fourth-century era of the creeds.

The River of God did not produce Christianity. It brought to Jesus and the early Christians the vast store of ideas and traditions that they used to form their unique expressions of religious truth. Religions do not arise out of rivers. They are formed by humans acting in the combination of crisis and inspiration. For a better understanding of how inspired people and communities form new religious expressions, we turn to a third model, that of "punctuated equilibrium," a modern view of evolution.

PUNCTUATED EQUILIBRIUM AS A MODEL

The biblical account of a creation some six to ten thousand years ago (depending on one's calculations)[3] is contradicted by the scientific evidence of the modern world. That evidence shows that the earth is some few billion years old and the universe somewhere near twelve billion years old. The human race evolved, as did every other species of life, from succeedingly earlier species. One arrives by theoretical backtracking at a single replicating string of molecules in the primeval ooze at the very beginning of life on earth more than three billion years ago, give or take several eons. God does not seem, according to our scientific evidence, to have actually created Adam out of mud on a particular Friday morning a few thousand years ago.

The theory of evolution itself has evolved since the time of Darwin. An older version of the theory held that evolution was a gradual and relatively uniform process requiring few or no outside pressures for a species to evolve. That early view, of course, played right into the hands of the Israel-alone understanding of the Bible, even after the great similarities between the religion of Israel and its surrounding cultures were recognized. Other nations were poly-theists, so the argument runs, no matter how close they may have come here and there to monotheism, and were therefore fundamentally different. Israel may have begun in Canaanite polytheism, but it was in Israel alone, without substantial contribution from outside, that monotheism and true religion developed by slow but traceable steps.

More recently, researchers have discovered that this earlier version of the theory of evolution does not fit the evidence. Left on its own, a species will not progress from a blob into a mastodon. It will not "progress" at all; it will simply remain much as it was, accumulating genetic mutations at random that have no particular use or direction. Sharks, for example, have remained substantially unchanged for millions of years because they have been "left alone" by their environment. Culture among human groups is similar: we still find "stone age" tribes in isolated jungle hideaways, and villages that still speak ancient Aramaic in isolated mountain areas. If the culture is open to the outside, however, it changes according to those outside influences. Villagers in mountain areas of the Andes still speak a Spanish closely related to that of sixteenth-century Spain, while Spanish in Spain itself, open to the influences of the Western world, has changed.

Thus a better understanding of evolution is that species change in some direction only when forced to do so by pressures in the environment: they adapt or die out. The new understanding has been termed "punctuated equilibrium,"[4] to describe long periods of near changeless equilibrium punctuated by moments of relatively rapid change brought about by crises in the environment. If the pressures are not global but limited to a particular area, then the new adapted form will coexist with the descendants of its non-adapted ancestor, each in its own niche of the environment. "Progress" happens not gradually but relatively quickly in response to some stress or crisis that requires adaptation. Between such moments, little or no change occurs.

If we apply this newer model of punctuated equilibrium to help in understanding the rise of Christianity, we again find major differences from the old Israel-alone model. Were it not for new crises, new pressures from surrounding nations, the religion of Israel would have remained that of its Canaanite origins, and Christianity would never have arisen in the form that it did. The religion of Israel did not develop on its own, in isolation. It progressed in stages, with long periods of stasis disrupted by moments of rapid change, most notably as it responded to the crises of successive national disasters. It was conquered time and again by superior cultures and was forced to adapt or die out. These adaptations, caused by political subjugation to other cultures lasting at times for centuries, account for the changes in religious conception that are visible over time, and for the coexistence of several varieties of Judaism during the Second Temple period (ca. 538 BCE–70 CE). The varieties of Christianity that arose after the death and resurrection of Jesus were again more or less successful adaptations to the new revelation and the new pressures of the Greco-Roman world.

THE VALUE OF NEW MODELS

These models for interpretation are useful in helping us ask questions about our religious history that we would not normally ask —

questions different from those raised by the older Israel-alone model of the history of salvation. Any Israel-alone model determines the results: Christianity arose from Israel alone. The legacy of this two-millennia-old paradigm still has influence today, even among scholars who are very well aware of the enormous debt that pre-Christian Judaism owed to various other cultures. The claim is still made that Israel had already absorbed and domesticated all the necessary elements that Christianity drew on for its substance. Jesus and the early Christians simply taught what Judaism was already teaching, but in their own selection and combination. This is surely scholarly progress over older ways of thinking, but note the result: it was still Israel alone in the background of Christianity.

With better models, however, we are led to ask different questions, and we discover quite different answers. Who were the parents and grandparents of Christianity? What was its genealogy? What were the cultures of the great River of God, and what were their contributions? What survived in the delta of diverse Christianities, one of which became orthodoxy? And how does Christianity show itself to be a new adaptation to its new environment of the first century? What was it doing different from other adaptations that allowed it to succeed and thrive, while others died out?

These models and the questions they raise carry fundamental theological implications of their own, just as did the older view of the history of salvation. They are based, however, not on religious conception, but on study of the actual histories of the cultures that lay in the long stream of pre-Christian tradition. One disturbing aspect of the study of religious history is the observation that succeeding religions tend to denigrate their forebears: Marduk, for example, the great god of Babylon, was "greater than" the Canaanite gods because he conquered them; Yahweh was "greater than" Marduk because Marduk was in turn conquered and eventually disappeared. The salvation-history model elevates the final form of Christianity as God's best religion over its precursors.

The models presented here, on the other hand, do not make judgments against former religious traditions. Children are not necessarily improvements over their parents; rivers tend to get more polluted as they grow larger and longer; evolution does not guarantee "progress" in *quality*, only in *survival*. Succeeding religions may be improvements in this or that area (the elimination of slavery, for example), or they may be steps backward toward intolerance (saying, "Convert to our religious opinions or become second-class citizens in our empire," or worse).

We tend to rewrite our own histories in order to say something to and about ourselves in the present: "We are legitimate; we are even better than those who went before." The early Christians were no exception. Jesus had given them something exciting, new, and real. But "new" was a major problem. To solve that problem, they appropriated the story of Israel as their own and added themselves as the final chapter, dispossessing the Jews.[5] Yet Christianity cannot in fact be derived from the Old Testament or Jewish tradition alone.

That the church claimed to replace Israel does not lessen its debt to the many cultures (including Israel) that made contributions to its worldview. What, for example, of the Greeks, Christianity's other immediate parent? Did Socrates go to heaven? It is not an idle question, for it was one that early church writers worried over for centuries. Educated Christians recognized the huge debt that Christianity owed to Greek philosophy, and especially to Socrates. They argued over whether he, a pagan Greek, could have been saved, having come so close to the Christian conception of the spiritual life. On the other hand, perhaps he had his inspiration from a personal "demon," the inner voice that he described as guiding him throughout his life.[6] The interpretive models used here would imply that not only Socrates, but also Hammurabi and Akhenaton and Zoroaster and many other "pagans" made real contributions to the substance of both Judaism and Christianity. Those contributions did not determine the actual form that Christianity would take. Its rise could not be predicted, nor was its specific content and conception determined ahead of time. That was the product of Jesus and the early church itself, their choices and adaptations. But the store of materials and traditions they worked with was determined by their place and time and provided to them by these previous cultures. What they did with those inheritances by their own inspiration is what created Christianity.

THE CONTENT OF THE RIVER OF GOD

In the following chapters, we will look at five major subject areas that make up the core of the Christian faith, the main content of the River of God: the rise of monotheism, the subsequent development of Christian Trinitarianism, the arrival of the Devil and ideas about eschatology, the development and consequences of the concept of body and soul for humans, and the advent of Jesus as Savior. Each of these subject areas had a long history of development. In no case were the initial stages of these ideas anything like what they turned out to be in their final forms in the church of the fourth century CE. In fact, it does not appear that these concepts existed at all (in the sense that we understand them) at the beginning of the period of our study approximately three millennia earlier: no one we have record of was a monotheist and certainly not a Trinitarian, there was no Devil, humans did not have souls, and there was no need for a heavenly savior. Nevertheless, there were here and there intimations of each idea—preparations, so to speak, for the eventual rise of the more complex and defined ideas of later times.

In their early histories, each of these concepts was understood differently from culture to culture, and some were completely absent. Each took many centuries to develop and was the result of contributions from several traditions. Inspired individuals and communities of believers melded together competing and often conflicting ideas time and again in periods of crisis. New forms existed side by side with older versions of the same basic ideas. Stage by stage, each progressed, transformed, or regressed to form the eventual Christian doctrines. Over time the ideas became intertwined and interdependent: one first needed a Devil to have an eschatology; one first needed a soul to require a heavenly savior. Even within Christianity itself, when each of these larger ideas was well in place, there was a wide variety of conception from one community to the next. It was not until the time of the creeds in the fourth Christian century and later, when definitions and orthodoxy became prime concerns, that these ideas became standardized. Yet the creeds and definitions bear the signs of long historical development from concepts born in non-Christian societies centuries, even millennia, earlier.[7]

In the following chapter, we will look at one of the most important advances in religion in human history: the development of monotheism from what was near ubiquitous polytheism. Polytheism, the belief in many gods, is the opposite of monotheism, the belief in one God. Several cultures surrounding Israel arrived at one or another version of monotheism, some long before Israel existed as a nation. Eventually a particular kind of monotheism arose in Israel itself, but it did not take hold for centuries. Surprisingly, no culture seems to have retained the singular view of monotheism of the inspired writer of Isaiah chapters 40–55. That view itself evolved quickly as his heirs added new insights to the flow of tradition, while older views continued in competition, eventually winning a place in the final formulations.

The single most important contribution toward the development of monotheism and our conceptions of God did not come from Israel or ancient religion at all, but from ancient science. New scientific understanding of the size and shape of the universe changed the way the gods and then the one God were viewed. The old, small universe was seen to be in fact much, much larger than ever before thought. The old, small gods who ran it became either expressions of the (newly conceived) one God beyond all gods or merely God's servants, angelic beings who did the will of the unseen One. Science again judged the material world to be something other than and foreign to the nature of the one God. In fact, the spiritual nature of the one God was so different in kind that the act of "creation" itself became a problem. This immaterial and unknown God did not, in fact *could* not, create the material world directly, but did so only through the agency of a second divinity, a being emanated from the One for the purpose of creating and managing the universe to be.

Ancient scientific discoveries and philosophical meditations on them were fundamental to later Christian understanding of the nature of God. Eventually, as a result of these scientific discoveries and the conclusions of theologians who developed their implications, the church defined the doctrine of the Trinity (the subject of the third chapter). At the inception of Christianity, however, neither the concept of the Trinity nor the terms necessary to describe the idea existed; there was not yet even language for such sophisticated formulations. The process took hundreds of years. Early Christians fought their most significant internal battles over how to define and understand the divine nature. What does a monotheistic tradition that believes in the one God do with Jesus the Lord, or later with the Holy Spirit?[8]

At a significant point in the religious evolution of the ancient Near East, at an important confluence of river and tributary, God gained an enemy in the Devil. The fourth chapter will examine the origins of this being, tracing how conceptions of the enemy of God changed from their beginnings in stories about the conflicts of the gods in more than one culture to become the Christian Devil. The most significant point was the time of the Exile, when Babylon, which had once again conquered the Israelites and exiled the upper classes to Mesopotamia, was itself conquered by the Persians. The Persians were a thoroughly foreign, Indo-European culture that brought a wholly new understanding of the divine to the Semitic Israelites. Zoroastrianism had been present in Persian culture for hundreds of years before Persia expanded into Mesopotamia. The basic position of Zoroastrianism was that God was opposed by a near equal but opposite being, the Devil. One early form of that theological dualism claimed that at the beginning there was but the One, the single God alone who contained all there is—all opposites, all things good or evil. This one God then emanated two roots or sources, the Holy Spirit and the Devil, who were destined to fight each other for a predetermined number of ages until the battle was won.

A major value of the concept of the Devil is its ability to explain evil in the world. If there is only one God at the beginning of all things, all-knowing and all-powerful, then where does evil come from? In real-life terms, it was the as-yet-unanswered question of undeserved suffering that provided the stimulus for change. In the Exile, the Israelites experienced undeserved suffering on a massive scale—and were confronted with a new answer. The old view of the central story of the book of Job, that one must be silent in the face of calamity caused by God, gained a new perspective: the calamity came from Satan, because God and Satan were using the innocent in a kind of contest over loyalty. Whose side was Job really on?

In time, this concept grew in sophistication in the light of the changes in ancient cosmology. Not only God and the Devil, but armies of spiritual forces were at odds, organized in ranks and levels of power, ruling territories, peoples, even the stars and planets. And how and when was the great cosmic battle to end? Early Christians were very concerned that the end would occur during their lifetime, and New Testament writers often warned that although the end might be soon, no one knew when it would occur. The end itself was conceived of as a final war between good and evil that included a great, fiery catastrophe that would destroy not only the enemies of God, but heaven and earth as well.

In the fifth chapter we will examine the idea of the soul and its importance for the preaching of Jesus and the Christian worldview. Monotheism has often been thought to be the great advance that brought the possibility of equality among peoples of different cultures and status, but this positive result has only rarely been the case. The scientific advance that was fundamental to the development of modern monotheism also contributed greatly to a new view of the human being. It was the development of the idea of the soul—the idea that a human being was not merely a clay pot into which God had breathed the breath of life, but a dualism of body and soul—that laid the foundation for equality among peoples. Historically, the two ideas, monotheism and the concept of the soul, are not related. Monotheists existed who did not know of the dualism of body and soul, and body-soul dualists existed who were polytheists. The dualism of body and soul is the single most important foundation on which Christianity is based; indeed, without it, Christianity would not exist. Jesus' own view of proper human life—right relationship with God and the world at large—stands on the idea of the dualism of body and soul. To cite Jesus' words in the Gospel of Mark, "What does it profit one to gain the whole world and lose one's soul?" (8:36). Here lies one of the greatest differences between Christianity and the religion of the Old Testament. Much of the difficulty within Christianity today, in fact, arises because of misunderstanding or neglect of this central doctrine.

In the sixth chapter, we will examine the role of Jesus as Savior. Where did the idea of the heavenly savior come from? How did it come about that human beings needed to be saved at all? Adam in Genesis, for example, is not "saved" in the Christian sense; he simply lives a very long time and then returns to dust. The concept of the universe in which human beings had been created underwent radical change from its beginnings as a small, good place that would last forever to become a world of darkness in which constant battle between spiritual forces was taking place. In the midst of that battle were humans, now with eternal souls that could be won or lost by loyalty to one side or the other. But we humans were overmatched, deceived, led astray. We were very much in need of a divine and powerful leader who could teach us what was true about the spiritual world and overcome our enemies. In earlier times, when the enemies were mere humans, armies at war for example, saviors were human military leaders like Joshua or David. Now, however, the kingdom was no longer that of the land of Israel in Palestine; it was the kingdom of heaven, a spiritual kingdom. We humans were in need now of someone from outside our cosmos of darkness who could lead us back to our true and eternal home. And then, at the final moment, he would return to defeat permanently the Devil and his legions, and to judge the living and the dead.

Finally, in Chapter 7, we need to ask about the implications of a River-of-God understanding of the history of our tradition for the present. Where will the River of God flow in the new century? Christianity arose out of the melding of thousands of years of interrelationship between God and humanity in many cultures. That relationship did not stop in the first century of the apostolic generation, or the fourth century of the creeds, or the sixteenth century of the Reformation. One of its main turning points was the scientific discovery of the much larger size of the earth and the surrounding cosmos, necessitating a revolution in the older conceptions of God and the soul.

Today people of faith face another series of scientific advances. We live in a universe inconceivable to the ancients, apparently infinite and random, perhaps destined not for destruction by fire but for continual expansion into frozen lifelessness. Those discoveries must again influence and change our understanding. Religious truth has been about making order out of chaos, about finding one's place in God's plan. But it has also been about the mystery of knowing a God who is ultimately unknowable, who is greater than mere human understanding. We have grown, we have changed time and again, but we are still faced with the mystery.

2

FROM THE GODS
TO THE ONE GOD

There do not seem to have been monotheists anywhere that we can find as few as 5,000 thousand years ago. Today western culture and much of the world's population claim to be adherents of one sort of monotheism or another. How did monotheism arise in the background as a fundamental inheritance of the Christian tradition? Philosophers and scholars of religion have theorized for centuries about the origins of the worship of one God alone in the worldwide polytheism of human culture. It is a surprisingly complex phenomenon with a wonderfully rich history of development.

Historians have observed in the cultures of the ancient Near East the appearance of several types of monotheism long before the founding of the kingdom of Israel. Monotheism appeared in many forms, often in highly charged situations of religious reform and conflict. It was used as a major tool for the building and consolidation of empires and, in contrast, as a solace for the loss of political independence. In Israel, there were a number of important critical steps taken toward the eventual development of a particular Jewish form of monotheism: the exclusive worship of the national God, Yahweh.

How many gods there are or ought to be, however, is only one facet of the larger problem—and not even the most significant facet. Whether God is many or one, while important, is in no way comparable to the problem of the very substance of divinity. The greater issue that the historical process had eventually to face was that of the divine nature itself: How was God to be conceived at all? What was God made of? Answers to these and other similar questions raised further questions: How big and where was God? What were God's characteristics?

The old answers—that God had a body, sat on a throne on top of the sky, and spent sleepless nights jealous of other gods and angry with humans—became inadequate as time went on. Culture was growing; humans were learning more and more about the world in which they lived. Science changed and grew in conception, and slowly religion responded and changed. The two together—culture and science—produced a new understanding of the very nature of divinity that became the foundation of Christian theology.

RELIGION IN THE ANCIENT NEAR EAST: GENERAL OBSERVATIONS

For all cultures in the ancient Near East, the process of creation began with "chaos," the Greek word used to signify the undifferentiated material out of which the universe was made. Chaos was imagined as water in darkness, much like a stormy sea at night, that filled everything. There was no concept of nothingness or empty outer space; there was not even the number zero. The concept of *creatio ex nihilo,* "creation out of nothing," did not yet exist. That idea was a much later invention, not gaining full expression until the Christian period. It was a concept that developed after and because of monotheism, in controversies about what was eternal: Was God alone at the beginning, or was the "stuff" out of which the world was made there also? Was there one eternal principle or two, God and chaos?

Earlier, however, no one seems to have asked where the stuff of the universe came from; it was simply there already. Even as eminent a philosopher as Plato thought that the world was made out of chaos, that God and chaos had existed together from the beginning. In Genesis, water and darkness are preexistent raw material out of which God makes the world. In Egypt, the process of creation begins when the primeval hill arises out of the water. In Greece, the poet Hesiod says, "Truly at the first chaos came to be, then next wide-bosomed earth, the ever sure foundation of all" (*Theogony* 115–117). In the famous creation epic of Mesopotamia, the *Enuma Elish,* chaos is alive. We are told that before there were heaven and earth, there was only water. Freshwater and saltwater mingled together and began to engender all the other gods. So the world arises out of preexisting material that has the power to generate the first gods.

The first primeval beings are usually personified aspects of the natural world who generate lesser and more specialized cosmic and natural entities. In one of the most widely spread stories in Egypt, Atum, the primeval hill, engenders all the other gods in a process that takes several generations. The early gods are the air, the earth and the sky, the sun, moon, and stars. In Mesopotamia, the primeval water produces pairs of gods: male and female river silt, the male sky horizon and female earth horizon, the male and female heaven, and the male and female versions of freshwater. Likewise in Greece, chaos engenders the earth and begins the process from which the gods, heaven, the underworld, air, day and night, and the ocean come into being.

These are the "olden gods," the original gods of nature who lie at the foundation of all that there is. These gods give birth to families that are related to one another and live in a kind of hierarchy. In general, the farther from the original gods on the scale of generation, the lower the duty of the deity. The gods of the sky produced eventually all the gods who were or controlled the winds, storms, and other aspects of weather. The sea produced all the various sea creatures and monsters of the deep. The earth engendered all the rivers and streams, mountains, volcanoes, and other earthly features.

The first gods, the olden gods, always held pride of place, but they did not generally interact with the human sphere. They were the original and greatest gods in size and power, but they were elements of the structure of the cosmos—too large, as it were, to deal directly with human beings. Thus there was the phenomenon of a huge god (or gods) standing behind and far from the gods who rule the human world. This idea gave foundation to the later philosophical idea of a God behind the gods, a God who produced the lesser gods, who in turn created the world.

Not all cultures looked at the world as something "created." As we have seen, the world for the Greeks arose of itself out of chaos. The earth, sky, seas, and other natural phenomena were not made, but were born into existence as the natural unfolding out of chaos proceeded. For other cultures, a particularly powerful deity "created"—that is, produced order out of chaos. The very idea of cosmos is order, and order is visible in the lights of heaven, the orderly movement of sun, moon, and stars, and the progression of days and seasons.

The gods who created were not themselves preexistent and eternal, as they would later come to be understood. They also arose out of the process that began with chaos. In the Mesopotamian epic *Enuma Elish,* for example, the original gods of the waters of chaos first bore and then came into conflict with their younger offspring. The younger gods, headed by Marduk, entered into combat with the primeval saltwater, named Tiamat. After a pitched battle, Marduk slew Tiamat and from her watery corpse created the universe.

In Egypt, there were several competing versions of creation deities and their methods. In most of these, the creator deities arose in the early stages of the unfolding process. Ptah, the god of the city Memphis, created by his word. Khnum, the primeval creator god in the cities of Antinoë and Esna, formed humans of clay on his potter's wheel. Remnants of these stories may be seen in the creation epic of the Hebrew Bible: in the opening verses of Genesis, God created the world out of preexisting watery darkness by his word and then formed Adam out of clay.

The original gods of the natural world eventually gave place to the high gods of civilization. The olden gods withdrew into the background and had little or nothing to do with the world of humans. In Greece, Zeus was in the third generation of gods and ruled the upper world of human habitation. In Mesopotamia of the second millennium BCE, Marduk of the fifth generation of gods ruled. These were the high gods who governed the world and doled out to humans both rewards and punishments for obedience or disobedience to divine laws. These were the gods who received worship and were recognized as "the God" of the Greeks or some other people. The younger gods who ruled our world were most often conceived of as being more powerful than their predecessors: Marduk was the youngest and strongest of the gods of Babylon; Zeus was the youngest of his generation and strongest of the gods of Greece.

Both gods and humans are seen as material beings. Gods and humans arise out of the same substance, out of the same primal matter though at different stages of the process. They are what might be termed different in density. The concept of "immaterial" is not invented until Plato in the fourth century BCE; there was not even a word for it earlier. In Homer, being "invisible" was not to be without visible form but to be cloaked in mist and therefore unseen and unrecognized. All the gods have bodies; recall in the Bible God walked in the Garden of Eden (Gen. 3:8) and showed his hand and back to Moses on the mountain (Exod. 33:23). Most gods are in the form of humans; others, especially those of the underworld or sea, are often monstrous beings; still others are of mixed nature, partly human and partly animal or something else out of evil imagination. It would be more proper to say that humans have the form of gods, and not that the gods are in human form, since traditionally humans are made in the image of the gods. Humans are creatures, made by the gods out of the heavy elements, earth and water. The gods are of heavenly elements, yet are nevertheless substantial and material beings.

The physical universe as the ancients perceived it was small, much like a sphere half filled with water, upon which floated the flat disk of the earth. There was water everywhere else—above the heavens, around the earth, and below, flowing around the under-world. According to an old myth, the Mesopotamians imagined the earth as a disk surrounded by a rim of mountains and floating on an ocean of freshwater. Resting on these mountains and separated from the earth by the atmosphere was the sky vault, along which revolved the astral bodies. A similar hemisphere under the earth formed the netherworld, where lived the spirits of the dead. This is known as the three-story universe: heaven above, the earth in the middle, and the underworld below. The whole universe was immersed like a gigantic bubble in a boundless, uncreated, primeval ocean of saltwa-ter. The earth itself consisted of nothing more than Egypt or Greece or Mesopotamia and its neighboring lands; in the center stood the city of Babylon for the Babylonians, Nippur for the Sumerians, Delphi for the Greeks, and Jerusalem for Israel.

Heaven was thought to be a dome made of a hard substance not far from the earth, above which dwelt the gods in their homes. Those homes were sometimes conceived as being on a high cosmic mountain, such as Mount North in Canaan or Mount Olympus in Greece. The gods "looked down" from heaven on human affairs and were close enough to hear human outcry. In Babylon, human commotion kept Enlil awake at night. In Israel, God "sits above the circle of the earth and its inhabitants are like grasshoppers" (Isa. 40:22).

Heaven could be reached by those on the earth: two sons of the Greek sea god Poseidon threatened to pile three mountains on each other and climb to the sky; for that threat they spent the rest of time in Hades (*Odyssey* 11.315–316). With a similar goal, the tower of Babel was to have its top in heaven (Gen. 11:4). A later text tells us that men built the tower of Babel and, "taking an auger, they attempted to pierce the heaven, saying, 'Let us see whether the heaven is [made] of clay or copper or iron'" (*3 Baruch* 3:7).

Below the earth was the underworld, conceived of as a kind of kingdom under the ground, roofed over by the disk of the earth. The living could occasionally enter the underworld at certain hidden points — at the base of the cosmic mountain (in Canaan), or in a special cave (Italy), or as Odysseus did, by sailing to the edge of the world-encircling ocean. Normally, one's shade descended to the underworld after death and could never leave. In Greece, for example, the gates of Hades' kingdom were barred and guarded by Cerberus, the monstrous three-headed dog who kept watch so that no one could escape. In the rebellion of Korah and his associates against Moses, "the ground under them was split apart. The earth opened its mouth and swallowed them up. . . . So they and all that belonged to them went down alive into Sheol; the earth closed over them" (Num. 16:31–33). In Mesopotamia, the netherworld was a city ringed by seven walls that must be entered through seven gates. The ruler of the Underworld was not evil or a devil, but a king reigning in a dark and misty realm of the dead.

These three domains — the sky, the sea, and the underworld — were spheres of divine power divided among the gods. In Greece, the three spheres were chosen by lot. Poseidon tells of the event in Homer's *Iliad:*

> We are three brothers born by Rheia to Kronos, Zeus, and I, and the third is Hades, lord of the dead men. All was divided among us three ways, each given his domain. I when the lots were shaken drew the grey sea to live in forever; Hades drew the lot of the mists and the darkness, and Zeus was allotted the wide sky, in the cloud and the bright air. But earth and wide Olympus are common to all three. (15.187–193)

The three brothers almost never came into conflict and in general respected each other's domains. They occasionally met and feasted together on the mountain of the gods in heaven, Mount Olympus.

Among the Canaanites, the upper world of the sky was ruled by El, who dwelt on the cosmic mountain, Mount North. The sea was ruled by Yamm, whose name meant "sea," and who seasonally battled the gods of the upper world. In the Bible, this was Leviathan, the monster of the sea whom the Lord battled and had to keep under control. The book of Isaiah looks forward to a time when "the Lord . . . will punish Leviathan, the fleeing serpent, Leviathan the twisting serpent, and he will kill the dragon that is in the sea" (Isa. 27:1). There was, in addition, under the earth the kingdom of a great dragon with the deadly tail of a scorpion, Mot, whose very name meant "death." His main function was to swallow forever all who crossed over from life. Again, the book of Isaiah foresees a time when the Lord will turn the tables and "swallow up Death forever" (Isa. 25:7). For the apostle Paul, this dragon "Death" was the last enemy to be defeated at the end of time: "The last enemy that will be abolished is Death" (1 Cor. 15:26). And so, in exaltation, he can boast that the swallower will be himself swallowed up: "Death will be swallowed up in victory" (1 Cor. 15:54). And then he asks, "O Death, where is your sting?" (15:55), showing that the terrifying tail has been vanquished.

Divine society was seen by the ancients as a mirror of human society, and the whole of heaven was populated by powerful humanlike divine beings who had both human appearance and human weaknesses: although highly intelligent, the gods could run out of ideas; generally righteous, they could act capriciously and even wickedly. They were subject to passion, hatred, love. They ate and drank and got drunk; they sometimes quarreled among themselves. They could even die—that is, go and live in the underworld. They engaged in sexual activity, bearing offspring who were lesser deities. In Canaan, El and his wife, Asherah, bore seventy children. Gods even occasionally mated with humans and produced heroic individuals far superior to normal humans.

The religious world was understood by the ancient Near East to be organized as a great hierarchy, from the oldest high gods of nature to the lowliest tree sprites, known as the Great Chain of

Being.[1] The greater gods ruled the cosmos by means of lesser gods and spirits. The world was full of spiritual life; everything in the cosmos had an associated deity, no matter how small. All major natural phenomena, such as stars, sun, and moon, were understood as divinities. Winds of every direction and intensity were spiritual beings. Every tree and bush had its dryad; every spring and well its nyad and water spirit.

These divinities were organized into different rankings and different functions. Some controlled the many aspects of nature — winds and rain, lightning and storm, crops and hunting, the sea and its bounty. Others were concerned with human political events — deities of war and peace, kingship, government, cities, and especially law. Others oversaw more personal aspects of human life, such as fertility, birth, coming of age, marriage, health or disease, wealth or poverty, and finally death. Every human act had its patron deity, and every failure or success, disease or recovery, had its cause in a spiritual being.

In the early period there was no devil or demons who tempted one to sin and go to hell; there were only spirits who oversaw things inimical to humans, as there were those who oversaw things healthful. There were no morally evil gods. The spirit of the desert storm or of the plague had its place and function in the larger scheme, as did that of the spring rains and puberty. Destructive spirits, spirits of calamity, served the will of the greater gods in bringing just punishments to those who deserved them, and when the time came, death to all. It was not until Zoroastrianism began its influence that the idea of a battle between good and evil divine forces arose. In the Christian period, the Romans still had no morally evil deities.

The word *pantheon* denotes all of the gods worshiped by a particular group of people. Thus Jupiter, Juno, Minerva, Vulcan, and the rest of the Roman gods, taken together, made up the pantheon of Roman gods. The word comes from two Greek words: *pan*, meaning "all," and *theos*, meaning "god." Each of the larger ethnic groups of the ancient Near East shared a pantheon common to themselves but distinct from those of neighboring groups. For example, the Canaanites, including Israel, had a pantheon that was headed by El and his wife, Asherah, whose seventy children ruled the seventy nations of the earth. In Greece the pantheon was traditionally that of the twelve Olympian gods, headed by Zeus and his wife, Hera.

Even though all of the major cultural groups had a pantheon headed by some particular high god, none was originally monotheistic. Each city and people had its own protecting deity who was part of a larger pantheon of gods. This is called "henotheism," or sometimes "monalatry"—the worship of one particular god by one people with the full recognition of the existence of other gods of other peoples. Henotheism was the standard mode of religion in the ancient Near East. In Israel, the commandment, "You shall have no other gods before me, . . . for I the Lord your God am a jealous God" (Exod. 20:2–5), presupposed the valid, though despised, existence of other gods. The point at issue in the passage is whether the Israelites would choose to worship Yahweh alone or one or more of the many other gods available to them in their culture. This was not monotheism as it came to be understood many centuries later, but henotheism, the worship of one particular god chosen out of many. At that early stage in Israel's history, the people were not yet monotheists.

From the families of these high gods came the so-called national or city gods. If a particular deity ruled a relatively large territory, lesser gods related to his family ruled the smaller political units that made up the larger territory. So, for example, while nearly all the Greeks worshiped the twelve Olympian gods headed by Zeus and his wife, Hera, cities often held one or another of the Olympians or their children in special regard. Athens was named after its city goddess, Athena; Delphi was especially devoted to the worship of Apollo. Similarly in Egypt, each city had its own special deity even though for much of its recorded history the whole country was united under the religion of the king, the religion of the sun god Re. In Palestine there was a widely shared pantheon of gods headed by El and his wife, Asherah. Each of the peoples that lived in the area had a national or main city god who was either a local version of El or a member of El's family.

Originally, before the rise of monotheism and the universalization of the god of the ruling class, gods belonged to a specific people and land. The gods dwelt in and protected a specific place; in turn, their people honored them with worship and sacrifices. When individuals moved, they worshiped the gods of the new land. The psalmist complains, for example, that he cannot worship Yahweh in Babylon (Ps. 137); he has been exiled and no longer lives in the land of the Lord.

In times of war, greater gods conquered lesser ones, or so it was claimed in the language of praise for the victor and shame for the subjected people. This arose from the fundamental tenet that the god of a people was the real ruler, and that events in the political sphere were religious events. The gods of the empires were the greatest because they conquered those of the smaller states that they absorbed. So the gods of Rome were the greatest, and the universal gods, for they ruled the world. The losing theologians, therefore, said that their own god had decided to allow their land to be conquered because of fate or the sinfulness of its inhabitants. Both claims were made after the Trojan war; the latter, after the Exile of Israel.

TYPES OF MONOTHEISM

Monotheism arose in more than one form in the cultures of antiquity, but the oldest conceptions never did die out; they continued to survive alongside (and even inside) the various monotheisms. The most common form of non-monotheistic religion was monarchical polytheism. In this conception, the pantheon of gods of greater or lesser function was overseen by a single high god to whom all other gods owed submission. Since nearly all views of the cosmos (outside of Egypt) were divided into arenas of power (upper world, waters, and underworld), this tended to produce more than one powerful high god with attendant servant deities. The high god of the upper world (the sky god), however, was always the most powerful and was the deity who ruled the human sphere. In more than one culture, these gods came into conflict in a great battle known as the "combat myth," and the upper-world god (who else?) gained victory.

The point of bringing up this clearly non-monotheistic world-view is that in the final expression of the great monotheisms— Judaism, Christianity, and Islam—the one God is served by innumerable lesser divine beings who do his bidding (the angels) and is opposed by an enemy god with attendant beings (the Devil and the demons) who will one day be defeated. For all the "progress" of the River of God, the oldest conception known to us of the divine hierarchies of heaven in conflict with other gods with their own servants survives in rough outline up to the present.

Inclusive Monotheism

Monotheism arose out of politics, either for the building and maintaining of empire or as an explanation for its loss. The most common form is what may be termed "inclusive monotheism." Greek writers of the fifth century BCE articulated a theory (certainly operative much earlier) known as the *Interpretatio Graeca*. That theory stipulated that the god of a particular function in one place was the same deity as a similar god of a different locale with a different name: our Zeus is really your Jupiter or Amon by another name. So one god may replace another with similar attributes without difficulty. Such gods may be formally identified with another and their names compounded, such as Zeus-Amon, a compounding of the high gods of Greece and Egypt.

Inclusive monotheism went one major step further: it sought not only to identify gods, but to absorb them. The basic theory was that the highest god of the conquering or ruling people was in one way or another expressed in the other gods or was in some way present in all the local deities of the cities or groups under political control.

Each of the lesser deities was not only a servant of the high god, but was an actual manifestation of some aspect of the god of the rulers. The fundamental motivation for making such a claim was for the king to be able to use religion to expand and solidify control over a wider territory. Thus the god of the new empire would absorb the qualities of the other gods, and the other gods would become expressions of qualities of the conquering high god.

That lesser gods could express qualities of their parents, the higher gods, was an old idea that found expression in more than one way. In Greece, for example, Apollo, son of Zeus, held the power of healing and disease; but in time, the power to heal devolved, especially to his son Asklepios. In Persia, God emanated archangels who carried even in their names qualities of God. So in Zoroastrianism one finds archangels with names such as "Immortality," "Love," and "Perfection." This way of naming archangels and angels found its way into Judaism, Christianity, and Islam. The archangels Gabriel, Uriel, and Raphael, for example, carry in their names the qualities of the strength of God, the light of God, and the healing power of God.

An Example: Monotheism in Mesopotamia

For more than three thousand years the gods of Sumer, a territory at the mouth of the Tigris and Euphrates rivers, were worshiped by Sumerians and Semites alike, and by the various other peoples who invaded Mesopotamia. The country was organized as a collection of independent (and at times warring) city-states. While each city had its own patron deity and its own set of legends, the whole country worshiped a more or less common pantheon of nature deities. Some deities, such as Shara of the city of Umma and Zababa of Kish, were known only in their own towns, serving as sort of divine mayors. Others, while worshiped particularly in a certain locale, had wider appeal, especially the deities of nature: Sin, the moon god, was patron of the city of Ur; Utu, his son, the sun god, was patron of Sippar and Larsa.

The pantheon was headed by three great figures: Anu, the sky god; Enlil, "Lord Wind"; and Ea, the god of subterranean fresh-water. Anu was a power far above and removed from human life. The place of main deity was occupied by Enlil. Enlil was ruler of the earth, but he had an ambiguous relationship with humans; he could be both gracious and harsh. It was he, for example, in the *Epic of Gilgamesh*, who brought the flood in an attempt to destroy the human race for its raucous behavior. Ea was the god most well disposed toward people. He taught the Babylonian Noah, in the same original flood story, to build the ark, thus saving a remnant of the human race.

Ea's son was Marduk, originally a midlevel god of magic. By the middle of the second millennium BCE, the city of Babylon had become the center of the Babylonian empire that ruled most of Mesopotamia. Marduk, the god of the city of Babylon, became the national god of the empire and was elevated to become the head of the pantheon: Marduk became high god in Mesopotamia.

As noted earlier in this chapter, the creation epic *Enuma Elish* gives an account of the battle between the primeval sea, Tiamat, and the younger gods of earth and sky. The younger gods in their commotion rile the primeval parents of all, Tiamat (the saltwater) and her husband, Apsu (the freshwater), who threatens to kill them. Ea instead kills Apsu and takes up his abode in the freshwa-ter. He and his wife bear Marduk. The younger gods, and espe-cially Marduk, again disturb Tiamat and her sea monster off-spring, and she resolves to avenge her husband and destroy the younger gods. They pale in terror at her threats.

Completely at a loss, they finally turn to the youngest and strongest champion, Marduk. To secure his services, however, they must grant him supremacy over everything. Marduk defeats Tiamat, thus saving the gods, and from Tiamat's body he creates the world. The gods rejoice and declare the fifty names of Marduk, which attribute to him many of the qualities and functions of the other gods. His father, Ea, even cedes to him his own place: "Let him be like me; let his name be Ea." The old high god, Enlil, is also replaced, and Marduk becomes "the Enlil of the gods."[2]

In Assyria of the first millennium BCE, a similar process occurred. The capital city, the land, and the high god were all called by the same name, Ashur, giving us the name of the Assyrian empire. A version of the *Enuma Elish* was found in the city of Ashur that tells the same story noted above, except that Ashur at each mention replaces Marduk. In another strategy to exalt the main deity of the Assyrians, Ashur was given an even more exalted position. The old Mesopotamian pantheon had been headed by An, the sky, whose father was Anshar, the heavens above. Assyrian texts applied the ideogram for Anshar to Ashur, making him the father of the oldest pantheon. In historical inscriptions and art of the period, Ashur was placed at the head of the processions of the gods. So a royal inscription of Sargon II began: "To Ashur, father of the gods, the great Lord."[3] Here a tribal god of northern Mesopotamia (Ashur) at a rather late date rose to take over the supreme position in a much older pantheon as progenitor of all the other gods.

Three stages in the development toward monotheism may be seen in these examples. First, Marduk and Ashur, the high gods of new empires, replace the old high god of the territory now under their control. Second, the new high god Marduk absorbs the names, qualities, and functions of the other gods. Third, Ashur replaces Marduk in myth, taking over the sacred story that once belonged to the god he replaced. The events and experiences of Marduk are told in identical fashion now of Ashur. This is not exclusive monotheism, of course, but neither is it merely henotheism. The other gods do not cease to exist: they retain their own individual functions and remain guardians of their cities. Nevertheless, especially in the case of Marduk, the other gods are absorbed. There is a conscious attempt to meld the pantheon into the high god.

Exclusive Monotheism

The other main type of monotheism, "exclusive monotheism," denies the existence or validity of other deities and appears in several varieties. In the first, the exclusive monotheism of worship, the high god is extolled in language that claims a "one and only" status. In the words of Morton Smith, exclusive monotheism "is often an expression of local patriotism, which achieved it by a chain of exaggeration something like this: Our god is the greatest of all gods, there is none like him, there is none other."[4]

A second form appeared in Persia at the end of the second millennium BCE. The exclusive monotheism of Persian Zoroastrianism demonized all other gods and all other religions. There was for them only one true god; all other gods were demonic powers with no rightful claim to divinity.

In Egypt, at roughly the same time, a third type of exclusive monotheism appeared during the reign of Akhenaton in the fourteenth century BCE. During most of its history, inclusive monotheism had been the normal mode of religion in Egypt. Under Pharaoh Akhenaton, however, the very existence of other gods was denied. Their names were even chiseled off monuments, and they were never mentioned in the literature of this ruler.

Perhaps the most famous example of this latter type of exclusive monotheism is to be found in the writings of the prophet known as Second Isaiah. In those writings, the Lord of Israel declares, "I am the Lord and there is no other; beside me there is no god" (Isa. 45:5). For some modern scholars, this last form is the significant one, and it is Second Isaiah who takes the final step of the "breakthrough into true monotheism."[5] But as we shall see, the development of monotheism did not stop with the formulation of Second Isaiah. The four great religions commonly described as exclusively monotheistic—Zoroastrianism, Yahwism, Christianity, and Islam—are all genetically dependent: Persia dominated the ancient Near East in the sixth century BCE and brought Zoroastrianism to conquered Israel; and out of Israel and the Greco-Roman world arose Christianity and then (after nearly six hundred years) Islam.

Monotheism, however, underwent its most important advances long after its appearance in Israel because of contributions by Greek science. Centuries later, Christians of many stripes discussed and argued until the great councils of the church arrived at the particular expression of monotheism that is Christian Trinitarianism. Judaism and Islam, of course (along with many Christian groups, as we shall see), rejected Trinitarianism as polytheism. Viewed from the outside, they had a point; from the inside, however—from the background of Greek philosophy, Christian Gnosticism, and the difficult texts of the New Testament itself—Trinitarianism was wonderfully defensible.

GREEK SCIENCE AND THE MONAD

The single most important step taken in the journey toward the Christian understanding of God did not come from religion at all, but from science. The view of the cosmos in the great civilizations and the Old Testament was that of the three-story universe described earlier. Because of the idea that the stars were servants of the gods and were "signs," revealing in their alignments God's will and human destiny, observation of the heavens had been important for millennia. At first, one surmises, the night sky seemed to constitute a sphere of fixed stars that moved in concert, as if the earth were covered by a kind of hemispherical tent or dome on which were affixed the lights of heaven. At some early time now lost to us, it was discovered, probably first in Babylon, that seven objects— the sun and moon, obvious to all, and five other heavenly lights— moved in regular patterns independent of the dome of the "fixed stars." These were termed the "wandering stars," and from the Greek word for "wander" (*planao*), we get our word "planet."

Greek mathematicians and astronomers made a number of important advances beginning in the sixth century BCE and later. Their discovery of the five planets (only five are visible to the naked eye) presented a major difficulty for astronomers. How did they move? New models for explaining not only the movements of the planets but also the very design of the universe were required: the three-story universe had to be discarded. What was required was a new view of the cosmos itself.

One of the most important discoveries, credited to Pythagoras, was that the earth was not a disk, but a sphere. Eratosthenes, in the third century BCE, calculated its circumference at approximately forty thousand kilometers, wonderfully close to its actual size. Scientific observation and mathematical calculation replaced the small disk-shaped earth of old tradition—the "circle" floating on water of the Bible—with a much, much larger spherical earth, very much as we understand the earth today.

If the planets move independent of the fixed stars, then the hemispherical "dome" of the fixed stars must be an entire sphere surrounding us. Observation and, interestingly enough, the discovery of the proportional intervals of musical scales led to the conjecture that perhaps the sun, moon, and planets were also affixed to concentric spheres of lesser, but proportional, diameters that rotated around the earth, independent of each other, whose proportions corresponded to the musical intervals discernible by mathematics. So there developed an entirely new understanding of the cosmos, never before conceived. The earth was a sphere at the center surrounded by eight concentric spheres—seven crystalline and invisible spheres to which the moon, sun, and five planets were attached, with an outer limit of the eighth on which were the fixed stars. The "music of the spheres," produced by the rotation of the proportionally spaced spheres of the planets, was discussed long into the Middle Ages.

The effects on religious conception of this scientific advance over the previous three-story universe were fundamental. One of the most important was the new view of the physical size of the universe. The distance to the dome of the sky, once thought to be just a few thousand feet, was increased enormously. The firmament of the "fixed stars" was no longer within the reach of a mud-brick tower, but had been removed by verifiable mathematics to an almost infinite distance. Where now was God? This new view of the cosmos removed God far away, beyond any previous position or conception. God could no longer be a humanlike being who could eat with Abraham and show his back to Moses. God had to be something else, entirely different, *qualitatively* different, from previous conceptions: God could no longer have a body.

From time immemorial, the high gods had been likened to light or understood as beings of light. The encounter with the gods "enlightened" the understanding. In Egypt for much of its history, God was the sun itself. The God of Israel was likewise often likened to the sun; accordingly, the prophet Isaiah declared: "Arise, shine; for your light has come, and the glory of the Lord has risen upon you" (Isa. 60:1). The implications of the new science for understanding the nature of God were almost inevitable: the cosmos below the eighth sphere, as all could see, was in darkness, lighted only by the sun and a few other ineffectual heavenly bodies, and these bodies were at best servants of God. Since this cosmos below the eighth sphere was in darkness, God as a being of light must be beyond the eighth sphere in a world of light.

Further thinking about the nature of the elements that made up the cosmos produced even more profound changes. Empedocles (ca. 492–432 BCE) theorized, as had others before him in Greece and elsewhere, that there were four basic "elements" that made up the material world: earth, water, air, and fire. He went on to apply this theory to the geocentric universe. Why was the earth in the center? It was because it was made of heavy elements, earth and water. It was surrounded by air, the next lightest element. All of this is obvious to us today, but that is because of Empedocles and his intellectual compatriots.

Above the lower air was a traditional fifth element, found in Homer (centuries before Empedocles) and established in scientific thought by Aristotle (a century after Empedocles) as occupying the cosmos above the moon: aither. For Homer, the allotment of Zeus was "in the clouds and the aither" (*Iliad* 15.192), which was the bright, clear air above the lower atmosphere. Aristotle, building on his philosophical predecessors, theorized that ether extended from the moon to the outer boundary of the eighth sphere and was the substance from which the stars and planets were made. If God was outside the eighth sphere, God must be enormous, Aristotle and his contemporaries concluded, and must be made out of light, or fire, or spirit, or ether—the ancients differed, and it is hard even now to answer the question as to the "stuff" God is made of. In any case, God could no longer have a body. The Aristotelian system of five "elements" held sway among scientists for nearly two millennia. It was not until Einstein in the early twentieth century that the concept of ether as a substance in space was finally overturned.[6]

So what now was God? Enlil and Marduk and Ashur, Atum and Re and Amon, El and Baal and Yahweh, Zeus and Jupiter and so many others—all these were impossible, even embarrassing. The geocentric cosmos required a fundamental change, a revolution to a wholly new understanding of God and the religious world. Greek philosophers took up the old question of the One and the many—the "one god who became millions," in Egyptian terminology. For all the brilliance of the Egyptian theologians in understanding the expansion of the One into the fullness of the cosmos, God could not be the Egyptian sun; the sun was itself a celestial object, another servant of God like the other planets, well below the eighth sphere. Nor could God have arisen out of water, as in all the oldest cosmologies, since water was a heavy element, restricted to the earth and impossible in the heavens. The old idea that there was water above the hard sphere of the sky that could be released to flood the earth, as in Genesis 6–8, was now known to be scientifically impossible. The new cosmology required God to be spiritual, made as we saw of light or fire or ether—"spirit," in the words of the Gospel of John. God was enormous, beyond human comprehension, hidden and infinite behind the veil of the vastly distant eighth sphere.

Meditation on the problem of the original cause of all things had long since brought religious thinkers to claim that at the beginning stood the one God as source. But here a wholly new basis for the one God, for monotheism, was found: in the new understanding of the structure of the universe, there was no place to put another infinite being. In the old cosmos, the gods (even the one god) had bodies and could be localized and even measured. "Where are the gods?" (or "Where is the high god?") was an easy question to answer: the gods sat on top of the sky on their thrones in their temples, or in the sea or underworld. Given the newly understood geocentric cosmos and its infinite God, the question had to be asked the other way around. It was not "Where is God?" but "Where is the universe?" If God was outside and infinite, then the cosmos must be inside God. Thus arose the idea of God as the container of the cosmos who was in turn contained by nothing. God was not in a place, but was the place in which all else was.

This God came to be termed the Monad, the "One" (from the Greek word meaning "one alone"), who was the source of all else. Plato and his followers had postulated that all things were made from patterns, ideas in the mind of God that existed in an eternal and immaterial divine dimension; the pattern of everything was "the Good," Plato's term for God. Aristotle considered the problem of movement and concluded that at the beginning of all things there must have been an "Unmoved Mover." The relevance of this to our discussion here is that the question of a single and eternal being at the source of all else had become a major philosophical issue, and the best minds of the ancient world had begun their inquiries.

The conception of Plato that God was "the Good" pointed to something fundamental about the nature of God that would become almost explosive in the controversies over the Old Testament view of God among traditional and Hellenized Jews, and among Christians of many denominations. Ethics had always been a prime concern among religious authorities from time immemorial; in fact, one of the prime functions of religion in society is and has always been to define and enforce ethical norms. Originally the gods had laws, based in nature and written on heavenly tablets, that humans had to obey. Both gods and humans, however, violated their commandments often for the reason that they had passions and appetites that the threats of laws could not overcome.

As the complex of ideas that made up the geocentric universe became more and more influential, ethics came to be seen in a wholly different light. Human beings were seen to be made up of two essentially different parts, body and soul. Passions and appetites, quite obviously, belonged to bodies. As long as Zeus, for example, was thought to have a body, no matter how beautiful and heavenly, he would be vindictive or wrathful or jealous or amorous. Thus the angers and antics of the gods, their meddlings with people, were dependent on the view that they had passions and desires—in other words, that they were material beings.

The Monad, however, the one God of all at the source of all, was wholly spiritual. The Monad did not even have a spiritual body—that is, a localized and measurable body made of some spiritual substance, like the bodies angels were later thought to have. No anthropomorphic terms were applicable. No expressions such as "the hand of the Lord was stretched out" or "may his face shine upon you" were permitted. In fact, the entire vocabulary developed over millennia for describing the gods and their actions had to be discarded. In a discussion of the biblical verse "And Cain went out from the face of God" (Gen. 4:16), Philo of Alexandria (ca. 20 BCE–ca. 50 CE) declared that

> in the books in which Moses acts as God's interpreter we ought to take his statements figuratively, since the impression made by the words in their literal sense is greatly at variance with truth. For if the Existent Being has a face, and he that wishes to quit its sight can with perfect ease remove elsewhere, what ground have we for rejecting the impious doctrines of Epicurus, or the atheism of the Egyptians, or the mythical plots of play and poem of which the world is full? (*De Posteritate Caini* 1–3)

God cannot have a face from which Cain can flee anytime he wishes. God cannot have a body. Epicurus (341–270 BCE), Greek philosopher and the founder of Epicureanism, had claimed that the gods had bodies and lived wholly apart from our world in bliss. The Egyptian gods likewise all had bodies; the "atheism of the Egyptians" in the eyes of the rest of the world lay in the fact that the Egyptians conceived of gods as animals. The "plots of play and poem" were the stories of the passions and immoralities of the gods of Greco-Roman epic and drama that were heard on stages everywhere. Philo shows that not only these "pagans" held "impious doctrines" about the divine nature; so did a literal reading of the Bible. The God of the Bible also had a body with its passions; it too had to be reinterpreted.

Even describing the Monad took considerable skill and sophistication. In place of the old anthropomorphic terminology, philosophers developed what was much later called "apophatic theology," or negative theology. This meant explaining God by saying what God was *not* (from the Greek word *apophasis*: "negation, saying no"), because God was so big as to be beyond human comprehension. According to this mode of description, God is infinite, immaterial, unknowable, invisible, immeasurable, and the like. Note that the words are all prefixed by a negative particle; that is apophatic theology. A wonderful example follows:[7]

> He Who Is is ineffable. No principle knew him, no authority, no subjection, no creature from the foundation of the world, except he alone. For he is immortal and eternal, having no birth, for everyone who has birth will perish. He is unbegotten, having no beginning; for everyone who has a beginning has an end. No one rules over him. He has no name; for whoever has a name is the creature of another. He is unnamable. He has no human form. . . . He is infinite; he is incomprehensible. He is ever imperishable and has no likeness (to anything). He is unchanging good. He is faultless. He is everlasting. He is blessed. He is unknowable. (*Eugnostos* 71.14–72.20)

But if the Monad is so far beyond the insignificant human sphere, so self-sufficient, where did the world come from? Why should the Monad do anything at all, let alone create this world in which we live? A second text, from a Jewish Gnostic group that had its roots in the second century BCE, addresses this very problem. God is again first described in apophatic language, and then the influence of Plato's "good" God is seen in an inspired statement of positives:

He is pure, immeasurable Mind. He is aeon-giving aeon. He is
life-giving life. He is a blessedness-giving blessed one. He is
knowledge-giving knowledge. He is goodness-giving goodness.
He is mercy and redemption–giving mercy. He is grace-giving
grace. . . . (*Apocryphon of John* 4.2–9)

Here is the motivation for the One to become many: it is its very
nature to overflow in joy. The Monad, who exists in depth and
peace and silent rest, bubbles over in its abundance.

Some process is clearly required for the one God to produce
eventually all the vast diversity of the cosmos. The process, however, is wholly spiritual among beings of light and spirit. Nothing
is said about the creation of the material world. There is no
primeval darkness or chaotic water at the beginning out of which
to make the world. In fact, as one can see from the very name used
of the Monad in the previous text, "He Who Is" (though we are
told that he has no name), we are on the way to *creatio ex nihilo*,
"creation out of nothing." The Monad simply exists alone; the
chaos material must later somehow come into being.

From a "scientific" viewpoint, the heavy elements out of which
the cosmos was made were different in quality from the Monad.
Earlier conceptions had essentially ignored the problem. The old
creator gods with bodies were made out of the same "stuff" as the
cosmos itself. They formed the material world out of preexisting
chaos directly with their hands, or they birthed it or spoke its form
into existence. In the new conception of the geocentric universe,
the fact that the cosmos was material and dark was taken quite
seriously; both qualities were the direct opposite of the Monad.
The dark material world did not and could not have contact with
this wholly spiritual, immaterial God of light. So someone other
than the Monad must have been responsible for the material
world; some mediator must have been the cause, either in accordance with or against God's will.

In either case, however—whether the material world began
good or not—it is still a problem; it is in fact a dark cosmos, while

the Monad is a God of light. Some account, therefore, of how it became dark must be told. In Persian Zoroastrianism, inherited by Christianity, the world was created good and was then defiled by the Devil; its destiny was that it would be destroyed and replaced with a new world. In Plato's system, especially as articulated by his later followers, the material cosmos was created by an intermediary good God, whom Plato termed the Demiurge (from the Greek word *demiourgos*, "skilled workman, craftsman"). This Craftsman created the good cosmos out of preexisting chaotic water according to the patterns designed by the highest God. People, however, were created by less skilled lower divinities, with material bodies that attracted the soul to the material world and away from its proper abode in heaven. Humans, in their heavy bodies, were "weighed down" with sins. Thus the problem was materiality itself; the spiritual soul belonged to the upper world and needed to escape even the good material world of Plato. A third view was that of an influential form of Gnosticism, which held that the material world came about by a mistake, a fall of one of the lesser divinities; it was not "good" at all. These three views—that of Zoroastrianism, Plato, and Gnosticism—were combined to form the worldview of Christianity.

In the classic Gnostic system of the *Apocryphon of John*, the Monad begins the process of creation by emanating a reflection of itself in the surrounding light of its own being, much like an image in a mirror. Eventually the Monad and this first image emanate further layers of deity until the Monad is surrounded by many levels of divine light, known as the "fullness" of God—in Greek, the *pleroma*. At the outer edge of this *pleroma*, its lowest and least member, Sophia (Lady "Wisdom") of intertestamental Jewish speculation, in imitation of the Monad tries to birth her own offspring without the consent of the One. She is so far from the divine light that she is on the outer edge: just beyond her is nothingness. She gives birth to a monster, and in her shame she throws him out into the darkness. The darkness congeals into materiality, which forms a veil between itself and the world of light.

Below the veil, the monster deems itself "god" and creates the lower geocentric cosmos from the dark matter. This it fills with wicked spirits as its servants to rule the seven spheres and the earth below the veil. The text names this monster Yaldabaoth, "Child of Chaos," which is a clear play on the name of the God of Israel, Yahweh. In a fit of hubris Yaldabaoth declares, "I am the Lord and beside me there is no other" (Isa. 45:5). At that point, a voice from above calls him "Sacklas" (Aramaic for "fool") and "Samael" (Hebrew for "blind god"). Later, when Yaldabaoth declares that he is a jealous god (Exod. 20:5), the text asks who it is that he could be jealous of, if he is the only god.

The origins of these Gnostic texts go back before the Christian era into times of controversy between traditional Jews and other Jews highly educated in Greek philosophy. The texts are difficult to interpret and potentially offensive to those who hold the biblical text in high regard. But the issues they point up in sarcastic denigration had to be faced by Jews and Christians alike as they struggled to determine the nature of divinity.

The Old Testament was written during times when essentially all gods lived in the small three-story universe. They had bodies and the passions to go with them, as we have seen; they were usually just, but they could also be extremely wrathful, showing little of the essential "goodness" that Plato thought necessary. The concept of the Monad—the infinite, immaterial One behind all things—did not arise until Greek science inspired Greek philosophers to rethink the concept of God and develop a revolutionary spiritual, passionless source of all, who "created" only by an intermediary.

Viewed against the Monad, the God of the Old Testament paled. The Jewish authors of the Gnostic texts applied Greek ideas to the Bible and found its God wanting. If "in the beginning God created . . . ," then this divine being could not be the Monad, since the Monad created only through a lesser intermediary. If Yahweh was jealous or wrathful, then he was not the One, for the One dwelt in unlimited bliss, untroubled by the passions of the gods with bodies.

These controversies among Jews of the pre-Christian era and Greek philosophy left their mark on Christian views of God. The fact that God is immaterial and spiritual is such a normal modern view that we hardly realize that the issue was still being argued during the era of the writing of the New Testament. The gods had been worshiped by food gifts, incense, and animal sacrifices for millennia in important cult centers run by large priesthoods all over the ancient world. The priests had considerable investment in the old views of the gods. If God were like the infinite and immaterial One, the priests were out of a job: What would the Monad do with the priests' sacrifice of a dead chicken?

Just such a situation arises in the conversation between Jesus and the Samaritan woman at the well. She brings up the controversy about which temple, Mount Gerazim of Samaria or Jerusalem of Judea, God should be worshiped in. Jesus retorts that neither temple is adequate, for "God is spirit and those who worship him must worship him in spirit" (John 4:24). Other texts illustrate the vacillation between spirit and light/fire used to describe God's essence. We read that "God is light" (1 John 1:5) and that Jesus is the "radiance of his glory" (Heb. 1:3). God as a spiritual being is the basis for the Christian rejection of animal sacrifice of any kind, whether in Jerusalem, Samaria, or any other cult center: God does not have a body and therefore does not, *cannot*, eat anything, let alone dead animals. The Christian argument against animal sacrifice was so obviously logical and persuasive that pagans were still trying to find some justification for their continuance of the practice in the fourth century (when they were finally losing out to the Christian majority).

The idea that the Christian God is the Monad and the original eternal and self-existent "One Who Is" is found in more than one important passage. First Timothy 1:17 declares God to be the "only God," using the Greek term *monos*, which lies at the root of the term *Monad*. First Timothy 6:16 adds, "It is he alone who has immortality." In the words of the Gospel of John, "the Father has life in himself" (John 5:26). He is therefore called the "living

Father" (John 6:57). Here God is the only one with life as a personal characteristic, the self-existent source of all other life.

That the Christian God as Monad is invisible, hidden, and unknowable is not often heard in churches, but it was required by the logic of Greek science and philosophy and is therefore often found in the New Testament. First Timothy 1:17 again declares God to be "invisible." First Timothy 6:16 continues that God "dwells in unapproachable light, whom no one has ever seen or can see." So also the prologue of the Gospel of John concludes with the statement that "no one has seen God at any time" (John 1:18).

The only way that such a hidden and unknowable God can be perceived at all by humans is through the process of the One becoming many. For early Christians this was the function of the Logos who became incarnate as the Son of God, Jesus, the mediator of the One to creation. So John 1:18 continues, ". . . the only begotten God [Jesus], who is in the bosom of the Father, has explained him." Jesus the Son is the explanation of the unknown Father. That is why later in the Gospel of John, when Philip asks Jesus to show him the Father, Jesus replies, "He who has seen me has seen the Father" (John 14:9). Recall that the Father has no body and is therefore invisible; no one has seen (or can see) him. The only way to "see" the Father is to see the explanation of the Father—that is, Jesus. Again in Matthew 11:27 (and Luke 19:22), Jesus declares, "All things have been handed over to me by my Father; and no one knows the Son except the Father, and no one knows the Father except the Son and anyone to whom the Son chooses to reveal him." The infinite and unknowable One of Greek philosophy, the One Who Is, is the Father of Jesus, who cannot be known except through his unfolding in the Son.

3

FROM THE ONE GOD
TO THE TRINITY

Christianity was born in controversy. It arose as a monotheistic faith, heir to the monotheisms of the River of God—of Persia and Egypt and Greek philosophy and later Israel. But it was complicated by early Christian reverence for Jesus himself, and later for the Holy Spirit, as divine Persons in their own right. During the second and third centuries, a number of powerful Gnostic Christian groups taught that there were far more than three forms of divinity. In contrast, at the beginning of the fourth century, Arius, a presbyter of Alexandria, taught a widely popular doctrine that there was one God alone—the Father—and all else, including Jesus and the Holy Spirit, were creations. In the crucible of such debates arose the theology of Trinitarianism.

When viewed against the background of the wider ancient world, the Christian concept of God is far more sophisticated than the mere problem of number of gods would indicate. The issue of whether God was a simple One or a Trinitarian unity, while important, was in no way comparable to the problem of the very conception of what constituted divinity. And that question depended, as we have seen, on science and a new and more accurate understanding of the universe itself. Scientific understanding of the cosmos grew—"progressed," in the modern sense—forcing religion to change and grow in response. Understanding of the divine nature had to change because the worldview on which the old gods with bodies depended was overturned. The old Three Story Universe was shown to be false. God was now something qualitatively different: God was infinite; God was immaterial; God was ultimately beyond human comprehension. We must view the development of the Christian conception of God, Trinitarianism, as the culmination of a long process that included not only the mere concept of number (how many expressions of the One there should be), but also the very being of God (how the divine nature should be understood at all).

PRE-CHRISTIAN DIVINE TRIADS

Triadic arrangements of gods were surprisingly common in the ancient Near East. As we saw in the previous chapter, the gods had bodies and were normally conceived in human form; their triads, therefore, reflected human family relationships. Statues from Jericho, for example, show divine triads of Father, Mother, and Son from the sixth millennium BCE. Similar triads were common in south Arabia. As historian W. F. Albright notes, "Early Hebrew popular religion was presumably similar, with a Father, El, a mother [Elah] . . . , and a son who appears as the storm god."[1] These triads were far from Trinitarianism, but the effect of such Semitic "families" of gods ran right into the second and third Christian centuries, as Semitic-speaking Christians attempted to formulate their own doctrines of God. Jewish Christian groups understood the divine "family" as God the Father, Spirit the Mother, and Jesus the Son. Because the word *spirit* in Hebrew and Aramaic is grammatically feminine, the Spirit-as-Mother conception came naturally.

Egypt had come closest to a doctrine of the Trinity in the pre-Christian era. Because of the fluid nature of their conceptions of the divine, Egyptians could create many different trinities (or binities, or monotheisms, or any other combination they desired). That fluidity arose out of the political necessity of melding the high gods of empire with the almost innumerable local gods of subjugated peoples.

One type of Egyptian trinity may be termed a "trinity of generation," similar in one sense to the Semitic triads: Atum, the primeval "Old One," becomes three by birthing from himself Shu and Tefnut, his son and daughter, representing the dry and moist air. So we read in one of the Coffin Texts (from ca. 1600 BCE and later, so-called because they were written inside coffins), "He was one and he became three."

A second form is a trinity of identification, where three gods are understood as one but retain their individualities. For example, three of the greatest gods of Egypt—Amon, Re, and Ptah—are conceived as summing up all the gods in themselves as one: "All gods are three: Amon, Re, and Ptah, and there is no second to them. 'Hidden' is his name as Amon; he is Re in face, and his body is Ptah."

A third trinity may be termed a trinity of aspect: the one sun god is worshiped in its three manifestations of morning, midday, and evening: "I am Khepri (one who rises), Re, and Atum (one who sets)."[2] Perhaps the closest parallel to certain outward aspects of the Christian Trinity is the very early trinity of the theologians of the Egyptian city of Heliopolis: the one god is expressed as the sun, the king, and the Horus falcon. This would be, in Christian terms, the Father (sun), the Son of God on earth (the king), and the Holy Spirit (as bird, the Horus falcon).

Yet this is not Christian Trinitarianism as it would later be defined. There was nothing exclusive about the Egyptian arrangements; the other gods continued to exist and were worshiped without losing their individuality. The genius of Egyptian conception was its very malleability. The trinities and formulations were not defined by philosophical debates to be written down as creeds that had to be signed and "believed."

Christian Trinitarianism arose instead out of the heated controversies over the nature of God among various Christian groups. Gnostic and other philosophically minded Christians championed the Monad of the geocentric universe against other Christians somewhat less well educated and tied more closely to a literal reading of the Old Testament. During the second century CE, great Christian Gnostic teachers arose, holding a religious worldview based not on the Old Testament, but on the "new wine" of the New Testament and Greek philosophy.

The old concept of a divinity who sat on a throne surrounded by angelic beings, and the cosmology on which that concept is based—the three-story universe—survived among some Christians into the New Testament period and literature. One finds in the book of Revelation, for example, a vision of the throne-room of heaven: "Behold, a throne was standing in heaven, and one sitting on the throne. And he who was sitting on the throne was like a jasper stone" (Rev. 4:2–3). This vision draws heavily on the similar vision in Ezekiel (1:26–27), where the heavenly throne and the humanlike being sitting on it are also described using the language of precious stones. In Ezekiel 10:20, this figure is named "the God of Israel." In Revelation 4:11, the one sitting on the throne is the Creator, not the Lamb; he is the Father, not the Son. The sky, as in Genesis 1, is made of some hard material, for there is a door in it to let the seer pass through from earth to the throne-room in heaven. It is not distant, for during a shaking of the cosmos, there is an earthquake, and as the sky shakes, it casts down to earth the stars fixed to it, "as a fig tree casts its unripe figs when shaken by a great wind" (Rev. 6:13).

Next, the sky is split apart, and through the opening those on the earth look up in terror and see "the face of the one who sits on the throne" (Rev. 6:14–16). Below the earth is the great abyss, the prison house of wicked spirits known as Tartarus among the Greeks. Here the angelic "sons of God" who sinned with human women, mating and bearing the giants of Genesis 6:1–4, were imprisoned. The Greek text of 2 Peter 2:4 even uses a verbal form of the word *Tartarus* to describe their prison. This prison is reopened in Revelation 9:2 and the wicked spirits are released, to torment humans again as they had in their original venture.

The point of these observations is that the move from understanding God as a small material being with a body in a three-story universe to understanding God as the infinite, immaterial Monad in the geocentric cosmos was still going on as Christianity was being defined. Both conceptions are to be found side by side in early Christian literature.

Other Christian groups, however, such as the community that produced the Gospel of John, had incorporated the geocentric universe of the Monad into their theology. The book of Hebrews has Jesus the Son of God, the one who created the world as an agent of God, "pass through the heavens" (Heb. 4:14) on his way back to the Father at the ascension, a clear reference to the eight spheres surrounding the earth. Another fundamental shift from the older conceptions of God to that in the New Testament is the role of the creator: in the Old Testament, Yahweh creates; in the New Testament, Jesus the Son of God creates as the Father's agent. So, for example, speaking of the Logos, the Gospel of John states, "All things came into being through him, and without him not one thing came into being" (John 1:3). Paul writes: "There is one God, the Father, from who are all things, . . . and one Lord, Jesus, through whom are all things" (1 Cor. 8:6). These texts illustrate the early Christian understanding of God as Monad, who created the material world not directly, but through the Son as intermediary.

MONOTHEISM CONFRONTED BY JESUS AND THE SPIRIT

We have traced the development of different types of monotheism from the third millennium BCE to the time of Jesus. Jesus himself was a monotheist. But Christians were called Christians because they followed Christ, not merely the monotheistic God alone; the point is inherent in the very name. For Christians God is God, certainly; but his Son is also someone greater than human, someone divine. What were Christians to do with Jesus? And further, what of the Holy Spirit? Jesus was clearly anointed with the Holy Spirit, and early Christian experience was filled with encounters of the divine, with Jesus himself and the Spirit. Yet many New Testament passages left the Holy Spirit out of the discussion. The last verse cited above (1 Cor. 8:6) indicates a problem that we barely recognize today: it leaves out entirely any mention of the Holy Spirit.

The reason for this lack is the fact that Christians had not yet developed their central doctrine of God, the Trinity itself. It is fair to say that no one in the first century was a Trinitarian as the doctrine was later defined in the creeds of the fourth century. Trinitarianism was stimulated by the worship of the one God, the worship of Jesus as Son of God, and the sense of the presence of God in the experience of the Spirit; in addition, Christians were baptized and blessed in the threefold name of God. Trinitarianism arose as a brilliant solution to a long series of questions that began to be asked in order to define the relationship of Jesus to the Father, and then the role of the Holy Spirit. Only a few of the questions and none of the eventual answers had yet been formulated in the first century.

First Corinthians 8:6 has been termed a "binitarian" formulation, and it clearly embarrassed scribes who copied the text in later times. In manuscripts stemming from after the era of the creeds of the fourth century, we find that scribes added a third article to the binitarian formula: "and one Holy Spirit, in whom are all things, and we exist in it." In the time of the New Testament, however, not only had the relationship between Father and Son not been clarified, but the very nature of the Holy Spirit had not been defined or even understood.

The main difficulty was that the River of God had not supplied a "doctrine" of the Spirit. There had not been a clear concept of the Holy Spirit before the Christian era; no such doctrine seemed necessary. In the old cultures of the ancient Near East there were two basic choices for fulfilling the function that the Christian Holy Spirit was later to fill: either the god or goddess in question did the job directly (that is, performed some mighty deed, such as creation or the flood, or filled some individual with power or skill or courage), or a lesser spirit was sent to do the same job.

For example, in classical Greece, Apollo himself would "possess" the Pythia, the prophetess at the Greek cult center of Delphi, and she would utter ecstatic language, "speaking in tongues." Her speech would then be translated and interpreted into Greek by the priests. Euripides described the process of ecstatic inspiration of the prophetess, writing that "wildly she flings her golden hair, as the god breathes in her soul the frenzy of foresight" (*Iphigenia at Aulis* 759–761). The "spirit" of the god was his breath; the basic meaning of the word *spirit* itself (in Greek, *pneuma*) is "breath" or "wind." Thus Apollo "breathed" out his inspiring breath into the prophetess.

On the other hand, a god or goddess might send a lesser spiritual being to fulfill a particular function. Socrates, for example, had a *daimonion* (Greek for a "lesser divinity") that directed him throughout his life. In the view of the Greek tradition, then, the enormous debt owed by Christians to Socrates and his pupil Plato is to be attributed, in part, to a lesser divine spirit sent from God to Socrates. Similarly, in the Old Testament God could act directly, or an agent—the angel of the Lord, for example, or another one of the heavenly host—could act at God's direction. God could even send a spirit to inspire prophets falsely, as he sent a lying spirit to deceive the prophets of King Ahab (1 Kings 22:23).

The choices available, then, were that God would act directly or that God would send an agent spirit. If God acted directly, that could be described as "the Spirit of God," meaning God's breath or power or influence acting. In Hebrew, the word "spirit" (*ruah*) is grammatically feminine, and so the male God Yahweh sent his female Ruah as agent. Far back in time, the male high god nearly always had a female wife or consort. In Israel this consort had become God's agent in creation, Lady Wisdom of Proverbs 8.

Philo of Alexandria, an older contemporary of Jesus, in applying Greek philosophy to the Bible, described the divine Logos as follows: "His Father is God, who is likewise Father of all, and his mother is Wisdom, through whom the universe came into existence" (*De Fuga et Inventione* 109).

By a process we cannot trace in specifics, but one that clearly continued, Jewish Christians of the early Christian period understood this Lady Spirit to be the mother of Jesus. Thus in the East among Jewish Christians, there was an early Trinity of Father, Mother (= Spirit), and Son. Origen (ca. 185–ca. 254), one of the church's most brilliant exegetes, quotes from the noncanonical *Gospel According to the Hebrews*, where the Savior himself says, "My mother, the Holy Spirit, took me by one of my hairs and bore me away to a great mountain, Tabor" (*Commentary on John* 2.6). Another text of the same era, the *Gospel of Philip*, uses the "fact" of the female gender of the Holy Spirit to attack the doctrine of the virgin birth: "Some said, 'Mary conceived by the Holy Spirit.' They are in error. . . . When did a woman ever conceive by a woman?" (*NHC* 2, 3.55.23–26). Early on there was no place for a male high god, his female consort, and a third separate entity, the Holy Spirit of the high god. If there was a third, as in Canaan, it was the main son who acted as agent, as Baal did for El (the Father) and Elah/Asherah (the wife/consort).

Such a Trinity of Father, Mother, and Son found among Jewish Christians in Syria can easily be understood as a development of this very old Semitic tradition. It contains one major element important for later times: that the Spirit is a divine being in its own right, less than but still of the same sort as the Father. A problem arises, however, because the Spirit is "older" than the Son, as the Mother who generates a child. The continuation of the quotation above from Origen addresses just this issue, that in this variety of Jewish Christianity the Mother generates the Son, while in his own understanding (which took centuries to become orthodoxy), the Son generates the "Mother" (= Holy Spirit). Origen observed that one who thinks the Holy Spirit is the Mother "will also be at a loss as to how the mother of Christ can be the Holy Spirit which came into being through the Word" (*Commentary on John* 2.6). Origen was reading the Gospel of John in the light of Greek tradition, in which the Son breathes on his disciples the Holy Spirit (John 20:22), just as the breath of Apollo, the son of Zeus, was given to his inspired devotees.

For the non-Semitic-speaking church, the issue of a feminine Holy Spirit never arose. The version of the Old Testament used by that church had been translated into Greek (the Septuagint), and later into Latin. In Greek, the Hebrew term *ruah* (= spirit) was translated by *pneuma*, which was grammatically neuter, an "it." In Latin the term was *spiritus*, grammatically masculine. In these languages—the two most important for the growth of the church in the Roman empire—a wholly new understanding of the relationship between the Father, Son, and Spirit had to arise. The old Canaanite models, with their families of gods, could not help; the Holy Spirit as "Mother" did not work if the Spirit was an "it" (in Greek) or a "he" (in Latin). For the Christianity of the empire, the Mother of God was to become someone quite different from the neuter or masculine Spirit. Isis of Egypt, queen of heaven, suckling her divine son, would become a symbol of divine grace and mercy far beyond her original national boundaries.

There were still other options for understanding the Holy Spirit. One possibility was to see the Spirit as Christ himself, Christ as spiritual being both before his incarnation and after he had become the resurrected one. Paul taught that Jesus was the "life-giving spirit," contrasting this heavenly being with the earthly Adam who was merely a "living soul" (1 Cor. 15:45). Perhaps the spiritual resurrected Jesus was now the Spirit of God. The book of Acts relates that the "spirit of Jesus" did not permit Paul and his companions to go into Bythinia (Acts 16:7). In addition, church writers often referred to the pre-incarnate Christ as the Spirit. So Hermas, a Christian author of second-century Rome, writes: "The preexisting Holy Spirit that created all creation, God made to dwell in flesh" (*Mandate* 5.6.5). Here the Holy Spirit, the agent creator, became incarnate as Christ. Commenting on Luke 1:35 (where Gabriel announces the coming birth of Jesus to Mary, saying, "The Holy Spirit will come upon you, and the power of the most high will overshadow you"), Justin Martyr (ca. 100–165) writes, "The Spirit and the Power from God cannot rightly be thought of as anything else except the Logos, who is also the firstborn of God . . ." (*1 Apology* 33). For Justin, what happened at the incarnation was that the Logos of God, the pre-incarnate Christ, simply entered into the womb of Mary to be born as Jesus. So the Holy Spirit was seen to be the Logos and not the third member of the Trinity. The *Epistle of 2 Clement,* in a wonderfully spiritual understanding of the relationship of the incarnation and the church, declares: "If we say that the flesh is the church, and the Spirit is Christ, of course, one who has abused the flesh has abused the church. Such a one therefore will not receive the Spirit, which is Christ" (*2 Clement* 13.4). The Spirit of God, according to the author, is Christ indwelling the church.

Another less exalted option was still available, inherited from the old tradition that God would often send a lesser divine spirit to accomplish his will. Speaking of the angels, the book of Hebrews declares, "Are not all angels spirits in the divine service, sent to serve for the sake of those who are to inherit salvation?" (1:14). It was a very old idea that every person—in fact, everything alive in the world—had a lesser divinity that oversaw its welfare, a guardian angel.

Jesus himself had warned in the Gospel of Matthew not to despise any of the "little ones, for, I tell you, in heaven their angels continually see the face of my Father in heaven" (Matt. 18:10). He likewise commanded John, in the book of Revelation, to send letters to the angels who oversaw the seven churches. The first letter in the series begins, "To the angel of the church at Ephesus, write: . . ." (Rev. 2:1). The letters themselves are of wonderful spiritual merit for any Christian reader, but the admonitions of each letter were for the original addressee, the angel who was responsible in the spiritual realm for the welfare of its church.

Higher-level angels oversaw whole nations. The book of Daniel describes a conflict between "the Prince of Persia," the archangel who was responsible for the rule of the nation of the Persians, and the angel who was sent to Daniel to reveal to him the answer to his prayer. An even higher angel, Michael, came to his aid (Dan. 10:13).

The angels as individual ministering spirits became one way of understanding the Holy Spirit in the life of the individual Christian. Justin Martyr, writing his first defense of the Christian faith to the emperor Antoninus Pius about 155, declared that Christians worshiped not the pagan gods, but instead worshiped "him [the Father], and the Son who came from him and taught us these things, and the army of the other good angels who follow him and are made like him, and the prophetic Spirit" (*1 Apology* 6). In the place where we would expect the Holy Spirit, we find first a list of angels followed by "the prophetic Spirit."

Another interesting example occurs in Paul's discussion of prophetic activity in the Corinthian church. There was, as we can surmise from Paul's polemics, a great deal of disorder in the church when individual members began speaking in tongues and prophesying. One church member would "receive a revelation" (1 Cor. 14:30) and begin speaking out what had been revealed at the same time that a neighbor was speaking in tongues or relating a previous revelation. Two or three or four people speaking at once produced cacophony, so Paul recommended that each speak in turn, whether in tongues or prophetically, "for the spirits of prophets are subject to prophets" (1 Cor. 14:32).

How one is to interpret the phrase "the spirits of prophets" is not entirely clear. The phrase is plural and therefore cannot refer to the singular Holy Spirit. From the point of view of later interpretation, the phrase is often taken to mean the human spirit of individuals. But we are looking at this text from the viewpoint of the ancients, and in their world such an interpretation would have been impossible. In their view of human psychology, the human spirit was one's highest faculty; it was the "you" to whom all else in one's life was to be subject. There was no other proper ruling entity within. From this viewpoint, Paul would be saying, "You are subject to yourself," which is nonsense. In addition, quite obviously, the "spirits of prophets" were what made the prophets prophesy. So the "spirits of prophets" had to be something other and greater than a mere human faculty.

What that something is may be seen in a highly respected work of the second century, *The Shepherd of Hermas*. Hermas was the name of a second-century Christian author, and the shepherd of the title was a guardian angel who revealed to Hermas visions of the condition of the church. The book had a wide currency and was used as Scripture in many Christian churches. In one important passage, false and true prophets are contrasted. The false prophet prophesies, the passage asserts, while inspired by a counterfeit spirit from the Devil. The true prophet prophesies only when prompted by the divine spirit. Yet, as in Paul, the individual prophet is given an individual spirit of prophecy: "Every spirit given from God is not to be questioned, but having the power of divinity it speaks everything from itself, because it is from above from the power of the divine spirit" (*Mandate* 11.5). Here a lesser spirit from the divine spirit inspires the individual prophet. The Holy Spirit, the angelic divine spirit, and the individual divine spirit are all mentioned together in the following:

> Whenever the one who has the divine spirit comes into the gathering of righteous men who have faithfulness of divine spirit, and intercessory prayer is made to God by the gathering of those men, then the angel of the prophetic spirit which rests on him fills the person, and being filled with the Holy Spirit, the person speaks to the crowd just as the Lord wants. (*Mandate* 11.9)

So the Holy Spirit sends an angelic, individual divine spirit to inspire the prophet. This passage may also help us understand why those speaking in tongues speak the "tongues of . . . angels" (1 Cor. 13:1).

The understanding of the Spirit as either Christ himself or an angel was clearly inadequate to explain passages that distinguished Jesus and the Spirit (as when the Spirit descended on Jesus at his baptism and inaugurated his ministry [Mark 1:10]) or that gave the Spirit much more exalted roles than those ascribed to angels (such as its role in creation: "The Spirit of God brooded over the face of the waters" [Gen. 1:2]). Even here there was no clarity: many Jewish Christians thought that the dove was the Christ that descended on the man Jesus and that the "Spirit" of Genesis 1:2 was what it seemed literally to be, a "wind" from God blowing over the ocean deep. There was no theoretical framework in Scripture that explained the relationship of the Father, Son, and Spirit. No Old Testament author addressed the issue of a separate being, the Holy Spirit, and its ("her," in Hebrew) relationship to the Father; the Spirit of God was God's "spirit" or breath that carried his power.

Likewise, no New Testament author addressed the interrelationship of Father, Son, and Spirit. There are triadic formulations in the New Testament, such as the command to baptize "in the name of the Father and the Son and the Holy Spirit" (Matt. 28:19), and the prayer of blessing that "the grace of the Lord Jesus Christ and the love of God and the fellowship of the Holy Spirit be with you all" (2 Cor. 13:14). But all of these have to do with how God relates to the church. None explains how the Father, Son, and Holy Spirit relate to each other in essence. That task fell to a particularly influential group of "heretics"—Gnostic Christians of the second century.

THE TRINITY AND INCLUSIVE MONOTHEISM

The story of the development of the doctrine of the Trinity is the story of monotheism confronted by Jesus and the Holy Spirit. For Christians, the obvious divine presence in Jesus and the Holy Spirit required a new understanding, required that a place be found for them in the one God; but where, and how? Three major complexes of ideas were at play on both a popular and a scholarly level, stemming from forces long at work in the religious development of the ancient Near East: inclusive monotheism, exclusive monotheism, and emanationism, the old answer to the problem of the One and the many. Let us look first at how inclusive monotheism influenced one concept of the Trinity.

Almost (but not quite) invisible to us today is one of the earliest and most common popular understandings of the Trinity—a perspective known as *modalism*—known to us only from a time when ancient scholars began to take it seriously. Modalism claimed that the one God had appeared in three successive stages as Father, Son, and then Spirit. Our New Testament and other early Christian texts were in general written by highly educated individuals more sophisticated in outlook than the majority of their uneducated contemporaries. The unsophisticated, however, made up by far the largest part of the early churches, and it was they who embraced modalism.

The constant propaganda of religious and political authorities for most of the three millennia of empire-builders had been that of inclusive monotheism: the one high God came in many forms, under many divine names, and held sway over all lands. In addition, stories had been told throughout the ancient world, including Israel, of the appearances of God or individual gods on earth in human form. In the most influential tales of the Greek world, Homer's *Iliad* and *Odyssey*, gods time and again took on human form and dimension and appeared on earth to influence human events, often changing their appearance to look like someone else. Athena, for example, changed herself into the form of Hector's brother Deiphobos in order to deceive him into fighting Achilles (*Iliad* 22.227).

Likewise in the Bible, Adam and Eve encountered "the Lord God walking in the garden at the time of the evening breeze" (Gen. 3:8). Three "men" appeared to Abraham in order to secure the destruction of Sodom and Gomorrah, one of whom was said to be Yahweh (Gen. 18). In the town of Lystra, Paul and Barnabas were taken for Hermes and Zeus because they healed a lame man;

the townspeople declared, "The gods have become like men and have come down to us" (Acts 14:11). Just so, Jesus, as God on earth, was worshiped by those whom he healed or who saw his miracles (John 9:38; Matt. 14:33). Two factors were at work in these accounts: the one God (of inclusive monotheism) could become human (at least in appearance) and walk the earth.

Tertullian, writing about the year 200 in his work *Against Praxias*, left us an important record of the viewpoint of the majority of Christians during his time. In his own presentation of the doctrine of the Trinity, he used the Greek term *oikonomia* ("economy, dispensation") to describe how the one God was "dispensed" or distributed in three Persons. Yet in trying to persuade his fellow Christians of this new view, he clearly came up against some rather hostile opposition. He responded:

> The simple, indeed,—I will not call them unwise and unlearned—who always constitute the majority of believers, are startled at the dispensation (of the Three in One), on the ground that their very rule of faith withdraws them from the world's plurality of gods to the one only true God. . . . The numerical order and distribution of the Trinity they assume to be a division of unity. . . . They are constantly throwing out against us that we are preachers of two gods and three gods, while they take to themselves pre-eminently the credit of being worshipers of the one God. (*Against Praxias* 3)

The majority view, if Tertullian's estimation is correct, was that God (the Father) transformed himself into Jesus (the Son) and walked the earth as a man, just as in the traditional stories of the gods. From the accusation against Tertullian and his cohorts that they were preaching "two gods and three gods," we see that again the Holy Spirit was at least at times left out of consideration. According to the more sophisticated of the modalists, the Father became Jesus at the incarnation, and Jesus at the ascension became the Holy Spirit. So for those who held this popular view, the entire time, there was only one God in three transformations.

The language "one God in three persons" would even work. The Latin word *persona* originally referred to the mask that an actor wore to mark the character being played on stage; it then became used for the role or character itself. So one God played three roles — not simultaneously, but successively.

This modalistic view of the Trinity was not only a natural deduction given the cultural traditions of the Greco-Roman world, it was also, apparently, the view prevalent in the church of Rome in the decades surrounding the year 200. We learn from one of the most educated members of the Roman church, Hippolytus (ca. 170–ca. 236), that both Zephirinus, bishop (the equivalent of "pope" in later terms) of Rome from 198 to 217, and his successor Callistus, bishop of Rome from 217 to 222, were modalists. Hippolytus called modalism "the heresy of Noetus" (*Refutation* 9.5). He reports that Noetus, a native of Smyrna on the west coast of Asia Minor, was called to defend his views before the presbyters of Smyrna. Noetus declared to them, "What evil, then, am I doing in glorifying Christ?" (*Against Noetus* 1). His devotion to Christ as God was the basis of his doctrine: Christ was his God.

Callistus, who according to Hippolytus was a follower of Noetus's teaching, made the counterclaim against Hippolytus and others that they were "worshipers of two gods" (*Refutation* 9.6). Callistus seems to have influenced one of the most important modalists of all, Sabellius, and modalism is sometimes called simply "Sabellianism." Tertullian wrote in anger of their fundamental claim about themselves: "We . . . maintain the Monarchy" (*Against Praxias* 3). Tertullian himself defined the term *monarchy* as "the single and individual rule of God" — that is, classical monotheism: the modalists were strict monotheists. Callistus's accusation points out the obvious difficulties that those who advocated one or another type of Trinity were facing: charges of polytheism. Note again the (near) absence of the Holy Spirit: Callistus's charge was against the Trinitarians advancing *two* gods, not *three*.

The great value of modalism was that not only did it meld readily with the stories of the gods in the popular mind, it also quite easily preserved the monotheism to which every Christian was committed. The difficulties, however, that the texts of the New Testament presented for modalism were legion, and they eventually proved fatal. Modalist teachers relied on such texts as "I am the Lord and there is no other" (Isa. 45:5), and "I and the Father are one" (John 10:30), and "Whoever has seen me has seen the Father" (John 14:9). Opponents asked questions such as, To whom was Jesus praying in the Garden of Gethsemane, if he was the Father? Modalism was sarcastically labeled "patripassionism," for if Jesus was the Father, then the Father underwent the suffering of the cross. That was ridiculous to the Trinitarians but readily admitted by modalists.

How was it possible, one may ask, that so many Christians as late as the 220s—perhaps the majority—could hold a view of God such as modalism? The answer lies in the fact that nearly all religion, especially ancient religion, was based in oral tradition. The gospel was spread and Christians were instructed in the faith almost entirely by the spoken word, with little or no benefit of text. Systems of interpretation and sets of doctrines were formed in discussions, preaching, exchanges between individuals, arguments, and reflection. There was as yet no authoritative church creed. There was no orthodoxy, no "true doctrine." Modalism was in the River and seemed to many—apparently to most—like the obvious solution to the "problem" of the three Persons of God.

Modalism was defeated because educated Christians read the written Gospels closely and found the modalist perspective impossible to reconcile with the texts. But few Christians could read. Only about ten percent of people in the Roman Empire could read in any case,[3] and those were generally in the upper classes. In the early period, Christian churches did not draw many from the upper classes: the apostle Paul wrote that "not many wise, . . . not many noble" were to be found in the churches (1 Cor. 1:26).

In addition, until relatively late in the second century, there was no New Testament. The "heretic" Marcion, teaching in Rome during the 140s, was the first to produce a New Testament, in which he included ten epistles of Paul and a shortened version of Luke's Gospel. Few churches had any authoritative texts at all. Texts of any sort were prohibitively expensive; a single sheet of papyrus (ancient paper) could cost two-thirds the daily wage of a common laborer. In addition, any texts a church did have could as easily have been "heretical" as not. We know of eighty Gospels that were written and used in the churches of the first two or three centuries. In the late second century, Irenaeus had to argue that only (our canonical) four were acceptable, indicating that more or fewer than four were to be found in use in various churches at that late date. By Tertullian's time, Christian teaching based on written Christian texts was still in its early stages. The date of the attack on modalism is instructive and significant: modalism could not be countered until there were authoritative New Testament Scriptures, and a New Testament did not begin to exist until late in the second century.

THE TRINITY AND EXCLUSIVE MONOTHEISM

Exclusive monotheism, developed originally in Persia and Egypt and then inherited by Israel after the Exile, also had a profound influence on early Christian conceptions of the Trinity. In the old world of Canaan, the idea that there was one high god, served by lesser divine beings or angels, had deep roots: El was high god served by one main son, Baal. In Israel, God was served by his great angel, the Angel of the Lord. The vision of God and "one like a son of man" in Daniel 7 is just such a picture, drawn from the imagery of El and Baal:[4]

> I kept looking until thrones were set up, and the Ancient of Days took His seat; His vesture was like white snow and the hair of His head like pure wool. His throne was ablaze with flames. Its wheels were a burning fire. . . . I kept looking in the

night visions, and behold, with the clouds of heaven One like a
son of man was coming, and He came up to the Ancient of Days
and was presented before Him. (Dan. 7:9, 13, NASB)

Here someone in human form ("one like a son of man") stands
before the God of Israel to receive a kingdom. One of the most
enigmatic designations of Jesus for himself is "son of man," a designation that clearly would have brought this passage to mind.
Based on this picture, by melding old Canaanite religion with
monotheism, many early Christians understood Jesus to be the
agent or servant of the one God, in a role clearly subordinate to the
Father. Exclusive monotheism would not allow that there be
another deity of the same rank as the Father, another God who
could stand beside the One.

On a popular level, this view also ran deep in the storytelling of
religious myth in several cultures. The fact that Jesus was also and
often called Son of God seemed to clinch identification with any
number of sons of Zeus or El, all of whom were divine, though
lesser than and servants of their fathers. In Israel the angels, too,
were often called sons of God (e.g., Job 38:7, Ps. 29:1). God's
agent did not even have to be divine at all: in Jewish tradition, the
son of God could be the King (e.g., 2 Sam. 7:14, Ps. 89:26), or the
people of Israel as a whole (e.g., Exod. 4:22, Jer. 31:9).

The idea that Jesus was not divine was furthered by a statement attributed to Jesus in the Gospel of Mark: when Jesus was
addressed by a questioner as "good teacher," he replied, "Why do
you call me good? No one is good but God alone" (Mark 10:18).
He seemed to say that he was not God. The very common, almost
ubiquitous, designation "Son of God" placed Jesus in a role less
than and subordinate to the Father. In his own words, according
to the Gospel of John, "The Father is greater than I" (John
14:28). Both of these verses were favorites of those who cast Jesus
in a subordinate, non-Trinitarian role.

The theology among second-century Roman and earlier Jewish
Christians of Palestine and Syria that understood there to be but

one God alone, served by a lesser "Son," was known as *adoption-ism*. The name came from their idea that the man Jesus was "adopted" by the Father to become the Son because of his personal righteousness. Hippolytus describes the opinions of one such group:

> They say that Jesus was justified because he accomplished the Law; therefore he was named Christ and Son of God, since none of the prophets completed the Law. For if some other one also accomplished the commandments in the Law, that one would be the Christ; they themselves are likewise able to become Christs, if they would accomplish the Law. For in fact they say that he was a man like all men. (Hippolytus, *Refutation* 7.32.4, trans. GJR)

Jesus was adopted by the Father to become the Christ because he was the first and only one to have fulfilled the Law. This was, in fact, the interpretation placed on a passage in the Gospel of Matthew where Jesus said, "Do not think that I came to abolish the Law or the Prophets; I did not come to abolish but to fulfill. . . . [N]ot the smallest letter or stroke shall pass away from the Law until it is all accomplished" (Matt. 5:17–18). Jesus was the only one who had been able to fulfill the entire Law, and was therefore, according to the adoptionist view, chosen to become the Christ.

One of the most unsettling aspects of these particular Christians is that they may have been the original conservative Jewish Christians of Palestine. Their name, the "Ebionites," was derived from the Hebrew term *ebionim*, which means "the Poor." They seem to have taken their name from the saying of Jesus, "Blessed are the poor" (Matt. 5:3). They may be those referred to when James, Peter, and John ask Paul to "remember the poor" at their historic meeting in Jerusalem (Gal. 2:10). It is impossible to imagine that up to that time, after more than a decade of apostolic ministry, Paul had forgotten to help poor people. In addition, the next significant addition to Paul's mission was to institute the collection for the Jerusalem church. Thus "the poor" in question may well have been these early Jewish Christians in Jerusalem and Palestine.

The signal doctrine of the Ebionites was that Jesus was a mere man, fathered not by God but by Joseph, and that he was elevated to become Son of God because of his personal righteousness. Eusebius of Caesarea plays humorously on their name in describing their views:

> The ancients properly called these people Ebionites, because they held poor and humble opinions concerning Christ. For they thought him a plain and common man, justified by the fact alone of his progress in ethics, born from intercourse of a man and Mary. (*History of the Church* 3.27.1–2)

Even more so than the inclusive monotheism of modalism, exclusive monotheism was championed by a long line of highly educated teachers and church leaders. For them, the Father alone was God; the Son was a mere man or an angel, even the highest of angels; and the Spirit—few had an understanding of the Spirit as a person as yet, no matter what their doctrine. Several such teachers were prominent figures in Rome, teaching in willful contradiction to the prevalent modalism that was supported or allowed to flourish by bishops Zephirinus and Callistus. But far more important than this teaching in Rome was a school of thought in Syria of the third century that continued the local early tradition of strict monotheism and subordinationist views of Christ.

Paul of Samosata was born of Christian parents in a major city on the Euphrates in the Roman province of Syria. Eventually he went west and by talent and pastoral skill became bishop of Antioch about 260. Antioch was the third-largest city in the Roman empire, after Rome and Alexandria, Egypt. The early center of Christianity outside Palestine, it was the home church of the apostle Paul and the likely place of the writing of the Gospel of Luke. It was here that followers of Jesus were first called Christians (Acts 11:26).

While bishop, Paul of Samosata was accused of reviving the

heresy of Artemon, one of the many teachers of adoptionist Christology, which had been current in Rome in prior decades. It is much more likely, however, that Paul's doctrine was indigenous to his eastern homeland and that he was teaching what eastern Christians had taught him. Palestine and Syria were the native land of Jewish Christians who had held similar views apparently from the beginning of the Christian movement. Paul was formally accused of heresy more than once by his fellow presbyters in Antioch. Eusebius of Caesarea quotes a letter written by the assembly that finally condemned him; in addition to denigrating his character, it describes his doctrines: "He will not admit that the Son of God came down from heaven, . . . not merely stating the fact but proving it from passage after passage . . . , especially where he says that Jesus Christ is 'from below'" (*History of the Church* 7.30).

That Jesus was called Son of God means today that he was divine, but among Jewish Christians of the early centuries, it meant that Jesus was a mere human, appointed to the high position of Son of God. The king of Israel was traditionally declared to be Son of God at his coronation: "You are my son; today I have begotten you" (Ps. 2:7). So Paul of Samosata, bishop of the third largest city in the empire, proved from verse after verse in Scripture that Jesus was "from below," a mere man who had been proclaimed and adopted as Son of God. He did so knowing quite well, one must assume, that he might lose his position in the church, and indeed that came to pass: in 268 he was deposed.

Paul of Samosata was accused of the many moral lapses that are almost requirements for the famous in religion today: pride, love of money, questionable practices with women (though he was not accused of sexual immorality). We do not have anything in his own words, nor did his (victorious) opponents preserve his personal defense. "Heretics" are almost always branded with a host of evils, but the branding tends to obscure the logic and historical derivation of their position. Paul was both an exclusive monotheist and a Christian, and his rise and fall were but another episode in a long line of Christians who attempted to defend the monotheism they had inherited from the River of God. He would soon be followed by others, more committed to personal piety than he and more heroic in devotion to the faith as they understood it.

The greatest challenge that the developing Trinitarian doctrine faced was that of a school of Christian scholars founded by Lucian of Antioch. Like Paul, Lucian was also born in Samosata and eventually settled in Antioch. He was ordained presbyter of the church, and it is tempting to guess that he was ordained by Paul himself. Lucian was martyred in Nicomedia, the imperial capital of the east, in 312, after being imprisoned in 303 at the beginning of the Great Persecution and enduring ten years of torture. Eusebius of Caesarea says of him:

> Lucian, a man of the highest character, self-disciplined and steeped in divinity, a presbyter of the Antioch diocese, was taken to Nicomedia, where the emperor happened to be staying. Before the ruler he put forth his defense of the doctrine he upheld, and was sent to prison and to death. (*History of the Church* 9.6)

Lucian had presented the faith to the emperor himself, and his courage cost him ten years of prison and finally life itself. As a result of his sanctity and faithfulness, he was elevated to the status of saint as a martyr of the church—a saint to whom the mother of Constantine, Helena, was especially devoted.[5] Nevertheless, he was a key player on the losing side in one the most important doctrinal crises the church ever faced.

Lucian founded a theological school that numbered among its students some of the most important opponents of Trinitarianism in church history, two of whom were Arius (ca. 260–336) and Eusebius of Nicomedia (died ca. 342). The most significant figure in the controversy was Arius, from whom the movement Arianism gets its name. Given the fact that his opponents never impugned his morals, Arius, like Lucian before him, must have led an exemplary ethical life. He was ordained a priest in Alexandria and was appointed preacher in the church of Baucalis, one of the principle churches of the city, where he achieved marked success as a popular teacher. Already nearly sixty years old, Arius espoused his characteristic subordinationist doctrines.

Arius and his fellow teachers were reacting to the growing Trinitarian movement that had begun at the end of the second century. They understood Trinitarianism to be a compromise of monotheism, if not outright polytheism. The doctrines that he and the others of the Arian party advocated were derived from traditions found in Greek philosophy and Judaism that had been developed in both Alexandria and Palestine. For Arius, God was the eternal and unknowable Monad of Greek philosophy: he alone was ingenerate, alone eternal, alone without beginning; he was the source and origin of everything. From the exclusivist camp they took the further step of applying Isaiah 45:5 ("I am the Lord and beside me there is no other") to the Monad, thereby eliminating emanation as a possible divine activity. For the Arians, the essence of God was incommunicable, lest he be diminished, divided, or changed. His nature was unchangeable, and therefore indivisible. The argument that a parent is not divided or diminished by bearing children held no sway, for if another were to share God's essence, there would be a plurality of divine beings (polytheism).

Christ, the Logos, was for the Arians not like God the Father by nature, but was a creature. God was not always a Father: in one of the Arians' favorite formulations, "There was when the Son was not." The Son was not eternal, but had been created by the Father out of nothing. Yet he was a divine being as one might speak of the angels—indeed, even higher; he was the "uniquely born one" (in Greek, *monogenes*), as the highest and firstborn of all creatures, and creator of all else. He was god and unchangeable, but unchangeable by choice, not by nature. As an incarnated being, Jesus was subject to temptations and free to sin, yet he did not sin by resolute action of his will. He learned righteousness and progressed to the point of unchangeability. Thus the core of the Arian controversy had in its background the exclusive monotheism of Jewish

Christianity presented in far more sophisticated philosophical terms.[6] Yet the continuity is unmistakable: there was but one true God, served by the Son, a creature promoted to the status of a god.

The controversy spread quickly, supported by other disciples of Lucian. Alexander, bishop of Alexandria (312–328), excommunicated Arius in 321 at a council of the clergy of Alexandria. Arius appealed for support in a letter to his friend Eusebius of Nicomedia, bishop of the imperial city of the east. The letter reads in part:

> To my beloved lord, the faithful man of God, the orthodox Eusebius. Arius, who is persecuted unjustly by the pope Alexander for the sake of the all-conquering faith which you too champion, sends greetings in the Lord. . . . [Alexander] the bishop is assaulting and persecuting us greatly and employing every device against us, so that he has expelled us from the city as atheists because we do not agree with him when he says publicly, "Always God, always the Son. At the same time the Father, at the same time the Son. The Son co-exists ingenerately with God; he is ever begotten; he is ingenerately begotten. Neither in thought nor by a single moment does God proceed the Son. Always God, always the Son. The Son is of God himself." . . .
>
> We cannot endure to hear these impieties, if the heretics threaten us with a thousand deaths! What we say and believe we have taught and still teach: that the Son is not ingenerate or a part of the ingenerate in any way, nor from any underlying matter, but that he came into being by God's will and counsel before all time and ages, full God, only begotten and unchangeable; and before he was begotten or created or founded he did not exist. For he was not ingenerate. We are persecuted because we said, "The Son has a beginning; God is without a beginning." For that we are persecuted and because we said that "he is from nothing." We said so, because he is not part of God. . . . For that we are persecuted. You know the rest.

Farewell in the Lord, remembering our tribulations, fellow
student of Lucius, truly Eusebius.

Arius calls Eusebius "orthodox" and the Trinitarians "heretics."
He says that Alexander has expelled him from the city as an athe-
ist, which he most decidedly was not; the real charge was that he
did not accept the full deity of the Son. The letter elsewhere
includes the claim that almost all the bishops of the east were in
agreement with Arius. It closes with a compliment to his friend,
"truly Eusebius": the name itself in Greek means "reverent, pious."

THE TRINITY AND THE FAMILIES OF
THE GODS: EMANATIONISM

Exclusive monotheism and subordinationist views of Jesus persisted, especially in the east, from the beginning of the church into
the seventh century and later. At the same time, the other main
lines of tradition from the River of God were both current and
developing in the now Christian tradition. Inclusive monotheism
was expressed in various types of modalism. The oldest of all, emanationism, (stemming originally from the old stories of the gods
producing families out of their own bodies) had been "upgraded"
by Greek science into the spiritual realm of the Monad, who
"emanated" spiritual offspring without a body at all. The church
was faced with an almost impossible—some today still claim that it
is impossible—task: how to understand the One and the Three.
The eventual solution availed itself of all three major ways of view-
ing the divine nature: God is exclusively One, but includes the
Three, because the One is understood to have emanated and
shares its very essence with the Two.

The third major way of understanding the divine nature, emanationism, was developed out of old family models of the gods by
Greek philosophers addressing the problem of the One and the
many. Their ideas had been taken up by pre-Christian Jewish

scholars who had directed Greek philosophy toward biblical religion. Some, such as Philo of Alexandria (a contemporary of Jesus), constructed a positive philosophical interpretation of Judaism; others, such as Jewish Gnostics, a negative one. Nevertheless, Greek philosophical understanding of the one God, the Monad, who emanated a series of divine beings around itself—beings known as the "fullness" (in Greek, *pleroma*) of God—was in place in the pre-Christian era.

It is in this stream of tradition that one must place the Gospel of John, the most important biblical text for the development of the Christian understanding of God. It is hard to overestimate the influence of the language and concepts in the Gospel of John for later orthodoxy: without it there would be no Trinitarianism. No other New Testament book except Hebrews contains the necessary conceptual framework—the idea of emanation, which became the very foundation of Trinitarian theology.

In John 8:42 Jesus states, "I proceeded forth and have come from God." In this and like verses, the origin of the Son of God is described quite differently from texts outside John. For example, in Philippians 2:6–8 Jesus is described as "being in the form of God" before his appearance on earth, rather than "proceeding forth from God" as John 8:42 has it. In other words, John describes the process of emanation of the Son from God, not simply the fact of his divinity. The presupposition of emanation is that the Son is in some way of the substance of the Father. The same idea is found in the unique emphasis on sonship itself in John, expressed in language from the families of the gods millennia old, now put to new Christian use: Jesus "was calling God his own father, making himself equal with God" (5:18). That is why it is possible in John (and only in John) for Jesus to say, "I and the Father are one" (10:30), or "He who has seen me has seen the Father" (14:9), or "I am in the Father and the Father is in me" (14:10). This does not mean that Jesus is the Father, as modalism claimed; rather, it means that the essence of the Son, the "stuff" that the Son is made of, is the essence of the Father.

There were, nevertheless, difficulties for Trinitarianism within the Gospel of John, as the centuries of controversy showed quite clearly: John could be used by "orthodox" and "heretic" alike. One finds in John a number of verses that identify the Father and Son, as noted just above ("I and the Father are one") — verses that were used by modalists. One finds, on the other hand, a strong tendency to subordinate the Son to the Father — verses that were used to advantage by subordinationists and Arians. For example, "The Son can do nothing of himself, unless it is something he sees the Father doing" (5:19), or "I do nothing on my own initiative, but I speak these things as the Father taught me" (8:28), or especially, "The Father is greater than I" (14:28). In addition, the Holy Spirit plays decidedly an even lesser role than Jesus. One finds, for example, that Jesus says that the Spirit "will not speak on his own, but will speak whatever he hears" (16:13), a description quite similar to the subordinate role that Jesus assigns to himself.

John calls the Holy Spirit the "Paraclete" (14:16, 26), the Greek word for "helper." The church so little understood the role of the Paraclete that in the middle of the second century a Christian prophet named Montanus in central Turkey claimed to be the Paraclete in person and founded a movement known to its members as "the New Prophecy" (denigrated by outsiders as "Montanism"). An inscription from Numidia reads: "Flavius, grandsire of the household. In the name of the Father and the Son [and] Lord Muntanus. What he promised, he performed."[7] Here the name of Montanus stands where we would expect that of the Holy Spirit. Similarly, Eusebius of Caesarea records that Mani (ca. 216–276), the founder of Manichaeism, "announced himself as the Paraclete, the Holy Spirit himself" (*History of the Church* 7.31). There was still far to go before arriving at Trinitarianism.

The Gospel of John was written near the end of the first century, probably in Syria. It is the one Gospel of the canon that shares most with Gnosticism, and is quite similar in worldview to its rough contemporary the *Gospel of Thomas*, also from Syria. Within a generation, other teachers of Gnostic philosophical orientation arose in Syria, Alexandria, and Rome. We do not know who their teachers were or the Christian schools in which they learned their doctrines, but their number and level of sophistication say much about the vitality of Christian Gnosticism of the late first and early second centuries.

Later Christianity owed much to these Gnostic teachers. Perhaps their most important contribution lay in further developing the concept and necessary language of emanation and applying these to Christian theology. Although no two of these figures taught identical doctrines or held to the same myths (something for which they were roundly criticized), common to all were the geocentric universe, the Monad, and the mechanism of emanation to explain the unfolding of the One into the many. Speaking of the personified Wisdom of God, the apocryphal book *Wisdom of Solomon* states that Wisdom "is a breath of the power of God and a pure emanation of the glory of the Almighty" (7:25). The word used here for "emanation" (in Greek, *aporroia*) means "an outflowing," especially of a stream from a spring or the like. The term was used by Gnostic teachers to describe the progressive devolution of the One as it surrounded itself with successive divine layers of the *pleroma* — that is, its "fullness." Followers of the Gnostic teacher Valentinus preferred the term *probole,* a "putting forth" (in an agricultural context, the "putting forth" by a plant of stems or leaves). Tertullian used the term *probole* with approval and adopted both images, adding a third from the book of Hebrews (1:3): "I would not hesitate to say that the Son is the growth from the root, and the river from the fountain, and the ray from the sun . . ." (*Against Praxias* 8, trans. GJR). He was here using the language of emanation developed among Gnostics to describe the relationship of the Father to the Son and Spirit.

As the One expanded, producing lesser and lesser divine beings in the *pleroma,* the layers of deity that surrounded the One were given names: in pre-Christian Gnosticism, the names were magical-sounding and derived from Hebrew, Aramaic, or Egyptian — Barbelo, Eleleth, Daveithai, Armozel, and the like. In Christian

Gnosticism, the names were often Christian names or concepts: Life, Truth, Church, and especially Jesus and the Holy Spirit. Often there seemed to be no limit to the number of such emanations. In one account of the myth-making of Basilides, an Alexandrian teacher of the first half of the second century, there were as many as 365 layers of deity surrounding the One; other texts spoke of far fewer.

The book of Colossians twice contradicts such Gnostic teaching about the unfolding of God with the claim that "all the fullness [*pleroma*] dwells in" Christ (1:19), and "in him, all the fullness of deity dwells in bodily form" (2:9). The point the author makes is that God is not surrounded by layer upon layer of lesser divine beings, but by one only, Christ; God has emanated only his Son. Note the complete absence of the Spirit; all the *pleroma* is in Christ. Nevertheless, here is the beginning of one important part of the eventual orthodox solution to the "problem" of the Trinity—the understanding that the Father emanated his divine substance, and the limiting of divine emanation to the Son and the Spirit.

We owe to these Gnostic teachers two other fundamental parts of the solution: creation out of nothing, and the use of the term *homoousios* (Greek for "consubstantial, of the same substance") to describe divine beings. Recall that ancient cultures everywhere believed that the cosmos had arisen out of chaos, out of primeval water in darkness. Even Plato thought that God, the fashioner of the universe, had formed creation out of preexistent matter. Gnostic teachers meditated on the problem of the *archai* (Greek for "first principles") and concluded that if there existed primeval chaos, then there must be *two* first principles, two eternal essences and the idea of the Monad was compromised: only the One could be eternal. Thus, they claimed, the material out of which the universe was made was not eternal, but must itself have come into being because of the Monad; it must have been emanated out of the Monad itself.

The process of emanation, however, implied a devolution of the divine substance; another meaning of the word *aporroia*, in fact, is "loss, falling away." In classic Gnostic texts, that is exactly the case: the material world is ultimately derived from the substance of the Monad—no other source could exist—but it comes into being by progressive devolution from what is spiritual and light to what is material and dark. To describe spiritual beings on the *same* level of emanation, Valentinus and his followers used (and perhaps coined) the term *homoousios* ("of the same essence"). They avoided using it, however, of the Monad and its emanations, since these devolved and were not identical in essence.

Basilides rejected this process of devolution of the divine substance as an explanation of the origin of the cosmos, in the first half of the second century. According to theologian Gerhard May, he became "the first Christian theologian known to us who speaks in the strict sense of a creation out of nothing."[8] In Basilides' view, there was but one "first principle," and the material world was not derived from the substance of the Monad; it was created from nothing at all by God's will. Thus Basilides was free to employ the term *homoousios* to God and the Son, since the Son was in fact an emanation of the substance of God. This idea spread rapidly in the controversies between Gnostic and non-Gnostic Christians. In fact, by the end of the second century, *creatio ex nihilo* had become standard Christian dogma and *homoousios* had entered Christian theological vocabulary.

THE ORTHODOX SOLUTION: THE TRINITY OF CONSTANTINOPLE IN 381

Constantine had marched victorious into Rome in 312, making him ruler of the western empire. Twelve years later, in 324, he defeated his rival in the east, Licinius, and became the sole master of the whole empire. Constantine was very much a Christian, as his letters and edicts demonstrate: he outlawed all sacrifices to the pagan gods, the creation of new statues of the gods, divination, and the consultation of pagan oracles.[9] At the end of 324, he set out to visit the territories in the east and planned then to turn south to

Egypt. While traveling he heard news of the raging Arian controversy in Egypt and its neighboring states; the crisis caused him to
cancel his plans and return to the capital.

The problem had long been smoldering in the eastern
Mediterranean. As Origen had pointed out nearly eighty years
earlier, writing from the same geographical area, "Many of those
who profess to believe in Christ differ from each other, not only in
small and trifling matters, but also on subjects of highest importance, as, for example, regarding God, or the Lord Jesus Christ, or
the Holy Spirit" (*First Principles* 1.2). By the time of Constantine,
the old fires of argument had grown into an inferno.

Constantine sent a letter to Alexander and Arius, the two main
antagonists. The letter not only attempted to heal the rift between
them, but also revealed his evaluation of the worth of their con-
tentions: "I find the cause to be of a truly insignificant character,
and quite unworthy of such fierce contention" (Eusebius, *Life of
Constantine* 2.68). The controversy is unworthy, he continued,
because such matters should be left in the obscurity they deserve:
"It was wrong in the first instance to propose such questions as
these, or to reply to them when propounded. . . . For how very few
are there able either accurately to comprehend, or adequately to
explain subjects so sublime and abstruse in their nature?" (2.69).

From Constantine's point of view, both Alexander and Arius
were quibbling because of competitive jealousy over things that
neither they nor anyone else could properly understand; by its
very nature, the subject of God's essence was "sublime and
abstruse," heavenly and hidden. According to the very claims of
both disputants, based on nearly a millennium of theological speculation, the one God was unknowable to mere human beings.
Arians claimed that the Father was unknown in his true nature
even to the Son. How could these two theologians argue so force-
fully over what they both admitted no one could know?

Unity among Christians for the sake of the progress of the
gospel (and, no doubt, political harmony) was of great importance
to Constantine. He complained that the Christian message was

being "exposed to the most shameful ridicule in the very theaters of the unbelievers" because of the public airing of dissension by partisans of both sides (2.61). Christians had until only recently been ridiculed in the arenas and then martyred, eaten by animals or burned alive. One can only guess at what kinds of ridicule the Arian controversy produced for comedians in the theaters, when potential martyrs released by Constantine's edicts of toleration were at each other's throats: "The animals weren't enough; now they're eating each other!" or, "We don't need to throw Christians to the lions; just throw them to other Christians!"

To heal the rift and bring unity to the faith, a council was held in Antioch in 325 and later that same year reconvened in Nicaea—a council that the emperor himself attended. Constantine's goal was to produce a creed that all present would agree on and sign.

Creeds: Defining the Faith

No official creeds existed in the first Christian centuries, not only because there was no doctrinal unity, but also because there was as yet no recognized central authority to oversee doctrinal formation. The churches in the early period had been founded by apostles and missionaries with differing ideas concerning the religious life: some emphasized continued obedience to the Mosaic Law, some the enlightenment of gnosis, some the walk of faith and grace. The target communities were also different: Semitic Jews, Hellenized Jews, pagans of several sorts, philosophical Greeks and Romans. So churches grew in relative independence from one another and only slowly began to draw together under the pressure of persecution and apologetic need. The teaching of the church developed over time, in response to the challenges of Judaism, paganism, and heresy. The doctrinal formulations of later generations would have seemed foreign and would certainly have been misunderstood by earlier generations. Later Christians developed new concepts and new technical language in historical contexts that did not exist early on, and as with all language, the context determined the meaning.

The term "creed" comes from the Latin verb *credo* (or *credimus*), with which many of the creeds begin: "I believe" (or "We believe"). When creeds first began to be used, the ancients themselves used the term "symbol" (in Latin, *symbolum;* in Greek, *symbolon*) to designate what we today call a creed. The term indicated a token or sign by which one could be recognized. *Symbolum* as a token of recognition was a current usage in the mystery religions: short formulae were often employed at initiations for members of the cult and were thereafter used as means of identification. Plutarch, a second-century pagan writer, referred to the "mystic symbols of the Dionysiac orgies which we who are participants share with one another" (*Consolation to his Wife.* 10.610d). Christians used various such signs: on grave markers, for example, one finds the fish, the anchor, the good shepherd, and many other non-explicit images signifying that the one buried was of the faith — images that were without Christian meaning to outsiders.[10] Among Christians, *symbolum* eventually designated the questions asked of the candidate for baptism by the officiating elder to confirm the content of faith.

Creeds developed into two forms. Baptismal (or catechetical) creeds were summaries of Christian teaching for the education of the church members themselves. They were used to separate not Christian from Christian but Christian from non-Christian, with the goal of producing educated and initiated church members. They often arose in the context of controversy with those outside the church: controversy with Jews and pagans, for example, as well as with Gnostics (who rejected out of hand much church teaching and were not considered Christians at all by many bishops).

Declaratory creeds, on the other hand, were summary statements of faith made for the purpose of defining doctrine against the background of heresy and schism. They are statements of doctrine made in controversy with other Christians, and had the function of distinguishing one type of Christian (the "orthodox") from another (the "heretic"). They were defined by authoritative bodies of bishops who championed one particular view against other leaders and bishops (who were to be excluded). Declaratory creeds did not even exist until the later third and early fourth centuries, when schism, "heresy," and unity were political issues of great importance. "Heresy" belongs in quote marks here because nearly every question of import was hotly disputed, and the winners—those who held political power at the time—were the ones who drew up the creeds and defined "orthodoxy." One group's heresy was always another's orthodoxy, and vice versa.

The Council of Nicaea in 325

Constantine convened what was the first "general council" of the church, attended by more than 250 bishops from all over the empire (Eusebius, *Life of Constantine* 3.6–7). Their task, according to Constantine's opening speech, was to become "united in one judgment" on matters of the faith. Almost immediately, "some began to accuse their neighbors, who defended themselves, and recriminated in their turn." Thus, "a violent controversy arose" at the very outset (3.12–13). Eventually, under Constantine's guiding hand, the council produced the Creed of Nicaea, which all participants were required to sign; only Arius and a few of his supporters refused, and they were immediately forced into exile.

The results of the council were a victory for (those whom we today call) the Orthodox and a heavy defeat for the Arians. The creed reads in part:

> We believe in one God, the Father almighty . . . ;
>
> And in one Lord Jesus Christ, the Son of God, begotten from the Father only-begotten, that is from the essence [*ousia*] of the Father, God from God, light from light, true God from true God, begotten not made, same essence [*homoousion*] with the Father . . . ;
>
> And in the Holy Spirit.
>
> But those who say: "There was when he was not," and "Before he was begotten he was not," and "He came into being from nonexistence," or say that he is from another substance

[*hypostasis*] or essence [*ousia*], or created, or mutable, or that the Son of God is subject to change, the catholic and apostolic church curses. (Bindley, *Oecumenical Documents* 26, trans. GJR)

The Son was now defined for the whole church as "true God from true God"—not a mere man, nor a created being, but "begotten from the Father only-begotten." The creed still uses the old language of the families of the gods: Jesus is the unique Son, a member of God's family. He is "*homoousios* with the Father"—that is, he is an emanation of the Father, begotten out of the "stuff," the *ousia* ("being, essence"), of the Father. As the essence of the Father is eternal, so the Son is eternal; thus the Arian contention that "there was when he was not" is directly contradicted. The word "only-begotten" is from the Greek word *monogenes*, which means "unique, only one of its class, one and only." That God had a unique, "one-and-only" Son would later become a problem for the Trinitarians: the council had defined *two* Persons who shared a single essence of divinity, but what of the third?

The creed says only, "and in the Holy Spirit," giving no further definition or explanation at all. In offering such a terse affirmation, the bishops followed an old precedent. Recall that the apostle Paul in the middle of the first century, when defining the faith in 1 Corinthians 8:6, made no mention of the Holy Spirit at all. The old Roman Creed, from late in the second century, concluded with "and in the Holy Spirit, the holy church, the forgiveness of sins, the resurrection of the flesh," classing the Holy Spirit with what seemed to be doctrines of lesser importance than the Father and Son. This third article of the old Roman Creed consists of seemingly miscellaneous things one should believe in, one of which is the Spirit.[11] Clearly, then, Nicaea had not finished the task.

Arianism After Nicaea

In spite of the creed of 325 and the efforts of Constantine, the Arian controversy would not go away. As with Scripture itself, group after group had its own interpretation of the creed, allowing them to continue to hold to what they had previously believed. All but a few Arians were thus able to sign the creed, and Constantine's subsequent efforts to unify the whole church eventually reconciled most of them. After Constantine's death in 337, the empire was divided between his sons, Constantius in the east, who sided with the Arians, and Constans in the west, who sided with the Nicenes. "Orthodoxy" (always the creed of those in power) vacillated between Arianism and the Nicene definition, depending on who held power: Arianism became orthodoxy in the east, and Nicene doctrine in the west.

When Constans was killed in 350, Constantius rose to power over the whole empire. He and a group of Arian bishops forced through an Arian creed after the Council of Rimini in 359 to replace the previous Nicene Creed. Jerome, rather sarcastically, wrote of the event: "The Nicene faith stood condemned by acclamation. The whole world groaned, and was astonished to find itself Arian" (*Dialogue Against the Luciferians* 19). After several more twists and turns, Theodosius, a supporter of Nicaea, became sole ruler in 379 and sponsored the Council of Constantinople of 381, the council that would define Nicaea as the basis of "orthodoxy" for the remainder of Christian history. The issues that this council faced were not only later versions of Arianism, but new controversies over of the nature of the Holy Spirit.

More than a generation after Nicaea, Gregory of Nazianzus (ca. 329–ca. 389), a brilliant exponent of the Nicene Creed, reported concerning the Spirit that, "of the wise men among ourselves, some have conceived of him as an Activity [in Greek, *energeia*, 'energy'], some as a creature, some as God; and some have been uncertain which to call him" (*Oration* 31.5). He describes here the views of "the wise men among ourselves," not the views of heretics. There was as yet no unanimity of opinion and little understanding; the question of the proper view of the Holy Spirit was only now becoming an issue. Athanasius (ca. 296–373), writing to the orthodox emperor Jovian (emperor from 363–364), complained that the

Arians were blaspheming "against the Holy Spirit, in affirming that It is a creature, and came into being as a thing made by the Son" (letter 56.1). The logic of the Arian position dictated that the Holy Spirit was a creature, just as they had asserted about Christ. Eustathius (ca. 300–377), bishop of Sebaste in Asia Minor and former disciple of Arius, became the leader of a movement known derisively by its opponents as the "Pneumatomachoi" (Greek for "those fighting [against] the Spirit"). The movement was divided into two groups: those who accepted the Nicene definition of *homoousion* for Father and Son but rejected it for the Spirit, and the more extreme Arians, including Eustathius, who rejected the term for both (Basil, letter 263.3). The Arian position was predictable. The first group, however, were Nicene Christians, some of Gregory's "wise men among ourselves," who, like the Nicene Creed itself, had no doctrine of the Holy Spirit as individual divine Person.

In 381, Emperor Theodosius convened a council of eastern bishops at Constantinople to settle, among other questions, the dispute over the Holy Spirit. Gregory of Nazianzus, who presided over the council for a time, described its work, in part, as "completing in detail that which was incompletely said by them [at Nicaea] concerning the Holy Spirit, for that question had not then been discussed, namely, that we are to believe that the Father, Son, and Holy Spirit are of one Godhead, thus confessing the Spirit also to be God" (letter 102). The thirty-six Pneumatomachian bishops present were heavily outnumbered and withdrew. The remaining 150 bishops and the emperor affirmed the Nicene position and extended the ascription of deity to the Spirit. The third article of the resulting creed reads in part:

> And in the Holy Spirit, Lord and Life-giver, who proceeds from the Father, who with the Father and the Son is together worshiped and together glorified.

Trinitarianism, one God in three Persons, has been the official teaching of the Christian church from the Council of Constantinople to the present day.

CONCLUSION

We have followed the development of ideas about God from the earliest times that we can trace, five thousand or more years in the past, to the fourth century—to the time of the definition of Trinitarian faith for all subsequent Christian history. As far as evidence allows us to discover, human beings began as polytheists; there were no monotheists to begin with, and certainly no Trinitarians. Religious development began with sacred stories that told of primeval chaos, dark and stormy water, out of which arose the olden gods of elemental nature, sea, earth, sky, and underworld. These primeval gods produced all else, not only the remaining aspects of the material world, but also the host of lesser and still lesser divinities and spirits who ruled every aspect of the cosmos, from sun, moon, and stars to the lowliest sprite of tree, bush, and stream. As human culture progressed, moving from villages to cities to city-states to empires, human understanding of the divine also progressed. The road to a more complete understanding of God as Trinity was the result of a long series of contributing steps, a large number of tributaries flowing into the River of God.

But why the long history of development, why the River? Why did God not reveal the whole of the Trinitarian faith right at the beginning, to Adam and Eve? The question demanded an answer, and an answer was required of the early Christians: pagans asked how Christians could deny the ancient polytheism on which their cultures had been based from time immemorial, and Jews asked how Christians could deny the Jewish version of monotheism in which Jesus himself had been raised. In other words, why did religion not simply stop where it started, or where some particular culture thought it best—that is, with its version of religious truth?

The fact that culture had advanced, and along with it human understanding of the divine, was clear. Why was the God of the Old Testament apparently so different, so small and material, so full of human characteristics, when compared to the God of the creeds? Novatian, in the middle of the third century, offered this explanation:

The prophet then was still speaking about God in parables according to the period of the faith, not as God was, but as the people were able to receive him. And thus, that such things as these should be said about God, must be imputed not to God, but rather to the people. . . . It is not therefore God who is limited, but the perception of the people is limited. (Novatian, *De Trinitate* 6)

Novatian realized that human culture in the millennia before the Christian era had not progressed far enough for people to be able to understand the immateriality of God and the Trinity. The prophets used analogies and allegories — "parables" that could no longer be used in his day, but were necessary in earlier times to accommodate the limited perception of earlier peoples.

So who was that God who appeared to Abraham and Moses and so many others? Educated Christian teachers claimed that the Father could not be seen: "No one has ever seen God. It is God the only Son, who is close to the Father's heart, who has made him known" (John 1:18). The one who appeared as God in the Old Testament was Christ, the visible "image of God" (2 Cor. 4:4). The purpose of the appearances was to educate, to bring people to a true understanding of God, as Paul had stated: "Now I know only in part; then I will know fully" (1 Cor. 13:12). God sent the Son, the Image of God, to bring humans to a full knowledge of God.

Novatian continues:

Gradually and by progression human frailty was to be strengthened by the Image to that glory of being able one day to see God the Father. . . . And thus the weakness and imperfection of the human condition is nourished, led up, and educated by him; so that, being accustomed to look upon the Son, it may one day be able to see God the Father Himself also as He is. . . . (Novatian, *De Trinitate* 18)

That, from the point of view of the early church, was the purpose of the River of God.

4

THE DEVIL, THE DEMONS, AND THE END OF THE WORLD

O ne of the most important developments in the River of God was the gradual move from monism to dualism, from the gods and their servants to the one God and his enemy, the Devil. This marked a revolution in the religious conceptions of the ancient world: for the first time, there was war in heaven and earth in the human present that would necessitate a final cosmic battle and an end of the world. Not all people or cultures accepted such ideas, nor did those who did agree with one another on how they should be understood. In fact, a large part of the conflict between the Christians and their Roman persecutors centered on this very issue. For the Romans, there was no Devil, and they worshiped the traditional gods in a monistic universe. For the Christians, the Romans worshiped demonic forces that empowered Roman idols as part of a vast conspiracy of the Devil.

MONISM

For old cultures like much of the Roman world, the whole of the universe, including both the spiritual and material worlds, was understood to be an integrated and cohesive system, with each member, divine and human, fulfilling a proper function. There was no Devil; there were no demons in the Devil's service; there was no heaven or hell for the eternal reward or punishment of the gods (angels and demons) or their human loyalists. The entire cosmos, from the stars on down to the bushes, was filled with spiritual beings, each of whom had a suitable role in the organization of the entire structure. This conception of the universe as a unified system may be called a "monism." Its opposite is a "dualism" of the cosmos at war, with God and the Devil fighting to a final "end of the world."

Such a cosmic dualism does not enter the River of God until the Persian invasion of Mesopotamia in the sixth century BCE. Before that time, all of the cultures of the ancient Near East lived in a world more or less at peace with itself. History had not yet become the history of *salvation,* but was merely a long sequence of events without deeper meaning. The early version of the three-story universe was eternal; we are told that the Lord "founded the earth forever" (Ps. 78:69) and that "the world is firmly established; it will not be moved" (Ps. 93:1). The cosmos was not slipping inexorably toward a fiery cataclysm of judgment that would bring its complete destruction, as in later apocalyptic visions: as yet, there was nothing wrong with it.

The monistic universe was divided into three spheres of divine authority: the gods of the sky who ruled the upper world, the gods of the great earth-surrounding sea, and the gods of the earth and underworld. Everything that happened was directed by the higher deities and carried out by lesser spirits: stormy winds were the work of the wind gods; diseases were the work of the dark spirits of death and calamity. Yet all spirits were part of the balance of the cosmos as a whole. Humans were required to obey the laws of the gods: for obedience, good spirits brought rewards; and for disobedience, destructive spirits brought punishment. In Exodus 12:23, for example, the "Destroyer," a spirit of plague, strikes down the firstborn of Egypt at the Lord's command. The battle is not between God and the Devil over eternal souls; people do not yet have souls separate from their bodily existence that survive physical death.

THE COMBAT MYTHS

The Christian idea that the kingdom of God is opposed by the king-dom of Satan, that God and the righteous angels face a great spiritual enemy (the Devil and his army of demons), had a long history and development in the ancient world. The creation stories in many of the cultures that influenced the biblical tradition contained accounts of conflicts among the gods—accounts known as "combat myths." One of the most famous is the Babylonian story *Enuma Elish*. In this story, as we saw in Chapter 2, the younger gods who eventually create and rule the human world must battle the primeval gods of chaos. Marduk, the high god of Babylon, battles Tiamat, the great primeval sea, who is a monstrous sea dragon. Though Tiamat creates a vast battalion of fighters for her cause, she is nevertheless defeated, and from her body Marduk creates the cosmos. (Tiamat's tail is still visible as the Milky Way.) The gods then labor to build for Marduk his temple-palace in the city of Babylon.[1]

In Egypt the great champion of death and chaos was the snake monster Apophis, who dwelt in the underworld. Each day the sun god Re has to defeat Apophis at the western mountains in order to travel through his realm of the underworld on his way back to the eastern sunrise. In another story (also introduced in Chapter 2), the Canaanite storm god Baal, chief son of the high god El, is forced to battle Yamm, the monster whose very name means "sea"; he is also called Lotan, which in the Hebrew Bible is Leviathan, "the twisting serpent, . . . the dragon that is in the sea" (Isa. 27:1). Baal fights and then defeats Yamm and gains a mountaintop palace, as Marduk had gained his temple-palace, from which he thunders forth against his enemies. He next must confront Mot (Death), the ruler of the shadowy underworld, a monster with a huge mouth and appetite who swallows the dead. For a time, Baal himself is swallowed—is "dead," in other words—and the earth experiences the drought of summer heat. Eventually Mot is defeated and Baal rises again to bring the rains and revivify the crops.[2]

Very much the same set of images is used to describe Yahweh in Israel, drawing upon these and other myths to portray the conflicts against his enemies, both divine and human, and his rise to sovereignty over the other gods of the nations.[3]

THE EXILE AND PERSIAN DUALISM

These great enemies of the gods had been defeated or at least put under control in the mythic past. There was as yet no Devil. The cosmos, however, had arisen out of chaos, and chaos was a constant threat that could break free and wreak havoc once again. Like the underworld monster Apophis of Egypt or Yamm (the Sea) of Canaan, it was an ever-present danger. The most important point in the history of Israel when chaos overcame goodness was during the experience of the Exile. There, Old Testament scholar Jon Levinson writes, "history, no less than nature, slips out of God's control and into the hands of obscure but potent forces of malignancy that oppose everything [God] is reputed to uphold."[4] In the Exile, chaos appeared to have overcome the Lord; his servants, the righteous on earth, suffered national catastrophe. The Israelites of the generation that were exiled had, in their own view, been faithful to the covenants (Ps. 44:17), but somehow the covenants had failed.

The ten tribes of the northern kingdom of Israel had been conquered in 721 BCE by the Assyrian empire and exiled. The two remaining tribes of the southern kingdom were overwhelmed in 586 BCE by the armies of the Neo-Babylonian empire under Nebuchadnezzar. The temple in Jerusalem was destroyed, and much of Israel's population deported to Babylon. "By the rivers of Babylon," the psalmist writes in despair, "there we sat down and there we wept" (Ps. 137:1). Israel remained exiled for two generations, until the Babylonian empire itself was overrun by Cyrus and the Persian armies in 539 BCE.

Unlike the Assyrians and Babylonians before him, Cyrus was remarkably tolerant of the customs of his subject peoples; he permitted the Jews in Babylon to return to their own lands and rebuild the temple in Jerusalem (Ezra 4:1–4). For that favor, the prophet Second Isaiah addresses a remarkable message to him: "Thus says the Lord to his anointed, to Cyrus, whose right hand I have grasped . . ." (Isa. 45:1). The word "anointed" used here of Cyrus would one day take on much greater significance: it is the Hebrew word *messiah*.

The Persians brought not only release from exile to Israel; they also brought an old and highly influential view of the spiritual world. The Persians were an Indo-European culture whose religion was based on a view of the world very different from the monistic cultures of the ancient Near East: theological dualism. We today call this religion Zoroastrianism, after the Greek mispronunciation of the name of its founder, Zarathushtra, a prophet who lived sometime in the second millennium BCE in an area near the border between Iran and Afghanistan. According to tradition, near his thirtieth birthday, Zarathushtra was granted a series of revelations from Ahura Mazda (the "Wise Lord"), a name for the one God of all.

Two forms of Zoroastrianism predate the Exile of Israel. Difficulties presented by the ancient sources have resulted in controversy among scholars over which of these two forms was the original. In one form, Ahura Mazda emanated twin offspring, the Holy Spirit and the Evil Spirit. In the second form, the two spirits were uncreated twins existing from eternity.[5] The first is reflected in the statement of the Lord to Cyrus, which rejects the eternal dualism of the second: "I am the Lord and there is no other; I form light and I create darkness; I make wholeness and I create evil" (Isa. 45:6–7). This idea that God created two divine spirits, good and evil, is clearly expressed in the Dead Sea Scrolls texts from Qumran (e.g., 1QS 3:25: "[God] created the spirits of Light and Darkness"). Whatever the ultimate source, God had gained a divine enemy in the Devil, a view that would shape all subsequent Christian understanding of the spiritual realm.

Zoroastrianism was a highly sophisticated religious worldview and included much more than merely a dualism of God and the Devil. That dualism had consequences for the whole of the cosmos. Before creation, both God and the Devil had each emanated armies of archangels and angels, archdemons and demons. God then formed the world as a battleground on which the Devil could be defeated. As soon as it was completed, the dark forces attacked and defiled creation, resulting in this present "evil age" of the mixture of good and evil. The two—God and the Devil—now had to fight over the loyalty of humans. In one important text, "the Evil One" declares to God, "I shall destroy you and your creatures forever and ever. And I shall persuade all your creatures to hate you and to love me."[6] Similarly, the adversary Satan states to God that Job "will curse you to your face" (Job 2:5). Someday, at the consummation of time, God and righteousness will prevail in a cataclysmic final battle. On that day, the Devil and his angels will be cast into an eternal hell of fire; the old heavens and earth will be burned up, and a new heaven and earth will be created as a home for the resurrected righteous.

With this perspective, the previous concept of history as the mere listing of events in sequential order, the successive reigns of kings and the record of their achievements, was completely transformed and the idea of "salvation history" was born: every event on earth and in heaven was now seen as part of a vast drama moving to an inevitable climax—the final defeat of the Devil and victory of the one God. The River of God had encountered one of its most important tributaries.

THE DEVIL

The term "devil" is a development into English of the Greek word *diabolos*, used in transliteration by Latin Christians as *diabolus*. In Jewish texts from the intertestamental period and in later Christian writings, the word designated the great adversary of God and righteousness, the Devil. *Diabolos*[7] was used to translate the Hebrew word *satan* in the Septuagint, the Greek version of the Hebrew Scriptures created in the third century BCE (e.g., 1 Chron. 21:1). Likewise, in the New Testament *diabolos* is a standard alternate designation for Satan.

In ancient Greece, however, and therefore in the Greek language, there was no "Devil." *Diabolos* and its related words denoted something or someone "slanderous." Socrates declared that the reason he had been condemned at trial was the "slanders" (*diabolai*) that had been spoken against him for years (Plato, *Apology* 37b). The Pastoral Epistles admonished women not to be "evil gossips" (*diabolous*: 1 Tim. 3:11; Titus 2:3). The Septuagint used the noun *diabolos* to mean "enemy" (e.g., Haman was the "enemy" of the Jews in Esther 8:1). It was in this sense that the Septuagint used the word *diabolos* to render the Hebrew *satan*, the superhuman adversary of God. Nearly a thousand years later, the Qur'an would reduce the word slightly to the Arabic name for the Devil, *Iblis*.

Greek religion did not have a "Devil" in the Christian sense. While the Greek gods could be morally ambiguous, none was wholly evil. The function, though not the person, of "divine evil" among the Greeks was filled by the concept of fate, personified as three weavers weaving the tapestry of life's events: as one cannot change the pattern woven into a rug, one cannot change what the Fates have decreed for humans. Fate lay at the heart of Greek tragedy and the worldview we often call "Greek pessimism."

Fate's evil function, and the ambiguity of the gods, is illustrated in the case of the hero Hippolytus. In the early prime of life, full of promise, Hippolytus was a devotee of Artemis, goddess of the hunt and a perpetual virgin; he thus was celibate and refused to give proper honor to Aphrodite, the goddess of love and sexuality. Aphrodite, angered, caused his young stepmother, Phaedra, to fall madly in love with him. As if in a harsher version of the biblical story of Potiphar's wife and Joseph (Gen. 39), Hippolytus refused her advances. Phaedra, driven mad by shame and passion-turned-to-anger, hanged herself but left a suicide note that accused Hippolytus to his father, Theseus, of attempted rape. Theseus declared: "Fate, you have ground me and my house to dust" (Euripides, *Hippolytus* 818). In outraged grief, Theseus called down divine anger on Hippolytus, invoking one of three curses promised him by his own father, the god Poseidon; against his will, Poseidon was forced to destroy the young man. Hippolytus was innocent, of course, but, as the chorus observed, "from what is doomed and fated, there is no escape" (1256). Even Artemis lamented to the dying youth: "Unhappy boy! You are linked to a cruel fate. The nobility of your soul has proved your ruin" (1389–1390).

The function of fate to destroy the innocent by means unknown or misunderstood by the actors was taken over by the Devil. Christians were persecuted and killed by those who thought that they were upholding the Law and ridding the world of a "pollution," just as Theseus thought he was destroying an incestuous rapist. Jesus in the Gospel of John predicted that "an hour is coming for everyone who kills you to think they are offering service to God" (John 16:2). Fate was written in the stars; and in the dark cosmos that was ruled by the Devil, the stars were the Evil One's servants, the "principalities and powers," the "spiritual forces of wickedness in the heavenly places" (Eph. 6:12). So Jesus, the one who would come to destroy the Devil, had to rewrite fate; he gave his followers a new destiny: in Paul's words, "God has not destined us for wrath, but for obtaining salvation through our Lord Jesus Christ" (1 Thess. 5:9).

Greeks were not the only ones not to have a Devil; neither did any of the other cultures we have surveyed, except the Zoroastrians. The idea originated in Persia, and only very slowly after the Exile, under the rule of the Persian empire, did the idea begin to take hold among some sects of Judaism.[8] The majority of Jews, however—especially those in authority—continued to understand God and his relationship to the people along the traditional lines of the Deuteronomist and the pre-exilic prophets: the cause of Israel's woes had been their own willful disobedience to the one God, who was now to be worshiped faithfully in his (second) temple even more strictly than had been done previously. One looks in vain for any mention of the Devil as cause of sin and suffering in important documents of the return and rebuilding of the second temple. There is no such mention in Esther or Ezra or Nehemiah, all of which could easily have used the new idea to explain their trials and opponents. They continued the traditional worship in the temple and used the Law faithfully, rejecting the new ideas of the Persians. There was no Devil to blame, no afterlife, no "world to come," to use their phrase for eschatology. The descendants of these traditionalists were those most in power in Jesus' own time, the Sadducees.

Stories of the Origin of the Devil

Gradually other Jews began to adapt the new dualistic concepts of the Zoroastrians into old Israelite traditions. In the New Testament, the Devil is called "Beelzebul, . . . the Ruler of the demons" (Mark 3:22). This title is based on the name of one of the old gods of Canaan who was the greatest competitor of the God of Israel: Baal. In the old Canaanite religion that was inherited by Israel, El and his wife, Asherah, had seventy "sons," the gods of the seventy nations of the earth. Chief among them was Baal, a name that was properly a title meaning "Lord." Since he was the ranking son of El, the king of the gods, he was also "the Prince," in Ugaritic *zebul;* hence the name Baal Zebul, the "Lord Prince," written in the New Testament as Beelzebul.

Baal was the Canaanite storm god, who rode the chariot of the winds, thundered at his enemies from his mountain palace, protected or persecuted with his lightning, and brought fertility to the earth in the rainy season. All of these were aspects of Yahweh of Israel, the "rider on the clouds" (Ps. 68:4). These similarities of function and shared characteristics brought Yahweh and Baal into direct competition and made differentiation difficult.

The cult of Baal was a large part of the religion of Canaan and Israel, and it continued right through Israelite history. Saul, for example, who lived in the eleventh century and was the first king of Israel, named one of his sons Mephibaal (meaning, in Hebrew, "from the mouth of Baal": 2 Sam. 21:8); Jonathan, David's closest friend, did the same (2 Sam. 4:4). Scribes altered the name to Mephibosheth ("from the mouth of shame"), in order to denigrate Yahweh's great competitor. Worship of Baal was so common, in fact, that Elijah, in the middle of the ninth century, declared to the Lord that the Israelites had turned against the worship of Yahweh entirely, destroying his altars and killing his prophets, and that he alone was left. God answered that there were still seven thousand in Israel who had "not bowed to Baal" (1 Kings 19:18). Later, when King Ahaziah had been severely injured, he sent messengers to the god Baal Zebul in Ekron to find out if he would die (2 Kings 1:3). Here again scribes rewrote the text to read "Baal-zebub," "Lord of the flies." Elijah declared to the messengers: "Is it because there is no God in Israel that you are sending to inquire of Baal-zebub, the god of Ekron?" (2 Kings 1:6).

The cause of the anger of Yahweh against Israel and the reason for the Exile, according to the prophet Jeremiah in the sixth century, was Baal. Jeremiah asked, "Why is the land ruined and laid waste like a wilderness, so that no one passes through?" The Lord answered, "Because they have forsaken my Law that I set before them . . . and have gone after the Baals, as their ancestors taught them" (Jer. 9:12–14). So Baal was the great rival and archenemy of Yahweh; and under the influence of Persian dualism after the Exile, he became identified with the Devil, the Beelzebul of the New Testament.

The writings of Second Isaiah and the Qumran community, drawing on one of the two strands of Zoroastrian tradition that we examined earlier, claimed that God was the source of both good and evil; God was not wholly righteous. The other strand of Zoroastrianism put God in competition with another power—a dark power—who was the cause of evil; God was not alone as God. Both strands presented difficulty for the view that God was good and that God was the sole sovereign of all. They called into question Deuteronomy's claim that "the Lord is God; there is no other besides him" (Deut. 4:35) and that "all his ways are just" (Deut. 32:4).

A solution to this difficulty was found again in the old traditions. The view everywhere had been that the highest God presided over a council of lesser gods (e.g., Ps. 82:1: "God has taken his place in the divine council"). In the combat myths, the upper-world gods ultimately defeated the forces of chaos; the enemies, though formidable, were weaker and lesser beings. In Zoroastrianism, these lesser beings were the archangels and angels, archdemons and demons. By melding Zoroastrian dualism with the old view of the divine council and the combat myth, believers could see the God of Israel as the one sovereign God of righteousness, presiding over the lesser divine beings of the heavenly council (the angels), some of whom were righteous, while others, by their own choice, were the cause of evil.

This solution removed the origin of evil in heaven one stage from God: evil was the result of a deliberate choice to sin by some of the angels. These sinful angels were led by a great adversary similar to the terrifying enemies in the combat myth, the Devil. He was understood in terms of the great mythic opponents of the heavenly gods: though at times an angel, he could also be a great dragon, a monstrous snake who ruled by death. Arrayed against him would be his righteous antagonist and counterpart, the Angel of the Lord (Zech. 3:1), or Michael the Archangel (Jude 9), or later, for Christians, Jesus.

A number of different stories were told in postexilic literature about how this powerful angel had become the Devil. An early story that originally had nothing to do with the Devil attempted to locate the cause of evil among sinful angels. Greek stories had for many centuries told of the gods mating with humans, producing the great heroes of epic, such as Herakles, Achilles, and others. Jewish writers adapted this theme, turning its positive Greek use into a negative.

In the Jewish version, a group of two hundred of the "sons of

God" (i.e., angels), known as the "Watchers," looked down from heaven, and, like the Greek gods, lusted after human women. After bribing the women with the "secrets of heaven," which included the making and applying of cosmetics in addition to more useful arts such as medicine and metallurgy, these angelic beings and their female consorts mated. Their union produced a race of lawless giants who, because of their violent sinfulness, were condemned by God to be destroyed by the Flood (*1 Enoch* 6–16; Gen. 6:1–4). The Watchers were then imprisoned in the vast underworld jailhouse known as Tartaros (Jude 8; 2 Pet. 2:4). It was to this powerful group of rebels that Jesus "descended into hell" to proclaim his victory over them (1 Pet. 3:19–20).

The leader of this band of fallen angels, Azazel, was branded as the cause of evil on earth: the Lord said to Raphael, "To Azazel ascribe all sin" (*1 Enoch* 10.8). The fact that Azazel (and not Satan) was the cause of sin became a problem, however, as Persian dualism began to have more and more influence. A later Enoch text therefore identifies Azazel as a *messenger* of Satan (*1 Enoch* 54:6), thus making the Devil ultimately responsible for bringing sin to humanity. In another story, Azazel is identified as the Devil himself (*Jubilees* 10.1–11). Here one should perhaps place one of the most unusual stories about the Devil and sex—one that sees sexual sin as a failing, as it had been of Azazel, of the Devil himself: the role of progenitor of Cain is assigned to the Devil—a role that later authors thought he accomplished by union with Eve in the Garden of Eden (cf. *4 Maccabees* 18:8, "the seducing and defiling serpent").

Yet if Azazel is the one who introduced sin to humanity, just prior to the Flood, who was the serpent in the Garden of Eden? Inevitably, Azazel also became identified with the serpent who deceived Adam and Eve (*Apocalypse of Abraham* 23). Christians have (apparently) always thought of the snake in the Garden as the Devil. Paul writes to the Corinthians, for example, that they not be deceived by false Christian missionaries, "as the serpent deceived Eve . . ." (2 Cor. 11:3). Quite surprisingly, though, the identification of the serpent in the Garden of Eden with the Devil seems to have arisen rather late in pre-Christian traditions. The serpent as a symbol in the ancient Near East meant many positive things before it became a symbol for the Devil after the Exile. It symbolized life, wisdom, and even resurrection.[9] Large (and harmless) snakes were ever-present denizens of the healing sanctuaries of Asklepios in Greece: their venom was the most effective antibiotic agent in antiquity, and the shedding of their skin represented renewal of life.

The writer of Genesis did not call the snake the Devil, as he could easily have done. Genesis 3:1–2 reads: "Now the serpent was more crafty than any other wild animal that the Lord God had made. He said to the woman, ..." The serpent in this depiction is an animal created by God; it does not seem to be a dark spiritual power in itself, nor is such a power mentioned as inspiring or motivating the serpent behind the scenes. The passage could have been written quite differently—"The Devil entered the serpent and said to the woman . . . ," for example—if the writer had wanted to indicate that the serpent was the Devil. Furthermore, Satan does not appear anywhere else in the Pentateuch (the first five books of the Bible). The only person described with the label *satan* is the Angel of the Lord, who goes out to oppose the pagan prophet Balaam, who is attempting to curse Israel: "The Angel of the Lord took his stand in the road as his adversary" (= *satan* in Hebrew: Num. 22:22).

The fact that, in the story of the Watchers, "all sin" is to be ascribed to Azazel shows that more than one source of evil in the human sphere was current in the sacred stories of the ancients. Chaos monsters, earth dragons, sea serpents, heavenly rebels, and of course the old standby, humans themselves, were all responsible (depending on the particular prophet) for evil in the world. There was, as we have seen so often, no orthodoxy, no definitive creed. The River was still flowing; ideas were still developing.

One of the most influential stories in the religious history of the origin of the Devil relates the "fall" of (the angel who is to become) the Devil to his relationship with Adam. Angels were created long before the material earth, out of spiritual elements much superior to dirt and water. Yet even though Adam was made of mud, he was made in the image of God, something far and away beyond the level of creation of the angels. "Through the Devil's envy," we are told, "death entered the world" (*Wisdom* 2:24). When God created Adam on the earth, the angels were commanded to reverence him as being made in God's image. Most of the angels did as required, but one high-level angel refused on the grounds that he was both greater and older than Adam; this angel became the Devil. He was followed in his rebellion by the many other angels who became his army of dark spiritual powers (*Adam and Eve* 13–15; Tertullian, *De Patientia* 5). This view of the origin of the Devil is the basis for the figure of Iblis in Islam (Qur'an 15:26–35).

For early Christians, the most important story of the origin of the Devil was found in the Old Testament prophecies against the king of Babylon (Isa. 14:4–20) and the king of Tyre (Ezek. 28:11–19). Isaiah 14:3–23 is a prophecy that condemns Babylon for its oppression of the nations it had conquered, centering especially on the arrogance of the king. It describes him in terms that seem to go far beyond a merely human king: "How you are fallen from heaven, O Day Star, son of Dawn! . . . You said in your heart, 'I will ascend to heaven. I will raise my throne above the stars of God. . . . I will make myself like the Most High'" (Isa. 14:12–14).

"This must mean the Devil," writes Tertullian (*Against Marcion* 5.17). Jesus, after his disciples returned from a mission that included exorcisms, declared, "I watched Satan fall from heaven like lightning" (Luke 10:18). That statement of Jesus was used to interpret the passage in Isaiah that says of the Devil that "at one time he was light" (Origen, *First Principles* 1.5.5), fell from heaven, and became darkness. The Latin translation of Isaiah 14:12 names this individual "Lucifer."

The prophet Ezekiel deals similarly with the king of Tyre, expanding the scope of his prophecy seemingly beyond the human sphere: "You were in Eden, the Garden of God. . . . You were blameless in your ways from the day that you were created until iniquity was found in you" (Ezek. 28:13–15). This passage was also interpreted as referring to the Devil. He had been "the highest rank-ing angel in heaven" (*Testament of Solomon* 6:1–2). Yet on the second day of creation, this archangel, through pride, attempted to set him-self up and be worshiped as an equal to God (*2 Enoch* 29.4–5).

Names for the Devil

Intertestamental and later Jewish texts ascribe to the Devil a vari-ety of names. In *Jubilees* "the Chief of the spirits" is Mastema, Hebrew for the "Hateful One" (literally, "animosity": 1:20). In *Martyrdom of Isaiah*, the leader of the hosts of evil is called Sammael (in Hebrew, "Blind God": 1:8), a favorite name in Gnostic texts. He is also Melkira, the "King of Evil" (1:8), and especially Beliar (a by-form of "Belial" = "Useless" in Hebrew: 1:8; 2:4). In a label that recalls his origins as fallen angel, he is also "the Angel of Iniquity" (2:4–11). In the *Testament of the Twelve Patriarchs*, he is the "Prince of Error" (*Testament of Simeon* 2:7) and the "Prince of the Demons" (*Testament of Solomon* 6:1–7). In a passage that recalls a verse in the New Testament epistle of 1 Peter, the Devil is the "wild old Lion" (*Joseph and Aseneth* 12:9). First Peter 5:8 reads: "Your adversary, the Devil, prowls about like a roaring lion, seek-ing someone to devour."

In the New Testament the embodiment of evil is called by sev-eral different names, reflecting the many traditions that were melded to construct the concept of the Devil in the intertestamen-tal period. In one remarkable passage we find "the great Dragon, . . . the Serpent of old who is called the Devil and Satan" (Rev. 12:9). The Dragon clearly recalls Leviathan, the great "dragon that is in the sea" (Isa. 27:1; cf. Tiamat and Yamm), while the Serpent is also the "serpent [who] deceived Eve by his craftiness" (2 Cor. 11:3; cf. Gen. 3:1–15). Just as in the intertestamental liter-ature, images and names of the great opponents of the gods of heaven in the combat myths are used of the Devil.

The names "Devil" and "Satan" are used interchangeably, without apparent difference in meaning. In Jesus' Parable of the Sower, for example, the one who steals the seed from the hearts of those beside the road is Satan in one Gospel and the Devil in another (cf. Mark 4:15 and Luke 8:12). In other passages, the antithesis of Christ is Belial (2 Cor. 6:15), and the spirit that he battles is Beelzebul (Mark 3:22). The Devil is called the Tempter (Matt. 4:3), the Evil One (Matt. 6:13), the Enemy (Matt. 13:39), the Accuser (Rev. 12:10), and the Ruler of This World (John 12:31).

Activities of the Devil in Pre-Christian Judaism

The concept of the "adversary" (in Hebrew, *satan*) is found in two senses in the Hebrew Bible: that of any (usually human) opponent, and that of Satan, the Devil. In the first sense, for example, Hadad the Edomite acts as a *satan* to Solomon: "The Lord raised up an adversary against Solomon, Hadad the Edomite" (1 Kings 11:14). In such cases, the *satan* is an "opponent" in politics or war or other earthly endeavor. In later biblical texts composed after the Exile, however, the concept manifests the growing changes brought about by the influence of dualism: the *satan* becomes the Devil (rendered, as we have seen, by *diabolos* in the Septuagint).

An interesting illustration of this change in meaning over time can be seen in a comparison of 2 Samuel 24:1, written before the Exile, and 1 Chronicles 21:1, written after. In the first passage, "the anger of the Lord was kindled against Israel, and he incited David" to count the people. In the second, "Satan stood up against Israel and incited David to count the people." The view was gaining ground that God was now wholly good and that the source of evil was the Devil.

God and the Devil were at war over the loyalty of humanity, the righteous belonging to God and the wicked to the Devil. The Devil attacked the bond between humanity and God, leading people to sin and blasphemy in an attempt to destroy their allegiance to God. So the Devil in Job (*satan*, "the adversary") slanders Job to God and then attacks him in an attempt to cause him to "curse" God "to his face" (Job 1:11; 2:5). This is not the action of a mere heavenly prosecutor in the divine council, appointed by God to accuse the defendant of sin (as appears to be the case in Zech. 3:1–2); no prosecutor destroys the property of the defendant, then kills the defendant's children and destroys his health, in order to bring about hatred for the judge. God and the Devil in Job are competing for Job's loyalty, which the Adversary calls into question. To settle the issue, God delivers Job over into the power of Satan for testing, "leading him into temptation" and "delivering him over to the Evil One," as God would later do with Jesus and his followers according to the New Testament (Matt. 6:13).

One of the chief activities of the Devil is to accuse Israel before God, as he had done with Job. This continues right into the New Testament: the Devil accuses the righteous "night and day" before God for their sins, attempting to prove that they belong to him (Rev. 12:10; Jude 9); yet Christians have an Advocate, a defense attorney, in Jesus (1 John 2:1). In order to make the accusations stick, the Devil causes people to sin: he traps and corrupts them that they be destroyed (*Jubilees* 1:20). As "the Angel of Iniquity who rules this world," he causes a host of evils: apostasy, sin, magic, and the persecution of the righteous (*Martyrdom of Isaiah* 2:4–11). He also causes the righteous to fall into promiscuity; so Reuben explains his sin with his father's concubine (*Testament of Reuben* 4:7–11). As the "Prince of Error," he blinds Simeon's mind so as to sell Joseph into slavery (*Testament of Simeon* 2:7) and causes Judah to go astray by love of money (*Testament of Judah* 19:4). As the "Prince of the Demons," he causes wars, tyranny, demon worship, violence, and lust (*Testament of Solomon* 6:1–7).

According to ancient pessimistic views of human nature, most people succumb to the Devil's influences, but resistance is the proper defense: "Resist the Devil and he will flee from you," counsels James 4:7. The Devil is able to enter into the hearts and minds of those who yield to him. He "inhabits as his own instrument" one who does evil (*Testament of Naphtali* 8:6), "dwelling in the hearts" of the rulers of Israel (*Martyrdom of Isaiah* 2:4–11). The biblical prophets had (nearly) always condemned these rulers; now the reason for their duplicity had become clear. Later, in the New Testament, Satan uses some of the Judean rulers to oppose and contradict Jesus (John 8:44), and later even Peter (Mark 8:33); eventually he indwells Judas Iscariot (John 13:27). Sinfulness is the door of opportunity and entry. The Devil is the master of the soul filled with wrath and falsehood, but he must flee from one who avoids anger and hates lying (*Testament of Dan* 4:7–5:1).

Occasionally some heroic soul resists the Devil even more vehemently. In the postbiblical Jewish story of Joseph and Aseneth, Satan is the father of the Egyptian gods, represented as idols; he attacks Aseneth for turning from him to the true God and destroying the images of the gods of her family (*Joseph and Aseneth* 12:9; 10:12). Retribution for attacking the Devil's idols is the basis for the plot of the *Testament of Job:* Job destroys an idol temple and must therefore undergo the wrath of the Devil (*Testament of Job* 4:4).

The view that God was good and sovereign over everything clashed with the idea that the Devil was free to attack and destroy the righteous at will. Some people therefore claimed that whatever the activity of the Devil, it was performed with the permission of God. Recall that God and Satan discussed Job's righteousness, and that Satan requested and received God's permission to ruin the life Job had known. In another story that gives something of a background to the story of Job, the Lord is about to imprison all the demonic spirits of the drowned giants after the Flood. The Devil pleads that he will not be able to fulfill his function without their help and is assigned a tenth of these demons; they are to test the righteous and demonstrate which among humanity are evil (*Jubilees* 10:8–12).

A reflection of this idea is to be found in the New Testament, where the apostle Paul writes about the quarrels that were rampant in the Corinthian church: "I hear that there are divisions among you; and to some extent I believe it. Indeed, there have to be factions among you, for only so will it become clear who among you are genuine" (1 Cor. 11:19). One with eyes to see would discern the activity of the Devil, stirring up strife that would test the authenticity of people's faith, separating the wheat from the chaff.

The Devil in the New Testament

By the time of the writing of the New Testament, conceptions of the Devil had grown considerably in scope and sophistication: the Devil had come to rule a vast kingdom of darkness that stretched from heaven through the seven spheres of the geocentric universe down to the air and onto the earth. This kingdom included the entire "world," the very cosmos itself and apparently everything in it: "The whole world lies in [the power of] the Evil One" (1 John 5:19). So the Devil is the "ruler of this world" (John 12:31) and the "god of this world" (2 Cor. 4:4). This is why the Devil, during his testing of Jesus in the wilderness, was able to offer him "all the kingdoms of the world" (Matt. 4:8–9) if Jesus would worship him. As members of this kingdom of darkness, all humans, until they turn to the true God, are under the "dominion of Satan" (Acts 26:18) and the "authority of darkness" (Col. 1:13), living "according to the spirit which works in the children of disobedience" (Eph. 2:1–2). People do not even know that they are Satan's subjects.

Zoroastrian teaching claimed that all the gods and religions of the world were demonic deceptions. One of the great controversies between Christian apologists and their Roman persecutors was that the Romans thought they were doing what was right in reverencing their traditional gods, while the Christians tried to show them their error in worshiping idols and demons. The Devil, in the Christian view, had blinded the Romans' minds to the message of the gospel (2 Cor. 4:4), for the Devil "deceives the whole world" (Rev. 12:9).

The kingdom of darkness that the world had become—a rebellion that was costing the souls of untold myriads of humans—was a direct affront to the sovereignty of God. So God sent an invasion headed by Jesus as champion of the kingdom of God. This was a mission with a dual purpose: the salvation of humans and the destruction of the rebellion. On the one hand, "God did not send the Son into the world to condemn the world, but in order that the world might be saved through him" (John 3:17). On the other hand, "the Son of God appeared for this purpose, that he might destroy the works of the Devil" (1 John 3:8).

Jesus found humanity beset by demonic powers; therefore, one of his most important activities was to cast out demons (Mark 1:21–28). This he describes as tying up the strong man, entering the strong man's house and plundering his property (Matt. 12:28–29; see also Luke 11:21–22). The strong man is the Devil, and the property that is stolen is people formerly oppressed by demonic powers. Jesus then sends out his disciples with the power to overcome demons, and he sees "Satan fall from heaven like lightning" (Luke 10:17–18). This is a sign of the eventual end: he predicts that "the ruler of this world shall be cast out" (John 12:31).

Jesus understands himself as a sower of good seed, the word of the kingdom of God. Satan is like a bird who eats the grains as they are sown; he steals the seed from the hearts of the unreceptive, that they not be saved (Luke 8:12). Jesus sows the seed of the children of the kingdom of God in the field of the world, while the Devil sows weeds, the children of the Evil One (Matt. 13:36–40). The Devil is able to influence or indwell those whom he uses as his instruments; eventually, as we have seen, he enters Judas Iscariot (John 13:27) to accomplish the crucifixion of Jesus (Luke 22:53). Nevertheless, it is through this death, which the evil powers had brought about in ignorance (1 Cor. 2:8), that the Devil would be "rendered powerless" (Heb. 2:14); the powers crucify themselves (*Treatise of Seth* 54.30–33).

The disciples were in trouble. They had dared to follow Jesus, the captain of God's most important attack on Satan's kingdom of darkness; they were therefore very much in the line of fire. Jesus prayed that they be kept from the Evil One (John 17:15) and taught them to pray that God not "lead them into temptation," as he had their Master, but "deliver them from the Evil One" (Matt. 6:13).

This was a prayer that was not always successful, for the very purpose of the battle between God and the Devil, from Zoroastrianism to the New Testament, was to test the loyalty of humans. Satan therefore demanded that he "sift" Jesus' disciples "like wheat" (Luke 22:31), which caused them to abandon him in the Garden of Gethsemane and run for their lives.

The Devil tested the loyalty (in Greek, *pistis*, meaning "faith") of Jesus' followers by any and every means, but especially by persecution. Having the power of death, he held people in slavery by the fear of death (Heb. 2:15). The disciples fled because they feared their own deaths, in direct contradiction of the teaching of Jesus that they give their lives for him and the gospel's sake (see, among other passages, Mark 8:31–38). Nevertheless, Jesus prayed for Peter that he should not fail completely, and he instructed Peter, when the latter recovered his faith, to restore his fellow disciples (Luke 22:31–32). So it is that by "the shield of faith" one extinguishes "the flaming missiles of the Evil One" (Eph. 6:16).

For early Christians the church was the main outpost of God in the kingdom of the enemy. Against it, the Devil was seen to employ several strategies. He raised up individuals as external enemies, such as Elymas the magician, who contradicted the preaching of Paul (Acts 13:10). He quite often used governing authorities: he used Roman officials to prevent Paul from visiting the Thessalonians, for example (1 Thess. 2:10). In addition, he instigated persecutions and imprisonments, that Christians "may be tested" (Rev. 2:10). Later he was also seen as enthroned in the Roman government (Rev. 2:13; 17:9).

Division and dissension within the church was a menace more threatening even than these, because it called the very truth of the gospel into question. Even pagans observed that if Christians could not agree with each other on their faith, their claim that it was God's truth must be mere pretense. In Paul's view, it was Satan who inspired false apostles to travel to Paul's churches and contradict his message (2 Cor. 11:13–15). False teachers were said to be in "the snare of the Devil, held captive to do his will" (2 Tim.

2:26; cf. Rom. 16:17–20). The Devil attacked individual Christians as well, leading them into sin by causing them to lie (Acts 5:3) or be sexually immoral (1 Cor. 7:5; 1 Tim. 5:15). He also used slander to destroy one's reputation (1 Tim. 3:7). (Recall that the Greek word *diabolos* meant "slanderer.")

THE DEMONS

The Devil was seen as the chief of a host of wicked spirits who made up "his kingdom" (Luke 11:18), ranging from the great "cosmic powers of this darkness" (Eph. 6:12) to the lesser demons on earth who plague humanity. One intertestamental text claimed that the "Prince of the Demons" resided in the evening star (*Testament of Solomon* 6:1–7), while a number of Gnostic texts placed not only this dark ruler but also his host of seven archdemons in the heavenly spheres of the geocentric universe. The "spiritual forces in the heavens" (Eph. 6:12) were the angelic astral forces, "the Dragon and his angels" (Rev. 12:7, 9), who had access into the very heaven of God (Rev. 12:10; Luke 10:18). These astral forces were called the "elements" (Col. 2:8, 20), the stars that were worshiped all over the ancient Near East as deities. Another text declared that "the heavenly bodies [were] the world rulers of the darkness of this age" (*Testament of Solomon* 18.3). The army of dark forces occupied not only the heavens, but especially the air, and thus the Devil was the "ruler of the power of the air" (Eph. 2:2). This idea was based on an old deduction of Greek science: the lesser the spirit, the more material it was, the less pure, the less righteous. So Eusebius informs us that Greek theologians assigned "the atmosphere to demons" (*Preparation for the Gospel* 4.5.141).

The term "demon" is the rendering into English of the Greek words *daimon* and the closely related *daimonion*. The original meaning of *daimon* was "divinity," designating either an individual god or goddess (e.g., Aphrodite in *Iliad* 3.420) or the Deity, meaning God as an unnamed unity (*Odyssey* 3.27: "The Deity will put it in your mind"). Most often it designated the class of lesser divine

beings arranged below the Olympian gods. Hesiod described
these beings as the souls of those who lived in the original Golden
Age of humanity, who now invisibly watch over human affairs
(*Works and Days* 122–124): "They are called pure spirits [*daimones*]
dwelling on the earth, and are kindly, delivering from harm, and
guardians of mortals."

The related term *daimonion* in the classical period meant similarly "the divine power" or "the Divinity" (Plato, *Republic* 382e). It
could also mean the lower divine beings who mediated between
the human and divine spheres (Plato, *Symposium* 202e: a "*daimonion* is halfway between God and mortals"). The famous *daimonion*
of Socrates directed him in God's will (Plato, *Apology* 24b, 40a);
Paul seemed to Athenian philosophers to be proclaiming strange
"divinities" (Acts 17:18) in speaking of Jesus. In classical Greek,
to be under the power of a *daimon* was often a blessing, granting
prophetic foresight or heroic courage; it could also be a curse,
however, driving one to insanity.

Spirits of Calamity: Demons in Monistic Cultures

Demons were not originally "demons as servants of the Devil,"
since originally there was no Devil. Everything in the world of the
ancients had a spiritual as well as physical cause. To enforce divine
laws, to regulate the balance of blessing and curse in the human
realm, and to ensure human mortality, the gods employed, among
other means, the *daimones*. Hesiod warned against evil doings,
because "Zeus has thrice ten thousand spirits, watchers of mortals,
and these keep watch on judgments and deeds of wrong as they
roam, clothed in mist, all over the earth" (*Works and Days*
252–255).

Just as *eudaimonia* ("prosperity, good fortune, happiness") was
brought by a benevolent spirit, so *kakodaimonia* ("ill fortune") was
caused by some dark but legitimate power. These powers were the
spirits of disaster, retribution, and death who performed the will of
the greater gods. The Greeks spoke of the Erinyes, underground

deities of vengeance, along with Ate (= personified "Delusion") and Nemesis (= personified "Divine Retribution"). In the Bible, Yahweh was attended by Resheph ("Flame," the Canaanite plague demon) and Deber ("Pestilence") as he descended in wrath against the earth (Hab. 3:5). The Destroyer who killed the firstborn of Egypt (Exod. 12:23) is mentioned in 1 Corinthians 10:10 as later having killed off the disobedient Israelites in their desert wanderings; he is perhaps the Abaddon/Apollyon of Revelation 8:11. The Mesopotamian story of Atrahasis relates that Lamashtu (the childbirth demon) and Namtar (the plague demon and henchman of Nergal, the king of the Mesopotamian underworld) had been created by the high god Enlil to keep down human population. *Sirach* 39:28–29 speaks of spirits created by the Lord for vengeance: personified "Fire and Hail and Famine and Pestilence, . . . these take delight in doing his bidding." One Mesopotamian text describes the function of such spirits as follows:

> *The shivers and chills of death*
> > *that shatter and waste the sum of things,*
> *The death guardians, beloved offspring of the storm god,*
> > *born of the queen of the Underworld*
> *They are the bitter venom of the gods;*
> > *they are the great storms let loose from heaven.*[10]

These spirits occupied the dangerous places: the desert wastes, the deserted byways. Rabisu, for example, the Croucher, lay in wait in dark corners and alleys (cf. Gen. 4:7). Lilith, the child-stealer, dwelt in the desert wastes. These spirits held power during dangerous situations and times: at night, during a windstorm or an eclipse, and especially in childbirth. Lilitu, a lascivious female demon, haunted men in their dreams. The desert storm winds, in Babylon headed by Pazuzu, king of the wind demons, were thought to bring calamity and disease. These seven evil gods of the winds attacked the moon and caused the eclipse, after which "they swept over the land like a hurricane."[11] The Midday demon attacked the unwary with various ills at the height of the sun.

Lamashtu, a terrifying specter, threatened women and newborns in childbirth and stole nursing infants; she was later identified with Lilith, who was the child-stealer at Ugarit and in later Jewish folklore.

These spirits were often personifications of dire situations, especially plague, and one of their main activities was to bring death:

From a man's embrace they lead off the wife,
From a man's knee they take up the child,
and the youth they fetch out of the house of his in-laws.
They are the numbness, the daze, that treads on the heels of man.[12]

Death was normally caused by disease, and one of the oldest functions of demonic forces was to cause physical disease: so *daimon* is used to designate a spirit of "famine and disease" (*Sibylline Oracles* 3.331). This inheritance explains the apparent anomaly that the main activity of demons in the New Testament ministry of Jesus is not to tempt to sin but to cause disability, disease, and insanity, even though these beings are clearly associated with the activity of the Devil. Just as Paul had a "messenger of Satan" to harm and humble him (Paul's "thorn in the flesh" of 2 Cor. 12:7), so he in turn delivered a sinful Christian "over to Satan" for bodily suffering, which he hoped would lead to repentance (1 Cor. 5:5).

Unlike the upper-world gods, these dark spirits were often not in human image but in animal (or other) form. They were the iconographic background of the images so often seen on medieval cathedrals as gargoyles. The *shedim* ("guardian spirits") of Babylon and Assyria were depicted as winged bulls. In Isaiah 34:14, Lilith as a carrion bird nested in the desert wastes and was joined by owls, hawks, and wild desert animals. Resheph was also conceived as a carrion bird (e.g., LXX Deut. 32:24). Jesus gave his disciples "authority to tread on snakes and scorpions" (Luke 10:19), referring to demons. The book of Revelation describes three demons as "unclean spirits like frogs" (Rev. 16:13).

These spirits were also often envisioned as composite beings—

made up of different parts of animals, for example, and sometimes including human faces or bodies. *Testament of Solomon* 18.1–2 speaks of demons "with heads like formless dogs, . . . [and others] in the form of humans or of bulls or of dragons with faces like birds or beasts or the sphinx." Pazuzu, the wind demon of Mesopotamia, was a horrifying winged creature with a humanlike face (cf. the Sirens of Greece). Revelation also describes the (demonic) "locusts" from the abyss, armed as battle-horses, with human faces (Rev. 9:7).

Demons could not only attack but could also indwell humans and cause many types of ills: epilepsy, insanity, disability. Against them one protected oneself by prayer and magic, calling in a magician to diagnose the problem and recite the appropriate incantation for exorcism. Incantations often used the form of an invocation of the higher gods and a verbal command to exhort evil forces to go away, and they were sometimes accompanied by magical aids. Josephus tells of a magic root that drove out demons when applied to the sufferer (*Jewish War* 7.185). Solomon, in Jewish, Christian, and Muslim lore, is said to have had "the skill against the demons for help and healing" and to have composed incantations and rituals of exorcism; in Josephus's own day, exorcism was performed in Solomon's name with a ring containing a magic root (*Antiquities* 8.45–47). These spirits could also be exorcised by providing a substitute host body, usually an animal but sometimes a figurine or even a reed of the same size as the human sufferer.[13] That a demon needed a host is an idea found also in the New Testament: demons cast out of the Gerasene demoniac ask to enter a herd of pigs lest, apparently, they be left homeless (Mark 5:12; cf. Matt. 12:43–45).

Demons as Servants of the Devil

For Hesiod, the *daimones* were wholly good and Zeus wholly just, but from a merely human viewpoint, nearly all deities in early times were morally ambiguous: they could be at one time wrathful and at another gracious, and one did not always know why. In a famous passage at the beginning of the *Odyssey*, Zeus declares, "Oh for shame, how the mortals put the blame upon us gods, for they say evils come from us, but it is they, rather, who by their own recklessness win sorrow beyond what is given" (*Odyssey* 1.32–34).

A great deal of Old Testament literature is an effort to defend the view that God is righteous against the apparent contradictions of the sufferings of Israel. There was evil in heaven that needed to be explained. After the Exile and the encounter with Zoroastrian dualism, that evil was understood to be caused by the Devil, and the terms *daimon* and *daimonion* began to bear among some groups of Jews the negative valuation of "demon in league with the Devil." As Zoroastrianism had demonized the gods of the nations, so "demon" in the dualistic sense designates pagan deities and spirits in the Septuagint. The national deities of other peoples, said to be idols (*elilim*) in the Hebrew, become "demons" ("All the gods of the nations are demons," Ps. 95:5). Likewise, the foreign divinities whom Israel worshiped are described in the Septuagint as "demons" (Deut. 32:17), rather than the *shedim* ("guardian spirits") of the Hebrew text; and we read that the Israelites "sacrificed to demons and not to God" (Deut. 32:17). In Isaiah 65:11 the Septuagint uses *daimon* to render the Hebrew name of the pagan god of Fortune (Gad), where the Israelites are said to have been "preparing a table for the demon."

This conception of table fellowship with pagan gods who are in reality demons carries over into the New Testament: Paul warns the Corinthian church that they may not eat sacrificial meals in pagan temples, for "that which the Gentiles sacrifice, they sacrifice to demons"—meaning, for Corinth, the Greek gods Asklepios, Serapis, and especially Demeter. So Paul sets in opposition "the table of the Lord and the table of demons" (1 Cor. 10:20–21). Likewise, the author of Revelation identifies the worship of idols with the worship of demons (Rev. 9:20).

Since the battle between God and the Devil is a battle over the loyalty of humans expressed in sinful or righteous behavior, the demons become tempters who lead one into sin. Previously, sin had always been the free-will choice of individuals, and demons caused such things as loss and arthritis; now—with the opposition between God and the Devil—they also cause immoral behavior, such as lying and adultery. They are even personifications of various sins. One finds the seven spirits of deceit (*Testament of Reuben* 2.1; 3.2ff.), which are named for and cause various sins. The "spirit of error" (*Testament of Judah* 23.1; 20.1) and the "spirit of falsehood" (1 QS 4.9ff.) are connected with licentiousness, idolatry, witchcraft, and lying. The names of the "spirit of anger" (*Testament of Dan* 1–2) and "spirit of envy" (*Testament of Simeon* 4.7) speak for themselves.

The Origin of the Devil's Demons

One ancient theory of the origin of the demons was that they were the souls of those dead who, having been unjustly treated or killed, sought retribution (as perhaps were the Erinyes in Greece). Tertullian echoes this popular idea of the time, affirming that the souls who "with violence and wrong have been hurried away by a cruel and premature death and have a keen appetite for reprisals" are demons (*De Anima* 57). Another theory was that they were the ghosts of the wicked dead, as the Jewish historian Josephus suggests: "Demons [are] the spirits of wicked people who enter and kill the living" (*Jewish War* 7.185).

Origen, the great third-century Christian writer, tells us that the church of his day had no clearly defined teaching on the genesis of demons; his view was that the Devil, after becoming apostate, induced many of the angels to fall away with him, and these fallen angels were the demons (*First Principles* pref. 6). Perhaps this is the explanation for an enigmatic passage in the book of Revelation: speaking of the Great Dragon, it reads, "His tail swept down a third of the stars of heaven and threw them to the earth" (Rev. 12:4). The "stars" would be the angelic astral "forces of evil in the heavenly places" (Eph. 6:12).

The most popular account, however, is found in scores of authors in the Bible, in intertestamental literature, and in the writings of rabbis and the church fathers: demons are the souls of the offspring of angels who cohabited with humans. This is the case in the story of Azazel (discussed earlier), in which a group of angels mated with human women and produced as offspring a race of wicked giants who conquered and defiled the earth with violence and bloodshed. To destroy them, God caused the Flood. The spirits of the drowned giants, neither angelic nor human, were trapped in the regions of the air, which they haunt as demons, seeking host bodies to inhabit. According to Justin Martyr, "the angels . . . were captivated by love of women and engendered children who are called demons" (*2 Apology* 5).

The Demons in the New Testament

The function of demons in the New Testament era was to defile and bring to evil their human subjects and hosts, in both physical and spiritual ways. Demons sought to indwell humans and were able to do so in large numbers: the Gerasene demoniac was indwelt, as he said, by "Legion, for we are many" (Mark 5:9). Mary Magdalene was said to have been healed of seven demons (Luke 8:2). The indwelling spirit seemed to "possess" the host, speaking through and casting the sufferer about as though animating a puppet from inside (Mark 1:24; 9:26). The main effect of demons on the host was to cause physical and mental suffering, along with antisocial behavior: the violent Gerasene demoniac, for example, lived in tombs and deserted places, continually crying out and gashing himself with stones (Mark 5:2–6).

Sickness was not always attributed to demonic activity by the early Christians. (The two sorts of sickness—demon-caused and not—are differentiated in Matthew 4:24.) Yet demons caused dumbness (Matt. 9:32), blindness (Matt. 12:22), deafness (Mark 9:17–29), epilepsy (Matt. 17:18; literally, "being moonstruck"), and apparently fever and other diseases (Luke 4:39; 8:2). The chief manifestation of demon possession, however, was insanity: the Gerasene demoniac, when healed, was said to "be in his right mind" (Mark 5:15). So common was this idea that people often claimed that one with whom they disagreed was "insane." John the Baptist was slandered as demonized (= "insane," Luke 7:33), for example, and opponents said of Jesus, "He has a demon and is out of his mind. Why listen to him?" (John 10:20).

As Captain of the invading kingdom of God, Jesus had come to "enter a strong man's house and plunder his property" (Mark 3:27); he had come into the Devil's world and was releasing those oppressed by demons. So, according to the New Testament, he cast demons out with a word of command. (In Matthew 8:32 the word is *hypagete*, "Go away!") The demons apparently recognized Jesus on sight, often shouting, "I know who you are, the holy one of God" (Mark 1:24). They seemed terrified (as in James 2:19), knowing of their coming judgment and knowing that Jesus would bring their demise; so they cried out, "Have you come to destroy us?" (Mark 1:24) or, "Have you come to torment us before the time?" (Matt. 8:29). God disarmed the demonic rulers and authorities through Christ (Col. 2:15), and Christ at his resurrection was given mastery over all—angelic and demonic—"rule and authority and power and dominion" (Eph. 1:21; cf. 1 Cor. 15:24–25). Jesus gave his disciples authority to cast out demons in his name (Luke 10:17), which they did with remarkable success for centuries.

For Paul, the competing gods of the Greeks and Romans were demons (1 Cor. 10:20–21; cf. 1 Cor. 12:2). Tertullian explained that exorcism of Roman gods "regularly makes Christians" of onlookers, because they see that "they are seized by the thought, by the foretaste of that fire, and they leave the bodies of men at our command, all against their will, in pain, blushing" at being exposed for demons (*Apology* 23.15–18).

THE END OF THE WORLD

One of the most important consequences of the move from monism to dualism, from the gods and their servants to the one God and his enemy the Devil, was that the Devil had to be judged and destroyed. For the first time, there was cosmic "eschatology." That word comes from two Greek terms: *eschaton*, meaning "end," and *logos*, meaning "account." Thus the word means an "account of the end," or one's doctrine of the end of the world. More than one kind of eschatology was current in the pre-Christian era and contributed to the eventual Christian understanding of the end of the world and the judgment of the Devil.

Originally, of course, there was no eschatology. There was no Devil with his army of demons who needed to be destroyed. There was no last judgment or heaven and hell; people did not have souls in peril of eternal damnation. The cosmos itself was not a dark system in rebellion against the good God. It had been created out of chaos, but chaos had been defeated and brought to order in the deep past. The universe was a system that worked according to divine laws. The upper-world gods of light were now in permanent control, or so it seemed. The world that God had created was good and was supposed to last forever: the psalmist declared that God had "set the earth on its foundations so that it shall never be moved" (Ps. 104:5) and said of the sun, moon, stars, and heaven that God "established them for ever and ever" (Ps. 148:6). The cosmos was not supposed to end; there was nothing wrong with it.

The "Eschatology" of Israel's National Restoration

Like the cosmos itself, Israel had been founded to last forever, but all was not well in Israel. Its relationship with God was based on a series of covenants that were designed never to end. God's covenant with Abraham, promising the land of Israel and vast progeny, was to be "an everlasting covenant" (Gen. 17:7). God's covenant with David, promising that one of his descendants would sit on the throne of the nation of Israel, was to last for all time: "I will establish the throne of his kingdom forever" (2 Sam. 7:13). Both of these covenants looked forward to times of blessing for the nation that would apparently last forever.

A third covenant, the covenant of the Law revealed to Moses at Sinai, entailed both blessings and curses, tempering the bright future with the promise of divine wrath at disobedience. The speech of Moses in Deuteronomy, which outlines that covenant, looks ahead as if prophetically to a time when Israel would undergo not only the blessings but also the curses. Yet even after Israel should experience all the curses of the Law, including military defeat and banishment, if Israel would but obey, "then the Lord your God will restore your fortunes and have compassion on you, gathering you again from all the peoples among whom the Lord your God has scattered you" (Deut. 30:3). Thus the Law promised national restoration after the experience of the Exile.

Prophets seeking to discipline Israel for its sins warned of disaster and doom, yet they too held out some measure of hope: "The eyes of the Lord are on the sinful kingdom, and I will destroy it from the face of the earth—except that I will not utterly destroy the house of Jacob" (Amos 9:8). The day would come, even after the national disaster of the Exile, when "the ransomed of the Lord shall return, and come to Zion with singing; everlasting joy shall be upon their heads" (Isa. 35:10).

The logic of the relationship between the Lord and Israel was that they had entered into a covenant that Israel would worship Yahweh exclusively. Instead, Israel did so only sporadically; most often it followed the cults and worshiped the gods of the surrounding nations. Because the Lord was a jealous God, as the first two of the Ten Commandments so clearly pointed out, he brought about a series of disciplinary measures, including famines, droughts, plagues, and military defeats. These measures worked only in part. Finally the Lord became exasperated and exiled first the northern and then the southern tribes.

He used the nations around Israel to accomplish his wrath, to punish Israel; but the nations were too harsh and their citizens ended up taunting not only the Israelites but also Yahweh, denouncing him as weak and worthless. Therefore, the Lord promised not only to regather and restore Israel, but also to punish the nations. The covenant of Sinai that had been the cause of Israel's sufferings would someday be replaced by a "new covenant" that they would forever obey (Jer. 31:31), and the covenants with Abraham and David were reconfirmed: "My servant David shall be king over them, . . . and they shall live in the land . . . forever" (Ezek. 37:24–25). Jerusalem would someday become the center of the world, prosperous and at peace forever.

This was the eschatology of national restoration. It was to a large extent a development that took place wholly within the religious thought of Israel alone. Whether there were similar prophetic hopes for subjugated nations elsewhere in the Near East, whether other Canaanite peoples in Ugarit or Moab had prophecies that they would one day be restored, we do not know; nothing to that effect has survived. Most commonly, defeated nations were absorbed and disappeared from history. Israel, because of its return under Cyrus, because it survived, was able to rebuild not only its temple but also its hopes for the future. Those hopes were not shared by all survivors in the same way; not all groups in Israel saw the future in like terms. The hopes were, however, unique because they were centered on Israel's own traditions: the temple at Jerusalem, David the king, the land itself, and the nations that surrounded the land. This combination of traditions specific to Israel and prophecy for the nations would have an important impact on eschatology in Christianity.

The New Heavens and the New Earth

In a late, postexilic portion of the book of Isaiah, the Lord declares through the prophet, "I am about to create new heavens and a new earth" (Isa. 65:17), an event that the seer of the book of Revelation affirms: "Then I saw a new heaven and a new earth; for the first heaven and the first earth had passed away" (Rev. 21:1). Here is one of the more remarkable changes in religious conception from before to after the Exile: the good and eternal (old) heavens and earth need to be replaced.

As we have seen, one result of the advent of the Devil into the stream of tradition was the effect of evil on the very fabric of the universe itself, on the material of which the universe was made. Zoroastrianism taught that the world had originally been created good and that immediately after creation it had been attacked and defiled by the Devil and his servants. One day, in the final age, it would be restored to its original purity.

Just as the prophet foresaw a new heaven and a new earth, this old tradition may be seen in Paul's epistle to the Romans: "Creation was subjected to futility, not of its own will but by the will of the one who subjected it, in hope that the creation itself will be set free from its bondage to decay" (Rom. 8:20–21). Very much as in Zoroastrian doctrine, Paul tells us that God allowed creation itself to be "subjected to futility" and placed in "bondage to decay" as the result of the attack of demonic forces on an originally good creation. The age to come, when all things will again be restored, is foreseen in a speech of Peter in Acts: the resurrected Jesus "must remain in heaven until the time of universal restoration that God announced long ago through his holy prophets" (Acts 3:21).

What was one to do with a creation that was now in decay, subject to the Devil? Here ancient Greek tradition also contributed to the Christian view of eschatology. A very old view of the universe was that it was really a cosmic *process*, an eternal succession of cycles. By the fourth century BCE, this cyclical view of the universe had been further developed by Stoic philosophy. For the Stoics, the original element of the universe was fire. Slowly fire had cooled and condensed into air, then into water, and finally into earth. Eventually, in a reverse of the same process, the entire universe would once again become fire, consuming the other elements in blazing heat. The cycle would then repeat, and once again fire would begin the process of world-formation in an endless succession of worlds.

The fact that the whole universe was to be destroyed by fire is related in an amusing story told by the Roman poet Ovid (43 BCE–17 CE). The Roman high god Jupiter hears that evil is widespread on earth, so he descends in human form to find out for himself. He finds wickedness rampant and is himself nearly murdered. He decides to destroy humanity, but just at the moment he is about to blast humans out of existence with his lightning bolts, he is stopped by the fear that he might set the whole universe ablaze: he remembers that "it was in the fates that a time would come when sea and land, the unkindled palace of the sky and the beleaguered structure of the universe should be destroyed by fire" (Ovid, *Metamorphoses* 1.254–258). Since the universe was going to be destroyed by fire eventually anyway, Jupiter instead decides to cause the flood.

This doctrine that the world would end in fire is reflected in the epistle of 2 Peter, where we read, "The heavens will be set ablaze and dissolve, and the elements will melt with fire" (2 Pet. 3:12).

The Signs of the End

The view that the world was degenerating and coming to a cataclysmic end was applied also to human history. As early as perhaps 700 BCE, Hesiod had written of the ages of humankind. "First of all," he began, "the deathless gods who dwell on Olympus made a golden race of mortal men" (*Works and Days* 109–110). These golden men are followed by a second generation of silver, and then a third generation of bronze. Fourth comes the generation of heroes, which is followed by the present generation of iron. The story of the degeneration of humankind, likened to a series of metals descending in value, is an old story not invented by Hesiod. Its point is that the human race has degenerated to a stage near its end. Hesiod expressed a desperate wish: "Would that I were not among the men of the fifth generation, but either had died before or had been born afterwards" (*Works and Days* 174–175). Underlying that wish was the belief that humanity, like the cosmos itself, was on a cycle: the iron age would one day be replaced by a new Golden Age.

Hesiod described a series of signs that would mark the close of the age of iron, "when Zeus will destroy this race of mortal men also" (*Works and Days* 180): there will be strife among family members and friends; children will no longer respect parents; evil and violence will increase, including war; "there will be no help against evil" (*Works and Days* 201). This is clearly the background for what we call "the signs of the end." That phrase is taken from the Gospel of Matthew, where the disciples of Jesus asked him, "What will be the sign of your coming and of the end of the age?" (Matt. 24:3). Jesus answered with a very similar, though much expanded, list of the progress of evils as the end approached.

The Antichrist

The final stratagem of the Devil at the end of the age will be to raise up the Antichrist, who in competition with God will claim the religious loyalty of all on the earth (2 Thess. 2:3–4; Rev. 13). This idea was constructed by Christian prophets out of two different sources: Jewish reaction to Greek persecution under Antiochus IV Epiphanes in 166 BCE, and Roman reaction to the death of Nero in 68 CE.

The armies of Alexander the Great had conquered the Persian empire that ruled Israel in a long campaign lasting from 334 to 323 BCE. That campaign brought all of the ancient Near East under Greek control. Alexander died in 323 and his empire was divided into four kingdoms, each led by one of his generals. The major significance for Christianity was that essentially the whole world in which Christianity would arise, Palestine included, now became heavily influenced—indeed, inundated—by Greek tradition and philosophy. Greek culture permeated nearly all aspects of life, not so much by coercion—Greeks were remarkably tolerant of the customs of others—as by allure. Greek ideas began to pervade all aspects of life: science, music, athletics, art, warfare, and especially politics ("Democracy" is a Greek word).

Unfortunately for again-conquered Israel, that sense of superiority of everything Greek was shared not only by Greeks, but came to be shared by many among the upper classes of the Jerusalem elite. By the second century BCE, many powerful Jerusalem families were beginning to support fundamental changes in Israel's religious traditions, moving away from the Semitic Yahweh toward the Greek philosophical Monad. The ruling and educated classes who shared the Greek worldview were inclusive monotheists, quite tolerant of others who accepted similar inclusivity. This had never been, however, the theology of the prophetic minority in Israel who had championed Yahweh as Israel's sole deity.[14] Among those who held power in Jerusalem were many less well disposed to Greek ways and far more devoted to the theology of the Deuteronomistic and Second Isaiah than to that of the Greek philosophers. In 166 BCE, tensions between the two groups, Greek rulers and their Jewish supporters against the Jewish traditionalists, ignited into open war.

The ruler of the Greek Seleucid empire (which included Palestine), Antiochus IV Epiphanes—an epithet meaning "appearance (of God)," an "epiphany"—decided that he no longer wished to tolerate, as had long been Greek policy, the old and exclusive traditions of Jerusalem. He entered the temple, from which all Greeks had been excluded for 150 years, and put an end to the Jewish religious observances ordained in the Law (see *1 Maccabees* 1:10–54). Against this affront arose the Maccabean revolution. These heroic Jewish fighters defeated the Greeks in 164 and brought back Jewish political independence after nearly four hundred years of subjugation. Independence lasted for just over one hundred years. It was lost again when Pompey and the Roman armies assumed political control of Judea in 63 BCE. Antiochus Epiphanes is described in the latest book of the Old Testament, Daniel, as one who would defile the temple and attempt to change the Law (Dan. 7:25; see chapters 7–11). Descriptions of his arrogance and ruthlessness would meld well with those of another arrogant ruler who persecuted God's people, the Roman emperor Nero.

Nero became emperor in 54 CE at the age of seventeen. At first he ruled well under the stewardship of counselors, especially that of his tutor, the famous philosopher Seneca. Soon, however, he began to show a darker side. In 59, he had his imperious mother, Agrippina, murdered for opposing one of his sexual affairs. In 62, after the retirement of Seneca, he had free reign and absolute power to indulge his vanities and his cruelty. He divorced and murdered his first wife, Octavia; and his jealous fear of all those with power who might be his rivals led him to various murders and persecutions of the nobility and of the military.

In 64, a blaze broke out in Rome that burned much of the city, including the imperial palace itself. Although Nero did much to help restore the city, the rumor persisted that he had ordered the fire set so that he could clear the center of town and build his infamous Golden Palace. Tacitus (ca. 55–120), a Roman patrician and historian, in his work *The Annals*, wrote that "to erase the rumor, Nero substituted as those responsible, and treated with the most exquisite tortures, those hated for their shameful deeds whom the people called Christians" (Annals 15.44). Thus Nero became the first Roman emperor to persecute the church.

Yet he was loved by many. He was a devoted Hellenist, competing in Greek games and festivals as a charioteer, a singer, and a poet to unanimous adulation. He granted Greece its freedom in 66 during an artistic "tour." By early in 68, however, many legions had revolted against him; later that year the Praetorian guard deserted him and proclaimed Galba emperor. Nero fled Rome and committed suicide on June 9, 68. Yet the belief persisted, especially in the Greek east, that he was alive and would "return." Suetonius, Roman historian and secretary to Hadrian (emperor 117–138) describes the expectation of his return:

> [Nero] died at thirty-two years of age. . . . Yet they did not desist who for a long time decorated his tomb with the flowers of spring and autumn, and now brought forth his images, clothed in togas, to the rostra, and now his edicts, as though he

were alive and would soon return with great calamity for his enemies. And indeed, Vologaesus, king of the Parthians, after sending legates to the Senate concerning the renewal of ties, asked earnestly for this also, that the memory of Nero be honored in cult. At length, twenty years later (while I was an adolescent), when a man of unclear station appeared who declared that he was Nero, so favorable was his reputation among the Parthians that he was supported vehemently and returned to Rome with difficulty [for punishment]. (Suetonius, *Nero 57*)

Several other texts by Roman authors and writers outside the New Testament likewise describe the expectation that Nero would one day return across the Euphrates with a vast army and attack Rome. The book of Revelation combines the traditions of Daniel concerning Antiochus Epiphanes as persecutor of faithful Jews and Nero as persecutor of the church, and speaks of the great and final opponent of God, the Antichrist, the number of whose name would be 666. (Since ancient languages used letters also as numbers, every name also had a numerical value.) One name that equals 666, in Hebrew letters, is "Caesar Nero."[15] Irenaeus, writing in the 180s, knew of several attempts to discover the Antichrist's name and gives examples of names that equal the proper number (Irenaeus, *Against Heresies* 5.30). He cautions that if we were meant to know the name, it would have been given in the text of Revelation, and perhaps he was right. If Nero inspired the idea of the Antichrist and stood as its first incarnation, Irenaeus and others looked still for its final installment in the future.

Constructing an Eschatology

We now are able to understand some of the different eschatologies of the early Christians. If we put together, as did many Christians, the eschatology of national restoration of Israel with the Zoroastrian and Stoic notions of new heavens and a new earth, we arrive at a rather widely held (though quite material) view of the end: there will be new heavens and a new earth with a new Jerusalem as its center. So the seer of the book of Revelation is taken to a high mountain, from which he sees "the holy city Jerusalem coming down out of heaven from God" (Rev. 21:10). A particularly influential Christian group of the later second century, the Montanists, garnered ridicule because they claimed that the new Jerusalem would descend in central Asia Minor, in the deserted ruin of the former small town of Pepuza near where they lived (Epiphanius, *Panarion* 48.14.1). An earlier writer, to be fair, states merely that they renamed Pepuza as Jerusalem (Apollonius, writing about 200, quoted by Eusebius, *History of the Church* 5.18.1). Even an author as highly educated in Greek as the writer to the Hebrews looks to "the heavenly Jerusalem" as "the city that is to come" (Heb. 12:22; 13:14).

Not all Christians held such material views of the future kingdom of God. Greek philosophical tradition held that the world of God was a spiritual one, and that to be in the presence of God required a spiritual existence. So a number of Christian texts understand the end in rather different terms. Jesus in the Gospel of John told Pilate, "My kingdom is not from this world" (John 18:36); there are no apocalyptic predictions of the soon-coming destruction of the cosmos in John—no new heavens and new earth. In the closely related, though noncanonical, *Gospel of Thomas*, the destruction of this universe is stated clearly, but no mention is made of a new material cosmos: "Jesus said, 'This heaven will pass away, and the one above it shall pass away, and the dead are not alive and the living shall not die'" (*Gospel of Thomas* 11). As in the Gospel of John, one gains eternal life while alive on earth: "Everyone who lives and believes in me shall never die" (John 11:26).

The church, for all the surety that exists today among some, had no clear teaching on the future of the heavens and the earth. According to Origen, writing in the third century, the church taught that

> the world was made and took its beginning at a certain time, and is to be destroyed on account of its wickedness. But what

existed before this world or what will exist after it has not become clearly known to the many, for there is no clear statement regarding it in the teaching of the church. (Origen, *First Principles* pref. 7)

Each one may have had this or that favorite text with which to argue for one or another opinion, but the church as a whole was wise in its restraint: there were too many contradictory traditions and interpretations, too many verses leading off into different directions to make a definitive statement. The major creeds of the church, composed later in the fourth century, reflected that restraint.

There were those who held, as did the book of Revelation, that God had a body and that the future kingdom of God would be an earthly and material one. In the second and third centuries, however, such believers were clearly in the minority. As time went on, the more spiritual conceptions of how the Scriptures should be interpreted and how the future of the world should be understood began to take hold.

Eusebius of Caesarea preserved a letter written on this point by Dionysius, bishop of Alexandria from 248–264, who later earned the title Saint Dionysius the Great for his acute scholarship and pastoral wisdom in the difficult times of persecution and schism in which he lived. Dionysius wrote concerning a controversy that had arisen because of "Nepos, one of the Egyptian bishops, who taught that the promises made to the saints in holy Scripture would be fulfilled more in accordance with Jewish ideas, and suggested that there would be a millennium of bodily indulgence on this earth" (Eusebius, *History of the Church* 7.24). The word that Eusebius chose for "indulgence" is no compliment: the Greek *tryphe* may mean, besides "luxuriousness," also "wantonness." This negative choice of words was not, of course, what Nepos was advocating, as the letter by Dionysius indicates; Nepos was a faithful and holy man, whose hymnody was still being used with profit by the church. The word "indulgence" reflects Eusebius's own disdain, as an educated bishop at the beginning of the fourth century, for any idea of a materialistic view of the future kingdom of God.

Dionysius encountered a group of Christian teachers south of Alexandria in the city of Arsinoe headed by a certain Coracion (otherwise unknown). These Christians championed the doctrines of Nepos and ignited a controversy such that "schisms and secessions of entire churches had taken place." Dionysius called together the elders and teachers of the group and held discussions that lasted for days. He described their teaching as follows:

> They put forward a treatise by Nepos, on which they rely completely as proving incontrovertibly that Christ's kingdom will be on earth. Now in general I respect and love Nepos for his faith . . . and I am most unwilling to criticize him, especially now that he has gone to his rest. But more than anything we must love and reverence the truth. . . . They do not allow our simpler brethren to have lofty noble thoughts, either about the glorious and truly divine epiphany of our Lord or about our own resurrection from the dead, when we shall be gathered together and made like him; they persuade them to expect in the kingdom of God what is trifling and mortal and like the present. (Dionysius of Alexandria, quoted in Eusebius, *History of the Church* 7.24)

Dionysius clearly advocated "lofty noble thoughts" against "what is trifling and mortal and like the present" in his understanding of the future kingdom of God. He did not mean by "mortal" to suggest that these teachers thought the resurrected would die again; rather, they thought that their lives would be "like the present"—the same kind of life that we mortals live now—no doubt better in every way, but still material and fleshly. Yet, in the words of the apostle Paul and the church as it was gaining in maturity, "flesh and blood cannot inherit the kingdom of God" (1 Cor. 15:50). Eventually, after long discussions, Dionysius convinced his fellow participants: they "accepted the conclusions to be drawn from the proofs and teachings of the Holy Scriptures" and in a spirit of concord abandoned their materialist teaching.

There was certainly cause for disagreement, given the disparity of the inherited traditions and the differences in conception among the early Christian teachers themselves. Eventually, during the contentious and wrenching controversies that gave rise to the creeds, the church would choose wisely either not to mention the future age at all or to describe it in rather general terms that did not require tendentious systems of biblical interpretation. The Creed of Nicaea of 325 stated only that Jesus "was coming to judge the living and the dead," with no comment at all about the future of the world. The Creed of Constantinople of 381 — the creed that is the basis for nearly all subsequent Christianity — added slightly more: that Jesus "is coming again with glory to judge the living and the dead, whose kingdom has no end." For the future, it stated only that "we expect a resurrection of the dead and life of the coming age." Jesus, for early Christians, would one day judge the living and the dead and would be the king in a kingdom that would have no end; there would be a resurrection, and there would be life in the coming age. The character of each of these beliefs — what *kind* of kingdom or resurrection or future life — was left to the individual Christian or teacher or local church to determine. Everyone, however, was required to sign the creed.

5

KEEPING BODY
AND SOUL APART:
TREASURE IN CLAY POTS

In Chapter 2 we traced the flow in the River of God from the ubiquitous gods of polytheism to the one God of monotheism, and then from the material gods with bodies (including Second Isaiah's one God with a body) to the Monad, the spiritual and infinite One at the source of all things. Chapter 3 followed that spiritual Monad into its expression as the Trinity. In Chapter 4 we followed the course from theological monism to dualism, from the high god and his subordinate divinities in monism to the dualism of God opposed by the Devil. These major changes were the result of a shift from a material view of the cosmos to a largely spiritual view, that God was infinite spirit and not measurable body, a concept not understood previously.

The new ideas flowing into the River inevitably had consequences for the way human beings perceived themselves. In the older views, human beings were basically material beings, clay pots with air in them. Human breath was "the breath of life," and when people stopped breathing, they returned to the clay of the earth and died forever. The new view was that humans were actually real and substantial souls that were separate and distinct from the clay bodies in which they were encased. People indwelt their bodies as they did their houses; they were no longer the houses only. When someone died, only the outer casing was buried; the real person lived on.

As a consequence of this new understanding of the soul, the reason that God made human beings was seen in an entirely different light; the new ideas transformed the very meaning of life. The understanding of what a proper human life was, what humans faced and were expected to accomplish in life, changed dramatically. But let us start at the beginning.

Why did the gods make human beings at all? It is not obvious that the world should contain human beings, given the fact that, in the oldest conceptions, the world had arisen out of chaos. The gods themselves originally came out of chaos, and they produced more and more gods, until there were gods for everything. What need did they have of clay humans?

One of the earliest answers to that question is found in the Babylonian creation epic *Enuma Elish,* cited in earlier chapters. That story concludes with a summary of its plot: "This is the song of Marduk, who vanquished Tiamat and achieved kingship."[1] As we have seen, Marduk killed the sea monster Tiamat, created the cosmos from her body, and became the god of gods for ancient Mesopotamia. After his victory, Marduk demanded that the vanquished gods who had fought on Tiamat's side should build him a huge temple-palace in a city to be called Babylon. To avoid personal destruction, they labored long and hard on his behalf. Marduk was so impressed by their humble and eager willingness to work that he was led to relieve them (and the gods in general thereafter) of such arduous earthly tasks: he created humans as replacement workers. Henceforth, humans would build cities and temples to the gods, and they would render service to the gods by worship and offerings. The original purpose of human life, therefore, was the care and feeding of the gods; humans were to replace the vanquished enemies in providing temples, rites, and offerings for the victorious and superior divinities.

The importance of this proper function of human beings—to offer food and drink, incense and prayers, to the gods—was seen in several ancient cultures and lasted well into the Christian period. Even though the gods had their own immortal food in heaven, the offerings were in some fundamentally important way their sustenance. In the *Epic of Gilgamesh,* for example, another very old Mesopotamian story, Enlil, the king of the gods, becomes angry with people and decides to destroy them by sending a flood, a story that many hundreds of years later would also be found in the Bible and Greek and Roman tradition. One man, Utnapishtim (the "Noah" of the story), is warned to build the ark and put on board his family and a representative number of the animals. When the flood comes and sweeps everything away, "and all of mankind had returned to clay," he and his family are saved. The ark lands on a high mountain; birds are sent out daily until finally they find something to nest on and things begin to dry out. Finally everyone disembarks, and, true to their purpose in life, the first thing they do is to offer sacrifice. "The gods," we are told, "smelled the savor; the gods smelled the sweet savor; the gods crowded like flies about the sacrificer."[2]

This is not a complimentary description of the gods, nor was it meant to be: they had just wiped out nearly all of humanity. It does, however, illustrate that the gods had almost starved themselves by depriving themselves of those who had been feeding them all along. That the offerings were food for God is again illustrated in Leviticus: speaking of the part of a sheep that was to be given as a sacrifice, the text commands that "the priest shall burn it on the altar as food offered by fire to the Lord" (Lev. 3:11, RSV). In a Roman version of the same flood story, when Jupiter declared that he was going to wipe out humanity with the flood for its wickedness, a much wiser council of gods wondered "who would bring incense to their altars?" (Ovid, *Metamorphoses* 1.248–249). The gods needed humans quite as much as humans needed the gods: everyone had to eat.

The rites were part of a contractual relationship between the gods and their human subjects. If the gods received their due ceremonies and offerings, they were obligated to protect and provide for their subjects by supplying rains and crops in due season. If humans broke the contract by refusing to make such offerings, they brought the wrath of the gods on the entire community. This was at the heart of the rationale for the Roman persecution of Christians: Christians refused to participate in the rites and sacrifices owed to the gods of the Roman empire. In 258 CE, for example, Cyprian, bishop of Carthage, was arrested and brought before the governing proconsul, Galerius Maximus. An account of his trial has survived:

> The proconsul said: "The most hallowed emperors have commanded that you perform the ceremonies." Saint Cyprian answered: "I will not." . . . Galerius Maximus, after conferring with his council, spoke with difficulty and regret: "For a long time you have lived with a sacrilegious mind, . . . and you have set yourself as an enemy of the Roman gods and holy religious rites. Nor were the pious and most hallowed rulers Valerian and Gallienus, the Augusti, and Valerian, most noble Caesar, able to recall you to be a participant in their rites."[3]

The issue was that the Christians refused to participate in the ceremonies and rites thought to be necessary for the welfare of the Roman state. The highest officials of the Roman government had tried to persuade Cyprian to reconsider. For his refusal, as the account goes on to report, Cyprian was beheaded.

THE COMMON FATE
OF DEATH WITHOUT AFTERLIFE

In the monistic universe of Mesopotamia, Israel, and early Greece, the great difference between gods and humans was that human beings were mortal. The *Epic of Gilgamesh*, referred to above, tells of a remarkable hero's search for eternal life. Gilgamesh is the greatest among his generation, much as Achilles of Homer's *Iliad* would later be among the Greeks who attacked Troy. He has but one near equal, his friend and soulmate, Enkidu. This friend, in the grip of hubristic bravado, kills the divinely appointed Guardian of the Forest, the monster Humbaba, and therefore is sentenced to die by the gods; there is no escape.

Gilgamesh mourns over Enkidu's body until it begins to decay, and then in anger and desperation begins a quest to defeat death, as he has defeated every other opponent in his life. He sets out on a long and perilous journey to the edge of the earth and beyond the world-encircling ocean, for he has heard that out there on a blessed island lives Utnapishtim the Faraway (the "Noah" mentioned above), who has been granted eternal life by the gods. When Gilgamesh finally arrives, he finds that such eternal life is not for anyone else, for there will never again be a flood; the gods have granted such life to Utnapishtim and his wife alone. Gilgamesh is told, however, how to gain a plant that will give him, not eternal life, but renewal of youth when he is old. By typical heroic effort, he obtains the plant, but on his way back home, he falls asleep in exhaustion and a serpent sneaks up and eats the plant. That is why snakes shed their skins and become once again young and vigorous. For Gilgamesh, however, and for the rest of humanity, not only is eternal life impossible, even renewal to youth is lost. He must, as representative of all humans, one day die.

In another Mesopotamian story with a similar point, Ea, the creator of humans and the giver of the arts of civilization, makes as his son and model of the human race the wise but mortal Adapa, to be priest for Ea in his city of Eridu. Yet, "to him he had given wisdom; eternal life he had not given him." Adapa, enraged because of a storm that sinks his boat, breaks the wing of the South Wind and incurs the wrath of Anu, the sky god. Anu summons him to heaven for judgment. Ea warns him not to eat or drink anything in heaven, for he surmises that Anu will offer Adapa the food of death. Because of the intercession of two of Anu's ministers, however, Anu changes his mind; he indeed offers Adapa food, but unknown to either Ea or Adapa, it is the food of the gods themselves, the food of life. Adapa, following Ea's instructions, refuses to eat and loses

the possibility of eternal life. Adapa, like Gilgamesh, is the arche-
type of humanity; again, eternal life is lost to all.[4]

Adam and Eve likewise lose any possibility of eternal life for all
subsequent humanity by disobedience in the Garden of Eden.
That story, though told of the earliest humans, is a relatively late
product in the sacred story traditions of Israel. That humans, obedient or not, were originally meant to be mortal in the oldest
Hebrew traditions, as in the Mesopotamian stories, is quite likely,
given the similar views of the surrounding cultures and the number of times in the Bible that death is spoken of as the normal
human destiny, without reference to sin or disobedience. When
the wise woman of Tekoa, for example, persuades David to allow
his banished son Absalom to return, she says, "We must all die; we
are like water spilled on the ground, which cannot be gathered up"
(2 Sam. 14:14). In another comparison of God and humans, it is
God's eternal life and human impermanence that is the point: "You
turn humankind back to dust and say, 'Turn back, you mortals.'
. . . You sweep them away; they are like a dream" (Ps. 90:3–5).
This is a common lament: humans are by nature and destiny different from and less than God; they are creatures of clay, transient
as dust and dreams.

In texts from a later time, humans lose the possibility of eternal
life by their disobedience in the Garden of Eden. As a result of eating from the tree of knowledge, Adam and Eve are told by God
that they will lose their privileges: they will suffer and sweat "until
you return to the ground, for out of it you were taken. You are
dust, and to dust you shall return" (Gen. 3:19). This story adds
human disobedience to a situation that is otherwise quite similar to
that of Adapa and Gilgamesh: weakness and foolishness demonstrate human unworthiness for life like that of God.

As in Mesopotamia and early Israel, death for humans was
originally God's will in Greece. Apollo, son and spokesman of
Zeus, explains that from the beginning it was not Zeus's plan to
overcome death:

Once the dust has drained down all a man's blood, once the man has died, there is no raising him up again. This is a thing for which my Father [Zeus] never made curative spells. All other states, without effort or hard breath, he can completely rearrange. (Aeschylus, *Eumenides* 647–651)

The depressing nature and finality of death is emphasized over and over in ancient texts. In the Homeric epics of Greece, the goddess Athena tells Odysseus's son Telemachos that "death is a thing that comes to all alike. Not even the gods can fend it away from a man they love, when once the destructive doom of leveling death has fastened upon him" (*Odyssey* 3.236–238).

Odysseus, wandering the world over to find his way home after the Trojan war, eventually descends while still alive to the house of Hades to learn how he is to gain his homecoming. There he meets the ghost of Achilles. Achilles questions him as to why he came to the underworld, "where the senseless dead men dwell, mere imitations of perished mortals" (*Odyssey* 11.475–476). As Odysseus tries to console him for his death, Achilles replies: "O shining Odysseus, never try to console me for dying. I would rather follow the plow as thrall to another man, one with no land allotted him and not much to live on, than be a king over all the perished dead" (*Odyssey* 11.488–491).

In the Bible, the world of the dead is Sheol, an underworld of silence and darkness where the dead "go, never to return, to the land of gloom and deep darkness, the land of gloom and chaos, where light is like darkness" (Job 10:21–22). In a prophecy of Isaiah against the king of Babylon, one finds again the ghosts of the dead in the underworld. The prophet foresees a time when the king of Babylon will die; in hyperbole he declares, "Sheol beneath is stirred up to meet you when you come; it rouses the shades to greet you" (Isa. 14:9).

Achilles' ghost declares that the ghosts of the dead are "senseless, . . . mere imitations of perished mortals."[5] There is as yet no substantial life after death. This is why Moses never threatens those who break the Law of God with eternal hell or promises eternal life in heaven to those who keep the Law. All rewards and punishments take place in this life, here on earth, and all the dead, righteous or otherwise, go to Sheol.

THE JUDGMENT OF THE DEAD
AND AFTERLIFE IN EGYPT

Unlike Mesopotamia or Israel or Homeric Greece, Egypt had a concept of life after death and a judgment of the dead. From about 2100 BCE comes a famous text known to us as the *Instruction to King Merikare*. It purports to be an instruction by the king's father to his son. In it Merikare is warned about the court of the gods that judges the dead; they are not lenient, he learns. He is told, "Do not trust in length of years; they view a lifetime in an hour. When a man remains over after death, his deeds are set beside him as treasure, and being yonder lasts forever. . . . [H]e who reaches them without having done wrong will exist there like a god."[6]

In the Coffin Texts of approximately five hundred years later, we find actual depictions of the judgment of the dead in the under-world, painted in vivid colors with explanatory texts. The soul of each dead individual is led before a tribunal of forty-two gods and makes a "negative confession," denying all sins, from sexual immoralities to theft, violence, and blasphemy. The heart of the deceased is then weighed in a balance against the dictates of Maat, the divine principle of Right and Order. If it passes, the soul enters into the blessed afterlife with the king of the dead, Osiris. If it fails, the soul is eaten by the composite monster Amemet, the "Swallower" of the dead, and ceases to exist.[7]

THE JUDGMENT OF THE DEAD
IN ZOROASTRIANISM

A view of the afterlife with many similarities to that of Egypt is found in the Zoroastrianism of Persia. In this view, humans are born pure and sinless, endowed with reason, and are wholly free to choose to participate with either of the two spirits, God or the Devil. (The world, one may recall, was created good and is to be enjoyed; asceticism is not part of Zoroastrianism.) Because the individual is thought to be entirely free to choose, perfect goodness is possible in this life. Ethics are therefore of central concern and are highly emphasized, based on good thoughts, good words, and good deeds. Included are truthfulness, works of charity, justice, compassion, honesty, education, and work. There is no means of atonement or need for forgiveness; no intercession is possible, and no offerings are able to cover sin. Humans make choices, and they pay a price or earn a reward based on what they choose.

At death, the soul travels to the judgment seat of Mithra, one of the emanations of God (beings similar to archangels), whose job it is to oversee justice. Mithra's judgment is based on the thoughts, words, and deeds of this life: those factors are weighed on a scale of balance, good against evil, and the way that the scale tips (even if only slightly) determines one's fate. After the weighing, the soul is led to the Bridge of the Separator. If the judgment is favorable, the bridge is wide and leads easily to paradise, a place of light, pleasant scents, and noble souls. If the judgment is for condemnation, the bridge becomes as narrow as a knife edge, and the soul falls into perdition. Hell is a dark pit, very deep and narrow, with noxious fumes and tortures. There the soul suffers torment until the End, the time of the last battle between Good and Evil. The righteous will be resurrected into bodies, and the wicked will finally be destroyed in the "second death," a concept later found in the book of Revelation (20:14).

BODY AND SOUL IN GREECE

Both Egypt and Persia contributed to the developing ideas surrounding the doctrine of the soul and its postmortem fate. But, in the words of the classical scholar Werner Jaeger, "it was the Greeks alone who were to determine for several millennia the way in which civilized man would conceive the nature and destiny of the soul."[8] Their ideas contributed much that was essential in forming the Christian worldview.

The Early Greek Tradition

Early in Greek tradition, just as in the Old Testament, there was no concept of the soul separate from the body, carrying the entire identity of the person. The Greek word for "soul," *psyche*, originally meant "breath" or "wind." In reference to human beings, it was the cold "breath of life" that was breathed out at death when one "breathed one's last." That final breath then assumed the form of the ghostly image that went to the house of Hades. The part of the person in the time of Homer that functioned as what we might now call the soul was in Greek either the *thumos* (the warm blood and breath of the chest and lungs, signifying the thoughts and passions) or the *ker* (the heart).

New conceptions of the soul appeared starting in about the sixth century BCE in Greece. The Homeric ideas of the various internal functions began to be combined so that the *thumos*, the *ker*, and the *psyche* were collected into the one word *psyche*, which now could be used of the whole inner person. Science again lay at the base of new understanding: the idea that the *psyche* was thought to be air helped in formulating a new conception of the human makeup.

Anaximenes, an important scientist and philosopher of the mid to late sixth century BCE, speculated as to what the original element might be—that element out of which all things came to be— and concluded that it was air. He declared that "air is the principle of existing things; for from it all things come to be and into it they are again dissolved. As our soul, . . . being air, holds us together and controls us, so does wind and air enclose the whole world" (*Aetius* 1.3.4). Since Anaximenes saw air as the first element of the universe, he believed that both God and the human soul were composed of air. The soul was no longer just "life breath"; in this new view it was much closer to what we today call the soul, for it "controls us."

In time, the essence of both God and the soul would be upgraded to spirit or fire or ether. Nevertheless, Anaximenes and other early Greek philosophers laid the foundation for what would become one of the most important principles in Christian teaching: that both God and the essential human being are spiritual entities.

Orphism

During the same century there arose an influential religious view known as Orphism — a view that lasted well into the Christian era. Orpheus was a mythical figure from before the time of the Trojan war, reputedly the son of Apollo and one of the Muses (usually Kalliope). He was known for his prophetic talent and wonderful ability to sing, mesmerizing his listeners. His songs could charm nearly anything: rivers would flow upstream to hear him; mountains and trees would move closer. To him was attributed a large body of literature (written under his name over centuries) containing revolutionary doctrines about the origin of the cosmos and about the soul and the afterlife. These were disseminated throughout Greece by wandering priests (often of questionable reputation) who held initiations into Orphic mysteries. Plato called them "begging priests and soothsayers" and described them as using spells and enchantments to force the gods to grant remission of sins and purification for injustices committed by both the living and the dead (Plato, *Republic* 364b–e).

Whether there ever was a distinct "religion" known as Orphism is in question, but a number of important religious ideas are found in texts attributed to Orpheus. In a description of the breakdown of civilized ways, Plato mentions "the Titanic nature of which our old legends speak" (Plato, *Laws* 701c). This is a reference to a fundamental Orphic myth about the origin of the universe and the place of humans in it. According to this story, the world came about in a series of six generations. Zeus, who ruled the fifth generation, fathered Dionysus by Persephone, the queen of the underworld, and then gave over the rule of the world to his son while Dionysus was still a child. The Titans, the older generation of earth deities from whom Zeus himself had wrested control, attacked the child and then dismembered, cooked, and ate him. Enraged, Zeus blasted the Titans into ash with his thunderbolts. From the ashes he made humans, who therefore partook of both natures: the divine Dionysus in their souls and the lawless rebellion of the Titans in their bodies.

The fundamental teaching inherent in this story is that of a dualism of body and soul. The soul is separate and different in nature from the body: the body is of the earth; the soul is divine. Aristotle relates an important aspect of this doctrine in a citation of the Orphic poems: "It is stated there that the soul, coming from the whole universe and being borne by the winds, enters the body when the animal inhales" (Aristotle, *De Anima* 410b). Again, as in Anaximenes' view, the soul is air; but in this passage, it is something from outside the body that enters the newborn at its first breath. The soul is a heavenly being in its own right that becomes incarnate in the body.[9]

The idea that the soul is divine, derived from the heavenly Dionysus, and that it is enclosed in the "Titanic" body, produced a new understanding of human origin and destiny: humans now, if properly enlightened and initiated into the Orphic mysteries, could claim to be on a journey back to their divine origin. This has been termed "the journey of the soul": the soul originated in God, became incarnate here on earth, and is destined to return to God.

Plato preserves one of the most famous Orphic sayings in antiquity. He writes, enigmatically, "Perhaps we are actually dead, for I once heard one of our wise men say that we are now dead, and that our body is a tomb" (Plato, *Gorgias* 493a). This statement lays out one of the quintessential Orphic doctrines—in Greek, *Soma sema* ("The body is a tomb"). We learn a great deal more about this saying in another passage:

Some say that the body is the grave (*sema*) of the soul which may be thought to be buried in the present life, or again the index of the soul, because the soul gives indications (*semainei*) to the body. Probably the Orphic poets were the inventors of the name, and they were under the impression that the soul is suffering the punishment of sin, and that the body is an enclosure or prison in which the soul is incarcerated, kept safe (*soma, sozetai*) as the name *soma* implies, until the penalty is paid. (Plato, *Cratylus* 400c)

The Greek word *sema* can mean both "tomb" and "sign," since a tomb "signified" who was inside: on the tombstone were written "the customary four hexameter verses in commendation of the life of the deceased" (Plato, *Laws* 12.958e). The Greek word *soma* could also be further interpreted: on the one hand, it meant "body"; on the other, if derived from the Greek word *sozetai* (meaning "to be safe"), the body could be understood to be an enclosure of the soul, a place that guarded the soul. Plato shows us in the above passage that the Orphic poets understood the soul to be in the body (which served as a kind of prison) as a punishment for some crime committed before its incarnation and believed that the soul would remain in the body until it had paid the full penalty. This clearly shows that, in the Orphic view, the soul existed before it entered the body and would exist after death.

Some indication of what crime humanity had committed is given in another text from the fifth-century poet Pindar (518–438 BCE). Speaking of the judgment in the afterlife, Pindar refers to those from whom "Persephone receives the blood-price for her ancient grief" (Pindar, quoted in Plato, *Meno* 81b). As we have seen, Persephone (according to the Orphics) was the mother of Dionysus; his murder by the Titans was the source of her "ancient grief." Human beings, as heirs of the "Titanic nature," were required to pay the penalty for their progenitors' heinous crime. Those who did so by ethical behavior and proper Orphic initiations and practices were restored to a blessed new life.

Another text, one of a number of thin golden plates found in Orphic graves in southern Italy from the fourth to third centuries BCE, instructs the deceased on what to say to the judges of the underworld and records their answer. The soul of the dead is to declare: "I avow that I am of your blessed race. And I have paid the penalty for deeds unrighteous." The judges reply, "O happy and blessed one, you shall be god instead of mortal." Here is quite visible the claim that the soul is from the race of the gods and that the individual, as heir to the Titans, has to pay through incarnation the penalty for wickedness. The judges then release the individual from the cycle of reincarnations and receive the soul into the company of the gods. So again, in a similar text, the soul is instructed to say, "I am a child of earth and starry heaven, but my race is of heaven alone."[10]

Pythagoreanism

Such ideas had a profound effect on one of the most important and enigmatic figures of the sixth century BCE. Pythagoras was born on the Greek island of Samos in the middle of the century and moved to southern Italy about 530. He was both a scientist and a religious teacher; we still use the famous geometric theorem that bears his name. He was founder of the movement known as Pythagoreanism, which strongly influenced Plato and later Greek philosophy.

As in Orphism, this movement advocated a specific lifestyle that included initiations, vegetarianism, and abstention from animal sacrifices. Perhaps its most distinctive teaching was that of reincarnation. Pythagoras, among his many other achievements, is said to have been able to remember his past lives. A roughly contemporary philosopher, Xenophanes, describes the following humorous incident: "Once they say that he was passing by when a puppy was being whipped, and he took pity and said: 'Stop, do not beat it; for it is the soul of a friend that I recognized when I heard it crying out'" (Xenophanes, *Diogenes Laertius* 8.36). Not only did the soul of Pythagoras go from body to body; so did that of his unfortunate friend. The point for Pythagorean eschatology was, of course, that the soul of his friend had failed the test of its previous life and was now being punished even further, both by "descending" incarnation (from human to dog) and by whipping.

The fate of the soul after death was a matter of deep concern for both the practitioners of Orphism and the Pythagoreans. In a poem commissioned by a patron who was clearly a committed Pythagorean, the poet Pindar writes:

> The sins committed in this realm of Zeus are judged below the earth by one who pronounces sentence with hateful necessity. . . . [B]ut in the presence of the honored gods, all who rejoiced in keeping their oaths share a life that knows no tears, while the others endure labor that none can look upon. (Pindar, *Olympian* 2.58–67)

For Pindar, the soul was a heavenly being temporarily incarnated in a body of the earth; it would one day face a judgment after death, for which it would either pay penalty or receive reward.

The Soul and Its Destiny in Plato

Orphic and Pythagorean teaching deeply influenced Plato (ca. 429–347 BCE), perhaps the most important philosopher in the entire stream of tradition that contributed to the formation of Christianity. He inherited from Orphism and Pythagoreanism the following ideas: that the heavenly and eternal soul was something separate from the perishable and earthly body, that the soul existed both before and after its incarnation, and that it underwent some type of judgment after death that determined its future state, either in another incarnation or, if purified, in a journey back to its heavenly home.

Plato had been a friend and disciple of Socrates until Socrates' judicial murder at the age of seventy in 399 BCE, when Plato was approximately thirty years old. Over the next more than fifty years, Plato wrote his famous dialogues, expressing not only the views of his teacher but also his own maturing ideas, most often using his teacher as spokesman. The Orphics and Pythagoreans had been secretive about their doctrines, requiring silence from their adherents and secret initiations. Socrates and Plato, on the other hand, were quite open about their ideas: Socrates spent decades publicly arguing and discussing his views on the streets and in the homes of Athens; Plato wrote hundreds of pages in beautiful Greek to be read by all, and founded a school known as the Academy in a public gymnasium in Athens. The Academy became the most influential philosophical school in the ancient world, contributing as much as any other source to Christianity.

Plato was faced with a situation in his society quite similar to that faced by Jesus and the earliest Christians: the vast majority of people of his era did not believe in an afterlife at all, but held to the traditional views of Homer. The case was quite similar with Jews in Palestine, the great majority of whom held to the view of life like that described in almost all of the Old Testament: people's "souls" were merely the breath of life in their bodies, and there was no afterlife. In the *Phaedo,* the famous dialogue that describes Socrates' last day of discussion with his friends before his death, the conversation quite appropriately centers on soul and body, death and the afterlife. His friends have come to mourn his fate, but Socrates, with typical good humor and calm, tries to console them. He is the one about to die, but rather than receiving comfort for his loss of friends and life, he has to console his companions for their loss of him. The difficulty that he must overcome in the minds of his friends is the common apprehension about death, well described by Socrates' follower Cebes. He tells Socrates that he fears

> that when [the soul] is released from the body it may no longer exist anywhere, but may be dispersed and destroyed on the very day that the man himself dies, as soon as it is freed from the body, that as it emerges it may be dissipated like breath or smoke, and vanish away, so that nothing is left of it anywhere. (*Phaedo* 70a)

The group converses for hours, during which Socrates argues against his friends' insecurities for the immortality of the soul. In a humorous final scene as the last hour approaches, Crito, one of the participants, asks Socrates, "How shall we bury you?" Socrates replies to the others:

He thinks that I am the one whom he will see presently lying dead, and he asks how he is to bury me! As for my long and elaborate explanation that when I have drunk the poison I shall remain with you no longer, but depart to a state of heavenly happiness, this attempt to console both you and myself seems to be wasted on him. (115d)

The cultural presupposition that there was no afterlife ran so deep that even Socrates' own disciples, like those of Jesus centuries later, had difficulty accepting their teacher's view.

Plato and his literary presentation of Socrates had quite a different conception from his society at large; in New Testament terms, it was "new wine" that required a "new wineskin." For him, "every soul is immortal" (*Phaedrus* 245c). Necessarily, therefore, "our souls had a previous existence, before they took on this human shape; they were independent of our bodies" (*Phaedo* 76c). Once, before their incarnation, our souls had a clear view of the divine light: "Pure was the light that shone around us, and pure were we, without taint of the prison house which now encompasses us, and we call a body, bound fast within as an oyster in its shell" (*Phaedrus* 250c). In addition, since our souls are immortal, they "will exist in the next world" (*Phaedo* 71e).

As to its essence, the soul is "most like that which is divine, immortal, . . . indissoluble, ever self-consistent and invariable." The body, in contrast, is "most like that which is human, mortal, . . . dissoluble, and never self-consistent" (80b). Here we see the strong influence of Greek science in its support of a dualism of the material realm, visible and ever-changing, opposed to "the realm of the pure and everlasting and immortal and changeless" (79d). The body and the material world are made of the heavy natural elements that decay and fall to pieces and are dissipated; the soul is made of heavenly elements that have no beginning or end. This pairing of religion and science carries with it a fundamental ethical imperative: the soul, so far as it is able, must keep itself pure from what is material and corporeal, for "purification . . . consists in separating the soul as much as possible from the body" (67c).

The Orphic myth of human origins derived the body out of the earthly and rebellious Titans, as we saw earlier. So Orphic and Pythagorean disciples lived a life of ethical purity and asceticism to fend off the "Titanic nature." In Plato's understanding of that nature,

> the body provides us with innumerable distractions in the pursuit of our necessary sustenance. . . . Besides, the body fills us with loves and desires and fears and all sorts of fancies and a great deal of nonsense. . . . Wars and revolutions and battles are due simply and solely to the body and its desires. All wars are undertaken for the acquisition of wealth, and the reason why we have to acquire wealth is the body, because we are slaves in its service. (66b–e)

One can almost hear the apostle Paul's outcry: "I am of the flesh, sold into slavery under sin. . . . Who will rescue me from this body of death?" (Rom. 7:14, 24). Here is the basis for the sustained polemic of Jesus, Paul, and the early church against the flesh and the "honors" of the material world.

The purpose of life, in Plato's view, is not the acquisition of wealth, or long life, or many children, but a kind of spiritual enlightenment that leads one to a "wisdom that makes possible courage and self-control and integrity or, in a word, true goodness; and the presence or absence of pleasures and fears and other such feelings makes no difference at all" (69b). The purpose of death, "the release of the soul from the body" (64c), is to give the soul a clear sight of that wisdom, and to arrive in the next world purified and enlightened to "dwell among the gods" (69c). To again quote the apostle Paul: "Now we see in a mirror, dimly, but then we will see face to

face. Now I know only in part; then I will know fully" (1 Cor.
13:12). Here on earth the soul is clouded in its vision of the divine.

An apt summary of Plato's position is found in one of his latest
writings:

> [T]he soul is utterly superior to body, and that which gives each
> one of us his being is nothing else but his soul, whereas the body
> is no more than a shadow which keeps us company. So it is
> well said of the deceased that the corpse is but a ghost; the
> real man—the undying thing called the soul—departs to give
> account to the gods of another world, even as we are taught by
> ancestral tradition—an account to which the good may look for-
> ward without misgivings, but the evil with grievous dismay.
> (*Laws* 12.959a–b)

As we saw in the discussion of Orphism, Plato denigrated the
begging priests who promised through rites and offerings to be
able to obtain remission of sins even for those who had already
died. This was to him a grand injustice: that one could act
wickedly and then pay priests to absolve one through "incantations," and even pay to have oneself or one's ancestors released
from the torments they manifestly deserved. The entire enterprise,
however, was based on a very well developed conception of
rewards and punishments of the dead in the afterlife that Plato
himself to a large extent shared. His concern was that the judgment in the afterlife be understood to be absolutely just, that it not
be thought susceptible to manipulation by religion. For him these
Orphic practitioners were crafty charlatans who promised what
they could never deliver: that they could subvert the judges of the
dead, and therefore that the wicked on earth could get away with
their sins. Recall that in Zoroastrianism there were no sacrifices
that could influence the judgment of the dead; much the same was
true for Plato. One's deeds were evaluated, and one paid the price
or reaped the reward.

Plato understood and accepted, nevertheless, the science and
logic that undergirded the Orphic and Pythagorean myths.

Science showed that the body was heavy and belonged to the earth; the soul was heavenly and its proper destiny was to return to its original home. In a parallel discussion of earthly existence and heavenly destiny, Paul said that "while we are still in this tent [of the body], we groan under our burden" (2 Cor. 5:4). Orphic myth, in addition, had declared the body to be "Titanic"—that is, rebellious against God—and an enemy of the purity of the divine nature. In Plato's understanding, this meant that the body was an ethical detriment; it led the soul into earthly and fleshly desires, distracting it from the wholesomeness of its true nature. The body "attached" itself to the soul, and the soul was weighted down by the body when the soul followed the body's passions and desires, becoming entangled in the material world. Thus there were two alternatives for the soul at death:

> If at its release, the soul is pure and carries with it no contamination of the body, . . . then it departs to that place which is, like itself, divine, immortal, and wise, . . . and where, as they say of the initiates in the Mysteries, it really spends the rest of time with God. (*Phaedo* 80e–81a)

Quite the opposite is true of the person who is devoted to the desires and dictates of the body. For "the corporeal is heavy, oppressive, earthly, and visible. So the soul which is tainted by its presence is weighed down and dragged back into the visible world" (81c). The soul cannot rise to its home because it is "burdened" by its attachment to things and desires of the material realm. This perspective is the source of the language behind a saying of Jesus in the Gospel of Luke: "Take heed to yourselves lest your hearts be weighed down with dissipation and drunkenness and cares of this life" (Luke 21:34, RSV).

Purgatory

Plato was somewhat less than consistent in his explanations of the destiny of the soul, but, as he tells us, how can one be sure about such things? (*Phaedo* 114d). Yet one aspect of his eschatology became the basis for a characteristic Christian doctrine, popular for most of Christian history until the rise of Protestantism: the doctrine of purgatory.[11]

The idea among many ancients was that suffering was sent by the gods not merely at random, but for a purpose: it was sent to discipline or educate one in righteousness and obedience. As the epistle of Hebrews declares, "God disciplines us for our good, that we may share his holiness" (Heb. 12:10). The fundamental principle underlying the theory of punishments in Deuteronomy was just that: that God would punish Israel for its sins in order to bring the nation back to proper worship and obedience. In Greece, the tragic poet Aeschylus expressed the idea in the simple phrase *pathei mathos*, "one learns by suffering" (*Agamemnon* 177). "It is impossible," clarified Plato, "to be rid of evils otherwise" (*Gorgias* 525b).

Both cultures had a particularly dark view of human nature: Paul quoted the Hebrew psalmist and generalized the meaning — that among Jew and Gentile alike, "there is none righteous, not even one" (Rom. 3:10). So all people needed the discipline of suffering. Even Jesus himself, as heir to human nature, "learned obedience from the things he suffered" (Heb. 5:8).

Plato understood the destiny of the soul to be, as in Zoroastrianism, blessed reward or punishment:

> The man who has led a godly and righteous life departs after death to the Isles of the Blessed and there lives in all happiness exempt from ill, but the godless and unrighteous man departs to the prison of vengeance and punishment which they called Tartarus. (*Gorgias* 523a–b)

But Plato also believed in the fundamental goodness of the divine nature, not its mere righteousness. God cannot be merely mechanically just, weighing deeds one against another, nor can God be vengeful. The punishments of the afterlife, therefore, must serve some curative purpose. Thus Plato's vision of the afterlife includes a third alternative, a place of temporary punishment for the healing of the soul of its ills and sins. There are not only those who succeed in finding their way to future blessing; there are also two categories of those destined for punishments in the under-world: the curable and the incurable. Both Plato's view of the value and necessity of suffering in the present life and his perspective on suffering's function in the next are seen in the following passage:

> Now, those who are benefited through suffering punishment by gods and men are beings whose evil deeds are curable. . . . But those who have been guilty of the most heinous crimes and whose misdeeds are past cure—of these warnings are made, and they are no longer capable themselves of receiving any benefit, because they are incurable—but others are benefited who behold them suffering throughout eternity the greatest and most excruciating and terrifying tortures because of their mis-deeds, literally suspended as examples there in the prison house in Hades, a spectacle and a warning to any evildoers who from time to time arrive. (*Gorgias* 525b–c)

The condemned but curable enter Hades' realm and undergo punishments that heal their souls of the ingrown evils that they acquired during life; they are further admonished by the terrify-ing examples of the incurable, whom they see being punished as warnings.

THE RESURRECTION

In Plato's view, those who succeed in overcoming fleshly desires and "have lived a life of surpassing holiness—these are they who are released and set free from confinement in these regions of the earth. . . . And of these such as have purified themselves suffi-ciently by philosophy live thereafter altogether without bodies" in the divine presence (Plato, *Phaedo* 114b–c). That both Greek sci-ence and Greek philosophy postulated a life for righteous souls with God in heaven "altogether without bodies" became a major point of contention for the church in the second and later centuries CE. The highly educated among the church writers understood quite well what science demanded: no earth-made bodies belonged, or could be tolerated, in the presence of the entirely spiritual Monad, in the heavenly world of light that was the home of the righteous.

But the church was not heir to the Greek tradition alone, nor were any but a few of its members highly educated. Its Scriptures were at first those of the Old Testament in Greek, with their decidedly this-world orientation. Only late in the second century did a collection of New Testament documents begin to take shape, and not all of them were written by the well educated. The writers of the Old Testament, and the vast majority of people in the Greco-Roman empire, lived in a distinctly material thought-world: for them, God (Yahweh or Zeus or Jupiter) had a body and sat on a throne on the top of the sky, a few thousand feet above us.

As the idea of an afterlife began to take hold among early Christians, the "resurrection" was conceived by some to be as materialist as Zoroastrianism had claimed: fleshly bodies would enjoy earthly, but upgraded and eternal, rewards. New bodies would be formed of the pieces scattered here and there of the old bodies. Nothing, these Christians claimed, was impossible with God: he would find all the parts of one's old carcass, even though eaten by birds or animals or scattered beyond the horizons. He would then construct a future body of the original flesh, though upgraded and blessed and no longer subject to corruption.

Against this view stood Jesus himself, and Paul, and the educated Greek Christians of the eastern empire, but to no avail. In an argument over the very issue of resurrection, a group of Sadducees (who denied the resurrection entirely) presented Jesus with the famous question about the woman who had seven husbands: Whose wife would she be in the resurrection? Jesus replied that "when they rise from the dead, they neither marry nor are given in marriage, but are like angels in heaven" (Mark 12:25). In other words, not only do they in fact rise from the dead, but they do so in bodies like those of the angels. One may assume from this and from the entire tradition about angels that whatever sort of bodies angels have, they are not bodies of earthly flesh, however upgraded. Thus Jesus did not believe in resurrection of one's original old flesh; indeed, he thought it important to teach the opposite to head off ridiculous ideas such as the question posed by his Sadducean opponents of people having sex in heaven.

Paul, in a very similar argument, responded to a question about "what kind of body" resurrected individuals would have (1 Cor. 15:35). He replied somewhat poetically that the earthly body is "sown a physical body; it is raised a spiritual body," for "flesh and blood cannot inherit the kingdom of God" (1 Cor. 15:44, 50). The early creeds of the eastern church therefore read, "[We believe in] the resurrection of the body," so that, as Jerome tells us, they could continue to believe in the resurrection of the soul without the flesh (Jerome, *Epistle* 84.5).

What the eastern church maintained was what Greek tradition had believed for a thousand years: that the body was of the earth and stayed in the earth where it belonged after death forever; it had no place in the spiritual, heavenly home of the spiritual God. It was the spiritual soul that ascended to heaven and lived with God (in Paul's terms), now clothed with a spiritual body (2 Cor. 5:1–10). There was no place in heaven for the earthly elements of clay that had constituted the flesh.

BODY AND SOUL IN PRE-CHRISTIAN ISRAEL

For the majority of their history, the Israelites shared in general the outlook of their Canaanite and Near Eastern culture: that human beings had no souls in the Greek or even Egyptian sense, and that afterlife was a descent into the underworld as an insubstantial ghost, if there was any survival at all. Yet slowly and inexorably, influences from the cultures that so often conquered and ruled Palestine began to find their way into the thinking of small groups of Jews—groups that were often quite at odds not only with each other, but also with the majority of their contemporaries. Most important were the influences of the empires of Persia and Greece, bringing the two major types of dualism: God against the Devil from Persia, and the opposition of body and soul from Greece.

The Israelite prophets were no mere imitators. They held tenaciously to a great deal of earlier storytelling and religious tradition. Yet neither were they impenetrable and immovable fundamentalists who could not foresee the value and inevitable success of the new and superior ideas of great empires. Inspired anew, they combined their native traditions with foreign and fresh ideas to produce unique, Israelite expressions of religious faith. They combined, for example, the ideas of the Zoroastrians, Egyptians, and Greeks with stories of Abraham, Moses, and David. In addition to the writings preserved in the Bible are a large number of writings that go under the names of Enoch and the patriarchs and Solomon—even Adam and Eve!—that combine traditional themes of Israelite culture with new ideas concerning the Devil and the demons, along with new ideas of the soul and its destiny.

A remarkable example, one among many, of the blending of the Old Testament and its monistic views with Greek science and religion may be found in Philo of Alexandria, a Jew wonderfully educated in Greek philosophy and a contemporary of Jesus. In a commentary on the story of Abraham in the book of Genesis, Philo attempts to explain an apparent anomaly in the text. God tells Abraham that after a long and successful life, he will die: "[A]nd you will depart to your fathers nourished with peace, in a goodly old age" (Gen. 15:15). "What fathers?" Philo asks, adding, "This is worth inquiring" (*Who Is the Heir* 277). The problem is that at the end of his life, Abraham is living in Palestine, and all of his "fathers"—that is, his relatives and ancestors—lived in Mesopotamia, where he originated. How could he be buried with any of his relatives when they were in another country hundreds of miles to the north and east? This problem led Philo into one of his characteristic "spiritual" interpretations of the literal text: the "fathers" must mean the four elements—earth, water, air, and fire. So when Abraham dies, his body will be buried with these "fathers"—that is, it will be dissolved back into the elements from which it was made. His soul, however,

> whose nature is intellectual and celestial, will depart to find a father in ether, the purest of substances. For we may suppose that, as the men of old declared, there is a fifth substance, moving in a circle, differing by its superior quality from the four. Out of this they thought the stars and the whole heaven had been made and deduced as a natural consequence that the human soul also was a fragment thereof. (*Who Is the Heir* 283)

The "men of old" to whom Philo refers are Plato and Aristotle, not anyone of Israel: Plato had written of the four elements out of which the Maker of the cosmos had formed all bodies, and into which they would all once again be dissolved (*Timaeus* 42e); Aristotle had taught that the four lower elements moved in a straight line, while the heavenly fifth moved with a circular motion (*De Caelo* 1.2–3). Philo well understood, although probably unconsciously, how far the River of God had moved from the thought-world of the writer of Genesis, and he applied his new understanding drawn from Greek science and religion to bring the text up to date.

THE COMMON FATE OF ALL

Traditional views were extremely difficult to overturn, even in the face of new ideas from philosophy and religion. By far the majority of people in the Mediterranean world at the time of Jesus still held to the old view of the finality of death. Those in the "entertainment industry"—that is, those participating in the plays and shows in the theaters of the major cities—occupied themselves with readings from the epics of Homer, with traditional tragedies, and with comedies based on the principle, "Let us eat and drink, for tomorrow we die." The apostle Paul actually quoted this popular saying in an argument against certain people in the city of Corinth who denied the resurrection of the dead (1 Cor. 15:32). He agreed that if there is no afterlife, then the pleasures of the body are all that remain, and his efforts as a Christian apostle would have been in vain: "If for this life only we have hoped in Christ, we are of all people most to be pitied" (1 Cor. 15:19).

Tomb inscriptions help us understand his sentiment. The vast number of inscribed gravestones that have been found throughout the Roman empire, including Jewish inscriptions in Palestine, show almost no belief in an afterlife. In fact, they show quite the opposite: that death was an unavoidable tragedy, the end of all life, all relationships of family, and all that is worthwhile. A kind of gallows humor is revealed in some of the inscriptions, reflecting the inevitable *Carpe diem* ("Seize the day") attitude that such a view of death fosters. A number of the inscriptions admonish readers to enjoy life while they can, since the time will soon come when all enjoyment will be impossible. One that occurs in several versions illustrates Paul's sentiment quite well, based on the observation that "You can't take it with you": "I have only what I ate and drank; everything else is lost." The only thing left to the deceased is the corpse, and that is made out of what the individual ate and drank during life—hence, "Let us eat and drink, for when death comes, that is all you will have."[12]

GALILEE OF THE GENTILES

Into this world came Jesus. His geographical homeground, Galilee, gave him a number of advantages, from the viewpoint of access to the richness of the River of God—advantages that were much less available in Jerusalem and Judah. Galilee had long been an important crossroads between the great empires of Egypt and Mesopotamia. It was easily accessible and on the main trade route north and south. In addition—and this is important in a desert land—it was rich in water and agricultural resources. As a result, Galilee was prized by the great empires and often occupied.

By the time of Jesus, it had been ruled by foreign empires for nearly 750 years. Even the Old Testament calls it "Galilee of the Gentiles" (Isa. 9:1).

Judah, on the other hand, was quite isolated. There were no major trade routes through Jerusalem or the surrounding areas. Because it was located high in the barren mountains and had few resources, most of the empires preferred to leave it alone. After the Exile, right through the entire period of the second temple, Jerusalem and its cult were dominated in the main by those who held to traditional Israelite conceptions as expressed in the Torah — that is, a this-world orientation of rewards and punishments with no afterlife. This was the view of the Sadducees, the sect that held most of the power in the time of Jesus. At the time of Jesus, then, these two areas — Galilee and Judah — were more nearly two different countries and cultures than we are used to thinking.

These observations help make sense out of an aspect of the teaching of Jesus that often goes unnoticed: he was preaching something new to his culture. There were certainly other Jews who agreed more or less with him in one or another aspect of his teaching: Pharisees, Essenes, Hellenistic Jews, and others. These, however, were but a very small minority of the people as a whole. In many other important areas, these groups held quite different views not only from the majority of their contemporaries, but also from Jesus and from one another. In the main, Jesus' message was something different from what his contemporary Jews believed. The vast majority of people of his day, Jew or Gentile, did not believe in souls or the afterlife; yet that belief is fundamental to the message of Jesus. The Gospel of Mark describes his message as a "new teaching" and (as noted earlier) as "new wine" requiring a "new wineskin" (Mark 1:27; 2:22). In a particularly contentious dialogue in the Gospel of John, in response to which many people leave Jesus, he asks his disciples if they also want to depart: "Peter answer[s] him, 'Lord, to whom can we go? You have the words of eternal life'" (John 6:68). The ancient world in general did not have such words.

BODY AND SOUL IN THE TEACHING OF JESUS

Fundamental to the teaching of Jesus was the dualism of body and soul. From the point of view of the field of religious studies, Jesus was a genius—what scholars call a master figure—and his dualism was unique. In many ways it was similar to that of Orphism, Pythagoreanism, and Plato, yet it is fair to say that the cosmos of Jesus had a darker side, for he was also quite conscious of the spiritual warfare inherent in the kingdom of God. No Greek philosopher believed in the Devil, nor did the Zoroastrians have a view of body and soul based in science (as did the Greek philosophers). Jesus brilliantly combined both traditions into something new.

The deaths of Socrates and Jesus illustrate their differences. Though both men were killed for fulfilling their divine commissions, the reasons for their deaths were quite different. Socrates was condemned to death, he tells us, because of the deep-seated hatred he had earned from his fellow citizens by constantly prodding them into caring for their souls instead of their bodies (Plato, *Apology* 18b). Jesus often did much the same, but he was killed not only because of the hatred of the authorities who opposed him, but because of the Devil: in the Christian story Satan entered Judas Iscariot, and Judas betrayed Jesus (Luke 22:3).

The dualism of Plato was based to a large extent on Greek science, as we have seen: the soul belonged to the world of spirit, while the body was heavy and weighed down the soul with its desires and worries for things in the material world. In the understanding of Jesus, the body could deceive the soul not only for these but for more sinister reasons. Not only was the material world a danger; so also was the Devil and his temptations.

In the first major parable of the Gospel of Mark (4:3–8, 14–20), Jesus the Sower casts the seed of the word on four types of ground: some seed falls beside the road, some on rocky ground, some among weeds, and some into good soil. Two forces are at work to prevent the growth of the seed on the first three types of ground. The first force affects the seed on the roadside: the birds eat up the seed sown by the road, which is interpreted by Jesus as Satan taking away the word. The next two groups are also doomed. The seed on the rocky ground represents those who easily fall away in times of suffering or persecution. The seed among the weeds is choked by "the cares of the world, and the lure of wealth, and the desire for other things" (Mark 4:19). This third group fails for exactly the kinds of reasons Socrates and Plato had warned against. The second group lands between both traditions. Suffering was a means for the training of the soul for Plato, requiring a firm resolve to hold to one's integrity. Persecution was also a device of the Devil, used to cause believers to abandon their faith, as in the book of Job. So Paul writes to the new Christians at Thessalonica, in the fear that the Devil had overturned their faith, that they not be "shaken by these persecutions," for "this is what we are destined for" (1 Thess. 3:3). So the two traditions are melded: the Devil and the material world work their evil to steal or choke or terrify the seed into uselessness. Only the good soil survives the tests to bear fruit.

In what is arguably the central passage of the Gospel of Mark, the dangers of the Devil and the material world for the soul are again combined. At the core of Jesus' dualism is his understanding of the reality of the spiritual dimension behind the visible world, and the surpassing value of one's soul in relationship to anything in the world of the body. In this passage (Mark 8:31–38), Jesus for the first time reveals to his disciples that he is going to his death. Peter, for reasons we will examine in the next chapter, takes him aside and begins to rebuke him. Jesus rebukes in turn: "Get behind me, Satan!" he says to Peter, "for you are setting your mind not on divine things but on human things" (Mark 8:32–33).

The "human things" come as something of a surprise, for they are the Old Testament promises of a restored nation of Israel and a renewed kingdom of David. Treasured though those promises are by his contemporaries, Jesus declares, "What will it profit one to gain the whole world and lose one's soul? Indeed, what can one give in return for one's soul?" (Mark 8:36–37, GJR). Not even the whole world, let alone the small nation of Israel, will suffice to buy back one's soul, lost because it has set itself on "human things."

One of those things is life in the physical body itself. In an early passage, Jesus warns his disciple not to "fear those who kill the body but cannot kill the soul; rather fear him who can destroy both soul and body in hell" (Matt. 10:28). In other words, governmental and religious authorities who may threaten one with death are in reality nothing important. They cannot, even if they carry out all their threats, do any real harm; they cannot touch the eternal soul. The only one to fear is God, who is a spiritual being capable of judging one in the spiritual realm, the only reality that matters; God alone can destroy the real "you."

That sentiment is very much in view in the above-quoted passage from Mark, which contrasts divine and human things. In that passage, Jesus has told his disciples that he is going willingly to his death. After the exchange with Peter, he calls the crowd to himself and declares, "If any want to become my followers, let them deny themselves and take up their cross and follow me. For those who want to save their life will lose it, and those who lose their life for my sake, and for the sake of the gospel, will save it" (Mark 8:34–35). There is a certain enigmatic quality to this: the only way to preserve one's life is to sacrifice it. Following Jesus will cost one's life, whether by martyrdom or by faithful discipleship until death, for "the one who endures to the end will be saved" (Mark 13:13). The contrast with older ways of understanding human life could not be greater. If one sacrificed one's life in the old monistic cultures, one died, went to the underworld, and was gone forever; long life was one of the promised rewards for a righteous life. Now the most righteous person ever (in Christian conception) is not only sacrificing his own life in his early thirties, but teaching others to do the same, saying that such sacrifice is the only way to survive death.

This helps us understand a mysterious but important character in the Gospel of Mark, the young man in a linen garment: "A certain young man was following along with him, wearing nothing but a linen garment. They caught hold of him, but he left the linen

garment and ran off naked" (Mark 14:51–52, GJR). At this point in
the story, Jesus had just been arrested by a group of soldiers in the
Garden of Gethsemane. The disciples, doing exactly the opposite
of what Jesus had taught, ran for their lives: "All of them deserted
him and fled" (14:50). He had told them to take up their crosses
and follow him; they took up their togas and ran like cowards in
the opposite direction. But one follower did not: the young man
lost his "garment" (that is, in ancient symbolism, his "body"—he
was killed—) and his naked soul escaped.

The young man has no name. In fact, *none* of the characters who
are positive role models in the Gospel of Mark has a name. The
"big names"—the disciples and famous women—are all failures
when it comes to faith. After seven and a half chapters of Jesus'
teaching and miracle-working, Mark sums up the disciples in a
depressing but insightful valuation of all who pursue a religion of
miracles and success: Jesus asks, "Do you still not perceive or
understand? Are your hearts hardened? Do you have eyes, and
fail to see? Do you have ears, and fail to hear? . . . Do you not yet
understand?" (Mark 8:17–21).

They do not understand because they are worrying about who
among them is the greatest. Jesus tells them, "Whoever wants to
be first must be last of all and servant of all" (Mark 9:36). But they
still do not understand. If we project that into the time of the writing of the Gospel, we see Mark's message: Christian ministers in
his day are competing with each other for name recognition, so
Jesus tells the disciples, "Whoever wishes to become great among
you must be your servant, and whoever wishes to be first among
you must be slave of all" (Mark 10:44–45). "Great among you":
they are trying to gain position in the church.

Jesus watches the rich put large sums of money into the temple
treasury. The widow who puts in her two cents—all she has to live
on—he declares to be the greatest of them all; she has no name
(12:42–44). Another woman has a costly vial of perfume and somehow, with prophetic insight, anoints Jesus before his death. He says
that she will be forever remembered, but she has no name (14:3).

Even Bar Timaeus, the blind man who would not be silenced in his calling out to Jesus for healing, has no name: Bar Timaeus means literally "son of uncleanness," clearly not the name his parents gave him at birth. It is a derogatory nickname given to him by his "friends," because he sits all day in the dirt begging. They call him "dirt bag," yet he is a hero (10:46–52). It is the humble, the meek — those who genuinely and from the heart seek after and serve God with all they have — who are the heroes in Mark's Gospel.

The big-name disciples, however, are quite the opposite. Peter denies Christ, after affirming vehemently that he would never do so (14:31). James and John, in their competitive spirit, ask to sit at his right and left hands in glory. Jesus asks them if they are willing to "drink his cup" and "undergo his baptism," which of course they affirm. Nevertheless, he tells them that they will not sit at his side; that is for others who are, one may rightly assume, more worthy (10:40). The famous women at the tomb, the two Marys and Salome, are too cowardly to tell their fellow disciples about the resurrection; they run away afraid and silent (16:8).

These are understandable stories of human failure and cowardice; few of us are martyr material. The disciples are competitive, boastful, willing to follow only so far, afraid to risk too much: "The spirit is willing, but the flesh is weak" (Mark 14:38).

TREASURES IN HEAVEN

The emphasis that Jesus placed on the dualism of body and soul, on the spiritual over against the material, had consequences in many other areas of life. One of the most common blessings promised to those who were obedient to God in the old monistic cultures was wealth. For Jesus, however, true wealth was not money but goodness and charity. In the Sermon on the Mount, he counseled his listeners: "Do not store up for yourselves treasures on earth, where moth and rust consume and where thieves break in and steal; but store up for yourselves treasures in heaven" (Matt. 6:19–20).

Treasures on earth, of course, are money and possessions; treasures in heaven are explained in the parallel passage in the Gospel of Luke: "[S]ell your possessions and give to charity, . . . an unfailing treasure in heaven" (Luke 12:33). Jesus illustrates this point in several ways. When he sends his disciples out on their first mission, he tells them, "Freely you received, freely give. Do not acquire gold, or silver, or copper for your money belts" (Matt. 10:8–9, NASB). He tells the Parable of the Rich Fool to make the point that "one's life does not exist in the abundance of possessions" (Luke 12:15). The rich man says to himself, "Soul, you have ample goods laid up for many years. Relax, eat, drink, be merry." But God replies, "You fool! This very night your life is being demanded of you" (Luke 12:19–20). Jesus concludes by saying, "So it is with those who store up treasures for themselves but are not rich toward God" (12:21). In the Gospel of Mark, when a man comes to Jesus and asks, "What shall I do to inherit eternal life?" Jesus tells him he must eventually "go and sell all you possess, and give it to the poor, and you shall have treasure in heaven; and come, follow me" (Mark 10:21).

NEW FAMILY

The emphasis on spirituality affects family relationships also. Again, one of the blessings on the righteous in the old cultures was a large family. So Deuteronomy promises, "The Lord will make you abound in prosperity, in the fruit of your womb" (Deut. 28:11). We hear of Jesus' mother, brothers, and sisters. In one situation, his family members come asking for him. Instead of responding to their request, he turns to those sitting around him and says, "Here are my mother and my brothers! Whoever does the will of God is my brother and sister and mother" (Mark 3:34–35). In another situation, Peter says to Jesus, "Look, we have left everything and followed you." Jesus responds by saying that all who have left their families and possessions behind will receive "a hundredfold now in this age—houses, brothers and sisters, mothers and children, and fields with persecutions—and in the age to come eternal life" (Mark 10:30). He cannot be referring to such things literally, for how could one literally have a hundred mothers? He is referring to the spiritual community of the church, in which all members are related as a spiritual family.

This helps us to understand the growing emphasis, especially in the eastern empire, on celibacy in the church. Jesus himself, apparently, never married and had no children. Paul describes a special gift that allows him to remain celibate (1 Cor. 7:7–8). Jesus in Matthew speaks of "eunuchs who have made themselves eunuchs for the sake of the kingdom of heaven" (Matt. 18:12). Eventually, by the fourth and fifth century, leaving behind one's physical family and choosing a life of celibacy in the spiritual family of the church or monastic community would become the ideal Christian life. The point was that nothing at all of the life of the body is of real value—not money or family or life itself—in comparison to following Jesus and the kingdom of God.

REVERSAL OF VALUES

Jesus proclaimed a spiritual kingdom of God, a kingdom "not of this world" (John 18:36). What one discovers in his teaching is in many ways a complete reversal of the values of the old monistic cultures. It is hard to avoid the inference that Jesus was quite consciously contradicting the materialist and this-world orientation of the dominant religious and cultural norms of his day. In the Gospel of Mark, for example, James and John want to be vice-regents of Jesus in an earthly kingdom. Jesus responds by overturning their underlying values. The old cultures, even Israel, were ruled by kings and the great, but not so in the kingdom of God: "Whoever wishes to become great among you must be your servant, and whoever wishes to be first among you must be slave of all" (Mark 10:43–44). There could not be a greater contrast: king and slave were at the absolute opposite ends of the social scale. One can hardly imagine any of the "famous" disciples asking to be slaves. But that is just what Jesus himself says that he is: "The Son of Man came not to be served but to serve" (Mark 10:45).

The kingdom of God proclaimed by Jesus overturned much more. The old covenant of the gods with their subjects promised prosperity, wealth, success, long life, progeny, safety from enemies, honor; all of that is also the substance of the covenant of Moses between God and Israel. Jesus, on the other hand, proclaimed the opposite: the curses of Deuteronomy were the signs of blessing for Jesus:

> Blessed are you who are poor, for yours is the kingdom of God. Blessed are you who are hungry now, for you will be filled. Blessed are you who weep now, for you will laugh. Blessed are you when people hate you, and when they exclude you, revile you, and defame you on account of the Son of Man. (Luke 6:20–22)

Slaves instead of kings; poor instead of rich; hungry instead of filled; hated, excluded, reviled, and defamed: these are the new blessings for the righteous, in direct contradiction of the old covenant. But Jesus did not leave it there; the formerly blessed were now endangered:

> Woe to you who are rich, for you have received your consolation. Woe to you who are full now, for you will be hungry. Woe to you who are laughing now, for you will mourn and weep. Woe to you when all speak well of you, for that is what their ancestors did to the false prophets. (Luke 6:24–26)

The point was, of course, that the material world was a kingdom of darkness, not what it seemed on the outside. All of its honors and blessings were not only transitory and subject to dissolution, but were deceptions that beguiled one into acceptance of a false set of values. The only reality and permanence was that of the spiritual world of the divine; that was the real origin and destiny of the soul.

Paul understood this well. He had given up his position in the world to become a follower who would not turn back. He was not ashamed of the cross or its message, and he would not be stopped by persecution. He recognized the value of the soul over against the body, that "we have this treasure in clay jars" (2 Cor. 4:7). He knew well that persecution and suffering were to be expected in a world of darkness, and that everything that was visible in the world of things was transitory. He told the Corinthians,

> Even though our outer nature is wasting away, our inner nature is being renewed day by day. For this slight momentary afflic-tion is preparing us for an eternal weight of glory beyond all measure, because we look not at what can be seen but at what cannot be seen; for what can be seen is temporary, but what cannot be seen is eternal. (2 Cor. 4:16–18)

Paul understood clearly what Jesus had taught and what the disciples of the Gospel of Mark had still to learn, what the church eventually mastered in its efforts to survive in the face of persecu-tion: "Those who want to save their life will lose it, and those who lose their life for my sake, and for the sake of the gospel, will save it. For what will it profit one to gain the whole world and lose one's soul? Indeed, what can one give in return for one's soul?" (Mark 8:35–37).

The fact that the Christians overcame the persecutions of the Romans and eventually won the empire was a demonstration that Christianity had learned this lesson. Christians learned to see themselves as clay pots inhabited by eternal souls, and that by endurance to death in faithfulness to their Leader, they would win eternal life.

6

SAVIORS AND THE SAVIOR
OF THE WORLD

In the previous chapter we followed the River of God as it redefined what it meant to be human from earliest times well into the Christian period. When the River first began to flow, people were merely clay images of the gods, filled with the breath of life. They understood their function to be proper religious observance; in Mesopotamia and elsewhere, people were created to worship the gods, build temples, and feed the gods with sacrifices. Human destiny, as they understood it, was permanent death: "Dust you are, and to dust you shall return," says God to Adam and Eve (Gen. 3:19).

As the River flowed on, tributaries from Egypt, Persia, and Greece brought the discovery to some that humans had eternal souls incarnated in fleshly bodies. The souls were made of heavenly elements and had a proper destiny in the divine world; if they could overcome the obstacles they faced in the body on earth and pass the test of the judgment after death, they might live with God forever. But therein lay a problem, one that is the subject of the present chapter: as the River flowed on, the obstacles people faced came to be overwhelming; no one was able gain a blessed afterlife on one's own, without divine assistance. If it truly was human destiny to return to God, how was that to be accomplished if it was humanly impossible? Thus people came to be in need of "salvation" and a "savior" in a sense never before conceived.

The old stories granted immortality to only a bare handful of special individuals, who gained either access to the realm of the gods or unending life on the distant Isles of the Blessed, in the western ocean at the edge of the world. Normal people had no hope at all for anything but a ghostly (non)existence in the underworld, "where the senseless dead dwell, mere imitations of perished mortals," to use Homer's expression (*Odyssey* 11.475–476). In Israel, the dead were simply gone in the underworld of silence and darkness, forgotten even by God (cf. Pss. 88:6–7 and 115:17). The situation was bleak, as evidenced in much of the literature of Mesopotamia, Palestine, Homeric Greece, and Rome: "All is vanity and chasing after wind," cries the preacher of the Bible (Eccles. 1:14). It is hard from the viewpoint of later times not to see these cultures open to other, more positive views of human destiny.

Christians affirmed that Jesus was the Savior of the world, but there was no such function in the older cultures; there was no such job description. If one claimed to be a new king or a prophet of God, at least people would understood what one meant. There had been kings and prophets from time immemorial; so now (big deal), here is another one. But there had been no saviors of the world. There had been kings and leaders and heroes who had delivered their peoples from oppression or disaster or some other emergency, and they were justly honored by later generations. There were even such leaders who were prophesied to come at some future time of need. But there had never been in the past a savior of the whole world, and no prophets of any culture had envisioned such a savior. The point of this chapter is to discover where the idea of a savior of the world came from and what it meant.

THE WORLD BEFORE THE SAVIOR OF THE WORLD: THE COMMON LOT OF DEATH AND HUMAN SUFFERING

It was not obvious that the world needed a savior originally (or, in fact, that it even could be saved). According to the myths and sacred stories of the old monistic cultures, before there were souls and the Devil, there was nothing particularly wrong with the way things were; the world was not lost and did not need to be saved. It was not in danger of ultimate demise; it was not at war with itself or on a path to self-destruction. Internal conflicts, such as they were, were more or less under control and not life-threatening on a cosmic scale. The world was a small, closed system controlled by the gods and designed to last forever just as it was. Moreover, before people came to understand that they had souls, salvation would not have been possible in the Christian sense: there were no souls to save. This was in no small part the substance of the gospel message itself: that people were not just clay pots full of air, but they had eternal souls that were in potential eternal danger.

The Christian gospel was preached to a culture that in the main held no such view. As we saw in the previous chapter, most people in the time of Jesus held to the old traditional ideas: neither Jew nor Gentile, in the vast majority, believed in souls that survived death or in an afterlife. In addition, before the influence of Zoroastrianism and the appearance of the idea of the Devil, the issues that people faced were quite different: there was no one to be saved from. Humans were not deceived by spiritual forces beyond their knowledge; they were not enslaved and controlled by unseen demons. They either were or were not obedient to the laws of God (or the gods) of their own free will. They received their rewards in the here and now, during earthly life, and then died forever. The only kind of "salvation" possible was deliverance from suffering in this short and miserable life, a concept very different from that which developed in Christianity.

"Short and miserable" is an apt description of real life in the ancient world; normal humans were, most often, in serious trouble. The sacred stories of the old cultures claimed that the gods rewarded the righteous and punished the wicked in this life. We read of the favorites of the gods who were blessed with health, wealth, and long life for their faithfulness and obedience to the divine will. The average lifespan in the stories of the patriarchs of the Old Testament, for example, was more than 150 years; these faithful ones died millionaires like Abraham, or in the prime of youthful old age at 120 years like Moses.

The average person in the time of Jesus, however, faced a much less optimistic future. Examination of ancient bones recovered from burial sites shows that about half of all humans died before puberty, women who survived to childbearing age lived about twelve more years, and men who survived childhood died around the age of thirty, depending on geography and social class. Some locales were healthier than others, and the higher the social class, the less vulnerable one was to malnutrition and famine. But whatever the locale or class, few people lived beyond forty, and barely one percent reached sixty.[1] Greco-Roman tombstones regularly recorded the length of life of the individual buried, giving historians another method of estimating average lifespan. From such statistics the averages are again low: between seventeen and twenty-five years of age, excluding infant mortality.[2]

Even for those who did survive into the "old age" of their forties or later, there was little to cheer. One of the most alluring aspects of the artful dialect in which the poems of Homer (the *Iliad* and *Odyssey*) were composed is its descriptive epithets. We read of "rosy-fingered dawn," "the wine-dark sea," and "swift-footed Achilles." The favorite epithet of the last phase of life was "hateful old age." Mimnermus, a poet of the century after Homer (fl. ca. 630 BCE), describes old age as follows:

When sorrowful old age comes on,
which makes a man an ugly and base thing,
evil worries continuously wear him out around his heart.

Even while looking at the rays of the sun, he has no joy,
but is hateful to children, and most dishonorable to women.
Thus God has made old age a grievous thing. (Mimnermus 1; GJR)

Old age in Mimnermus's day made one ugly and hateful to others because of the stresses of life itself and the almost complete
lack of medical remedy. The damage caused over time by trauma,
malnutrition, disease, and lack of dental care showed up in one's
physical appearance. People may or may not have grown wiser
with age, but they certainly grew uglier. One hears today that
there is a "youth culture" and that the world caters to the young;
that is no innovation.

In another poem, Mimnermus describes what economic, social,
and health challenges one so unlucky as to reach old age was likely
to face:

Sometimes one's house is consumed,
and the painful toils of poverty arise.
But another, again, goes lacking in children,
and yearning especially for them,
goes under the earth to Hades.
Another has a heartbreaking disease.
There is no one of humans to whom Zeus does not give many evils.

(Mimnermus 2, trans. GJR)

The three things listed, in order, are poverty, childlessness, and
disease. The old stories of religion held out promises for exactly
the opposite: the righteous would have wealth, numerous progeny,
and health. Yet remarkably few people were ever rich. Wealth was
concentrated, as always, in the hands of a few, but in antiquity the
percentage of wealthy people was far smaller than today, and the
possibility of upward mobility far more restricted. Horatio Alger
in antiquity would have achieved a brave (though always youthful) death for his efforts, not success and wealth. There does not
seem to have been any realistic possibility, no matter how pious
the aspirant, of a wealthy, healthy, long life, surrounded by admir-

ing great-grandchildren. In real life, sometimes the good were rewarded and the wicked punished, but more often ethics did not seem to matter much at all. In Mimnermus, certainly, the gods gave everyone "many evils," regardless of behavior. The belief that God would give the righteous a healthy millionaire's 150-year life was out of the question, something of legend, restricted to the heroic past of traditional tales.

The actual world was in fact a far more inimical place than many people today realize, blessed as they are with the benefits of medical science and a much more abundant food supply. Most people then lived but one or two droughts or crop failures away from severe hunger and even starvation. Even without the dubious reliability of nature, the depredations of tax farmers, bandits, and military campaigns had devastating effects on food supplies. And a poor diet was not only for the poor; ancients barely understood the need for variety and balance in diet for optimal vitamin intake. Wine and bread were thought to be the basic foodstuffs.[3]

Ancient philosophers and physicians, in order to explain rampant disease, pointed to the soft and seductive pleasures of "modern" city life as compromising the health of society. The sumptuous banquets of the upper classes and the "cook shops" (the common street-corner fast-food establishments of antiquity), with their sweet and rich foods, became easy targets for those who attempted to account for the poor health of their contemporaries. They were in part correct: as cities grew, access to the wide variety of foods available to hunters and gatherers, with their greater variety of vitamins and minerals, diminished.

Malnutrition made people more susceptible to disease in a world where disease was the common lot of the masses. Serious disease affected everyone; if one did not die of disease early, then one was living on borrowed time. Malaria, tuberculosis (or "consumption," as it was termed), and pneumonia were ubiquitous in the Mediterranean basin. Certain locales, of course, were healthier than others. Colder climates did not support "tropical" diseases. Warm and well-watered areas, on the other hand—areas that were good for much-needed crops and wildlife—bred mosquitoes and an overwhelming range of other parasites, rashes, and infections.

There was only rudimentary medical care. Because doctors had almost no medication to offer, prescriptions for change in diet and exercise were common types of medical advice. Aeschylus writes that to cure, "we must use medicine, or burn, or amputate" (*Agamemnon* 848–849). Cautery and amputation were almost the only means available for fighting infection. There were no antibiotics. "Medicines," such as they were, would as likely cause harm as help in curing a malady; often they did nothing at all. The mechanism of disease was attributed wrongly to an imbalance of the various bodily fluids: one had too much black bile in relation to yellow, or green in relation to white. To cure the "imbalance," doctors would bleed patients of the very fluids they needed to survive, cutting veins or arteries and causing blood loss, thus hastening their demise.

The actual causes of disease were almost entirely unknown. Microbes were, of course, invisible; the real reasons for infection and plague were thus opaque and completely misunderstood. The spread of contagious diseases was attributed to divine wrath. The abrogation of religion, not rats, unclean water, or poor hygiene, was thought to be the cause of plague. *Miasma*—religious "pollution"—was declared to be the cause of fatal sickness in epic storytelling, dramatic performance, and religious dogma.

But during a plague, not only did the thief or robber die; so did the schoolteacher and the streetsweeper. If one were a priest to whom it fell to explain such things, how was one to account for the fact that the innocent died alongside the wicked? Two reasons were invented: either the individual who died had secretly sinned and was not in fact "innocent," or someone else in the community had caused a "pollution" in the eyes of the gods and had brought down upon everyone the wrath of heaven. Hesiod tells us that

> [o]ften even a whole city suffers for a bad man who sins and devises presumptuous deeds, and the son of Cronos [= Zeus]

lays great trouble upon the people, famine and plague together, so that the men perish away, and their women do not bear children, and their houses become few. (*Works and Days* 240–244)

In one famous Greek tragedy, the great city of Thebes, second only to Athens, was beset by a plague that caused the death of crops, animals, and human children because of the presence of a great *miasma* in the person of Oedipus, who had killed his father and married his mother (Sophocles, *Oedipus Rex* 25–30). God in Israel sent a plague that destroyed seventy thousand people because of the sin of David in numbering his troops instead of trusting in God's military protection (2 Sam. 24:15).

The Christians were persecuted by the Romans for just this reason, as we saw earlier: they were a "contagion" in the body politic because they would not sacrifice to the Roman gods. The Romans were trying to cure themselves of the Christian "plague" before the gods sent a *real* one. They feared punishment on the whole society for allowing the Christians to break the contract between gods and subjects. People were especially vulnerable in the cities and wherever they were together in groups. Thronging to the temples of the healing god Asklepios for cures or to the temples of the other gods to repent and beg for deliverance only spread the contagions more effectively.[4]

As if to make real life contrast even more starkly with the "ideal" life promised in the venerable religious texts, the old stories also promised national peace and security from invading armies to those who obeyed the laws of God. Reality was quite the opposite. Even during times of international peace, the depredations of wild animals, thieves, brigands, and local warlords were common. One must recall that people lived much closer to the edge of life and death, and that "survival at any price" is a biological imperative not only for vermin. Those who could not "make" a living (given the hardships of nature, government taxation, and human environment) "took" a living from their neighbors and others; not everyone would simply sit down and die when the cupboard was bare.

There was little security. Effective police forces existed only too seldom, and often in only widely scattered areas. Governments were too often occupied elsewhere: at the level of statehood, international war was the normal condition of human affairs. In Palestine during the two and a half centuries from Alexander to the advent of Roman rule (63 BCE), there were nearly two hundred military campaigns.[5] Until the reign of Augustus, the Romans were continuously at war for nearly two centuries. International chaos was the rule. War was able to break in and upset the balance, to overturn the social order, seemingly at any time. Humanity, not the gods, nor the cosmos as a whole, was in obvious need of help from the divine world; it needed saviors.

DIVINE SAVIORS IN THE OLD CULTURES

Real human life was precarious. Humans were weak, disobedient, and dependent on the gods' care. In sacred stories, therefore, the idea that people needed saviors was present from the beginning. In many tales of the old cultures, humans were created as rather helpless beings (something like children), without the knowledge or skills properly to feed, clothe, or defend themselves. Once they lost their original blessedness, humans were naked and defenseless. The gods, or their lesser divine offspring, had to bring to them the skills of civilization: the use of fire, metallurgy, agriculture, astronomy, and the like. Those who brought the arts of survival are known today among scholars as "culture heroes." That phrase is somewhat deceptive, however, because such "heroes" were seen in antiquity in diametrically opposed roles: they were benefactors in some stories, deceivers and culprits in others.

The need for culture heroes depended on an idea quite unfamiliar and almost completely lost today. We think of God as a positive figure, gracious and in the main "on our side," disposed to help and save wherever possible. In the view of the church, the Devil has relieved God of the duty of causing random evil or calamity that makes no moral sense. God today is "heaven's all-gracious king," to quote a Christmas carol.

But in the absence of an evil entity, if God were all-gracious, then what made the plague or storm or other natural disaster kill the innocent? And more commonly, what made the Gauls or Assyrians or Romans enslave us? Before the idea of the Devil took hold, the claim that God was all-gracious was not only contrary to human observation; it was a logical impossibility. The only possible causes for random evil were the gods themselves; there was no one else up there to blame. The gods, even the God of the Old Testament, were often other than gracious. In the old stories, there was a certain tension and competitive animosity between the gods and their mud-servants. Thus, depending on the culture and the point of view, the gods could be seen as either positively or negatively disposed to their human subjects.

The Gods as Benefactors

How and why human beings were created was explained in more than one way in the varied story traditions of different cultures. No one, of course, actually *knew* how or why people came to be, but that fact was no deterrent to the invention of a variety of inspired myths offered as authoritative explanations. Some stories were more credible than others, but not because of their objective truth. "Truth," in the modern scientific sense of something verifiable by experiment or evidence, meant little in this context. The antiquity of the story was the most important criterion; the older, the "truer."

Philo of Byblos, a Phoenician writer of the late first and early second century CE, translated a particularly old and, for him, authoritative account of the origins of the world and human culture from an ancient sage known as Sanchuniathon.[6] The Greeks, in Philo's opinion, had in the intervening years embellished that true, older account and added much of their own invention, producing a mythology that, although false, had become the standard story of the origins of the cosmos. Philo's purpose was to present the "truth" of the older account of Sanchuniathon as a correction to the prevailing myths of the Greeks. Yet the task was not an easy one, for Greek "mythology, being aided by time, has made its hold difficult for us to escape from, so that the truth is thought to be nonsense, and the spurious narrative truth" (quoted in Eusebius, *Praeparatio* 1.10.40a). Philo's point is well worth taking seriously. The old stories, factually true or not, had the advantage of venerability and popularity. They answered the hard questions and gave security to generations; therefore, they *had* to be true—and the older, the better.

Christianity suffered from this ancient prejudice because it was patently an "invention" of the time of Tiberius, emperor from 14 to 37 CE. It therefore worked hard to show that it had been predicted in the ancient Jewish writings, that it was really "old" in the plan of God and not merely a new contrivance. Its actual success, however, had nothing whatever to do with the antiquity invented for it by its educated defenders. These defenders tried to make it "old," when it was in fact the first and best at what it really was. It was a new and inspiring message of heroic Christian discipleship: for faithful and ethical obedience, it promised eternal and accessible blessedness to all, regardless of social class or educational training or ethnicity. One did not need to be royal or philosophical or Jewish; one could be slave and uneducated and Gentile.

In the old stories, humans were unworthy failures; almost no one had a chance at the eternal life of the gods. The uneducated, the unphilosophical, the lowest classes, the wrong ethnicity—these had never before been given any chance at all at eternal life. No one but the very children of the gods, or at least their special favorites, garnered the attention of the divine world. Christianity succeeded because it gave every person, every single person without distinction at all, both a better way to live and a better way to die.

Many people today have stopped asking why humans came to be; to the modern scientific community, such existential why-questions are beyond the scientific mission. We are still working on the problem of *how*, and a basic evolutionary hypothesis is the foundation for all credible modern theories. Exactly the opposite view lay at the base of ancient thought. People did not evolve from lower life forms to higher, from the primeval ooze to humanity over billions of years. Instead, humans devolved a bare six or eight thousand years ago from an original high ideal to the very low level at which we find ourselves in the present. The ancient stories told of an original time when people lived hundreds of years without disease and without the "benefits" of civilization. Humans, so the stories explained, were created by the gods on a particular day near the beginning of history in an ideal state, in the very image of the gods themselves, from which we have subsequently fallen farther and farther away.

In an account written in the first century BCE, the Roman poet Ovid (*Metamorphoses* 1.89–112) describes this original state as the Golden Age from which present-day humans have degenerated, an old idea found six hundred years earlier in the Greek poet Hesiod. As we saw in Chapter 4, Hesiod tells of the degenerating ages of humankind, beginning with the original generation of gold, when people lived long, without toil or pains. From that Golden Age, people degenerated through the ages of silver and bronze to the present harsh and unfeeling age of iron (*Works and Days* 109–201).

The idea of human history as degeneration had an even older pedigree. From Mesopotamia in the second millennium, the Sumerian King List recorded the reigns of early kings who had lived before the flood and ruled for tens of thousands of years; after the flood, their lifespans became what was seen as normal for humans.[7] Similarly, Adam and Eve, even after their "fall," lived nearly a thousand years, as did their immediate descendants; then, after the biblical flood, human lifespans became normal in length.

Humans were, however, like newborns, created naked and without the benefits of civilization that would help them survive. To serve that need, stories were told of several individual gods who granted knowledge and skills to benefit humanity. Demeter, the elder sister of Zeus, was the great goddess of the produce of the earth and center of a very old mystery cult. Isocrates, a long-lived and justly famous Greek rhetorician of the fifth century BCE, describes the two gifts of Demeter. He writes of her double benefits, lauding "the grains, which are the reason why we do not live as beasts; and the [mystery] rite, in which those who partake have more pleasant hopes both for the end of life and all [present] lifetime" (*Panegyric* 4.28). Many works of ancient art show Demeter sending out her agent, Triptolemos, in his chariot to teach humanity the art of the cultivation of grain. The gift of grain—that is, the making of bread—was seen as one of the things that distinguished humans from the beasts.

Basic food was not merely the grain that made bread, but "grain and wine." The Bible includes wine among the blessings that God gives to the righteous. When Isaac was deceived into blessing Jacob, for example, he said, "Now may God give you of the dew of heaven, and of the fatness of the earth, and an abundance of grain and new wine" (Gen. 27:28). The book of Proverbs warns against wine's overuse several times (Prov. 20:1 and 23:20, among others), but it nevertheless commands one to "give strong drink to him who is perishing, and wine to him whose life is bitter. Let him drink and forget his poverty and remember his trouble no more" (Prov. 31:6–7).

The god who gave the discovery of winemaking in Greek tradition was Dionysus, who was not only the god of wine but also, like Demeter, the center of secret rites. The function of wine as the divinely appointed anesthetic for life's harshness is found quite explicitly in Greek tradition. Euripides, sharing the perspective of the author of Proverbs, writes that "filled with that good gift [of wine], suffering mankind forgets its grief; from it comes sleep; with it oblivion of troubles of the day. There is no other medicine for misery" (Euripides, *Bacchae* 279–283). While drunkenness was looked down upon, wine was seen as a blessing and gift from God.

Perhaps the most critical gift from the gods was that of the art of medicine. In *Prometheus Bound*, the fate of humans before the gift of medicine is aptly described: "If anyone fell sick, there existed no defense, neither food nor drink nor salve, but through lack of medicines they wasted away ..." (Aeschylus, *Prometheus Bound* 476–480). Several deities and heroes were credited with the ability to heal, but by far the most famous and influential was Asklepios. There were hundreds of cult centers all over the Mediterranean world devoted to this god of healing, whose popularity was at its peak from the fourth century BCE until the rise of the Christian empire. For nearly eight hundred years he was one of the most important deities in the real lives of his worshipers. Because of his healing gifts, he earned the description "of all the gods most loving of humans." He was "lover of the people," "gentle and kind," "the one who listens to prayer."[8] His most common epithet was "Asklepios the savior." His type of salvation was, of course, the physical healing of human ailments, not the salvation of souls; that would have to wait for further theological development.

The Gods as Jealous Enemies

In these and many other stories, the gods are seen as gracious and willing to share their knowledge with humans for their benefit. In other stories, however, the high god is seen in a negative light, jealous of the prerogatives of heaven and inimical to humans. In the old Mesopotamian story of the flood, for example, found eventually all over the ancient world, people were so despised at one point that God or the gods "had to" flood the earth with water, killing all but a small remnant of people.

The idea that most people were evil and only a few would be saved from divine wrath was not confined to the flood story. Only a very few were somehow worthy. Elijah had run out into the desert and declared that he alone of all Israel was still faithful (1 Kings 19:10). The prophets spoke of the "remnant" that would be saved, a small minority of Israel (e.g., Ezek. 6:8). It was an old idea: Homer spoke of deceptive and thievish scoundrels, "the sort that the black earth breeds in great numbers" (*Odyssey* 11.364–365). The idea survived into Christian tradition: Jesus warned his disciples, "Enter through the narrow gate; for the gate is wide and the way is broad that leads to destruction, and there are many who enter through it. For the gate is small and the way is narrow that leads to life, and there are few who find it" (Matt. 7:13–14).

On the other hand, the common ancient idea that God was somehow too harsh, or bordering on evil, is today nearly lost. Christian theology grew at a time after it was discovered that God was the eternally blissful Monad, whose character was entirely just and good; it was the Devil who carried the burden of evil. But the old stories were composed long before that discovery. Christians do not normally complain against God, shouting up to heaven, like Job or the characters of Greek tragedy, at the fundamental injustices of life. Ancients now and again dared to voice the complaint that the Plan was flawed, that innocent people should not be dying for "fate" or for the sins of others at the hands of the gods. Others were careful not to utter a single word against the heavenly powers. Later, in Christian theology, one could be seen as hazarding the penalty of eternal hell for such blasphemy.

Earlier, before there were eternal souls and the idea of the Devil—at a time when everyone, no matter how righteous or wicked, went to the same dark underworld—such complaints were the only defense of human dignity. One had to state one's complaint, because after death, there would be no opportunity; there would be only silence. What did it matter? The one who shouted about the injustices of the gods went to the underworld; the one who remained silent and hoped that there was some "reason" for the injustices also went to the underworld. In either case, one's destiny was the same.

In many early stories, the gods looked upon humans with suspicion. They were jealous in guarding divine prerogatives generally, but they were especially protective of the secrets of heaven that allowed them to live as comfortable divine beings at continual leisure. They did not want humans to have any similar culture. Their unique existence was somehow threatened or compromised, apparently, if the secrets of their existence were known. Human beings were forever to have their lesser and subservient place.

They were made of mortal clay and had to die when the gods and fate determined their limits; they were not to gain immortality any more than they were to know what the gods knew.

A reflection of this idea, though softened, is to be found in the biblical Genesis story of Adam and Eve: God forbids his new creatures the tree of knowledge of good and evil, and when they eat the fruit of that tree, there seems to be some kind of threat: God says to the other heavenly beings, "Behold the man has become like one of us, knowing good and evil" (Gen. 3:22). God greatly increases human suffering in consequence and denies Adam and Eve the tree of life. We do not today read this text in a light that is negative toward God, but neither do we read it as did the ancients. The point of the story was quite clear to all who heard it in antiquity: humans had no right either to the knowledge or to the life that God had. Some Jews in the pre-Christian era, and their Christian Gnostic heirs, saw the God of this text as the typical "jealous God"—that is, the world-ruling divinity who stood against human enlightenment. There were similar stories, especially among Mesopotamians and Greeks, that cast God in a comparable negative light.

The biblical writer plays the storyline so that responsibility lies with human weakness, of course, not divine harshness. That was an old strategy. Homer had taken the same approach hundreds of years earlier in the opening book of the *Odyssey*, in a passage cited in Chapter 4. Zeus complains to the other gods "how mortals put the blame on us gods, for they say evils come from us, but it is they, rather, who by their own recklessness win sorrow beyond what is given" (*Odyssey* 1.32–34). Again the fault really lies with the humans—but not all of it. In the Greek story, humans gain for themselves "sorrow beyond what is given"; that is, they are given a measure of sorrow at the outset, and then they make it worse by reckless behavior.

In these stories of the gods as enemies of humans, Prometheus was the reputed creator and perennial champion of mankind. Prometheus was one of the Titans, the generation of gods who fathered Zeus; and therefore the humans he made and the gods of the generation of Zeus were of the same era, both descendants of the Titans. In other words, as Hesiod declares, "gods and mortal men sprang from one source" (*Works and Days* 108). Zeus and his siblings defeated the Titans to rule the world, while humans populated it. Because humans were the same age as the gods, and were made in their very image, there was good reason for competitive jealousy to guard the divine prerogatives. Zeus, in this version of human origins, was jealous of the secrets of heaven and unwilling that humans should have the privileges of the gods.

Prometheus was forced to contend with Zeus for the sake of human beings. In an attempt to aid humanity, he stole fire from heaven and brought it to earth that people might warm themselves and cook their food. For this crime, Zeus "immediately contrived an evil thing for men in recompense for the fire" (Hesiod, *Theogony* 570). He commanded the other gods to create Pandora and send her to earth with her infamous jar of disasters and diseases. Pandora, like Eve, was thus the cause of the many human sufferings. In the much later Genesis story, Adam blamed God for his downfall, for Eve was "the woman that you gave me"; it was she who caused his disobedience and got him cast out of Eden (Gen. 3:12).

Prometheus did not give up after Zeus sent Pandora, however. He continued to help, teaching humans to predict the seasons and instructing them in the art of writing and mathematics. He helped them learn to domesticate horses and make chariots, to build boats and sail the seas. Finally, he gave them the ability to mine for copper, iron, silver, and gold and passed on the skills of metallurgy; in short, "all arts come to mortals from Prometheus" (Aeschylus, *Prometheus Bound* 506).

Prometheus's very name means "forethought," and in his wisdom he discovers a terrifying secret: he learned who it would be in the next generation of the gods that would overthrow Zeus. To defend his rule, Zeus had Prometheus impaled on a rock and commanded an eagle to daily eat his liver, which regrew each night. Zeus inflicted this punishment in the hope that Prometheus would be forced to tell the secret, and "that he might learn to bear the sovereignty of Zeus and abandon his love and championship of man" (*Prometheus Bound* 10–11).

THE BIBLICAL PATRIARCH ENOCH
AND THE FALL OF THE ANGELS

Greece, Asia Minor, Mesopotamia, Persia, Palestine, and Egypt had maintained more or less substantial contacts through trade, cultural exchange, and outright warfare for hundreds of years before the era of Alexander the Great. Persia had conquered the Middle East in the 530s BCE, and as a result, Persian Zoroastrian views of God and the Devil began to influence a small minority of the educated elite of subjugated Israel. In the 330s BCE, Alexander conquered most of the ancient world, beginning in Greece and moving east and south to rule the very nations that had previously ruled Israel. He conquered Asia Minor, Palestine, Egypt, Mesopotamia, and Persia; he also went even farther north and east, into countries that had never had any interest in the lands of the eastern Mediterranean.

The old stories in these regions that told of the power of God or the gods — stories claiming that "our God is supreme" — were decisively contradicted by the conquests themselves. These various "supreme" gods had been conquered just as their lands had been. The defeated gods could at best claim through their prophets that they had allowed themselves to be bested because of their people's sin. But they could continue to claim superiority only with great difficulty.

By the time of Alexander, of course, all of Israel had been ruled for more than two centuries by the Persians, and most of Israel (the ten northern tribes) had been ruled by Assyria for the two centuries before that. Some Israelites, especially among the educated classes, began to meld their old traditions with those of their new overlords (as they had time and again before). In general, that process was a creative and positive one: the River of God produced new constructions out of the flowing together of older traditions. The gods of the empires changed and grew as their cultures were influenced by new ideas through contact with others. The smaller nations either were assimilated completely and disappeared, or underwent the same process of growth and change, but at an even more profound level. Israel had been ruled now and back again by Mesopotamia, Egypt, and Assyria, then by Persia, and now Greece. Only rarely did it have independence, and that most often by paying tribute. Its religious traditions necessarily changed time and again as it faced the new influences of new overlords.

One effect of Alexander's conquests and the hundreds of years of Greek rule after his death was that all things Greek—the stories, language, and culture of the ruling elite—became the required curriculum of any ambitious and upwardly mobile individual. Israel was ruled by Greeks and immersed in a world overrun by Greek culture. The Greek rulers were in general quite tolerant of the religious traditions of their subjects. In a positive acceptance of the new ideas, a number of Jewish writers produced a significant body of literature in Greek that represented their Israelite traditions as the finest example of Greek philosophy. Some of these texts are "apologetic" literature (from the Greek word *apologia,* "defense"). The very fact that such literature was produced at all shows that there was felt a need to maintain Israel's identity in the face of a new world situation. The Jewish writers were seeking to "defend" their old traditions in the face of the far superior empire and the god of the Greek philosophers; the tribal warrior God of the Israelites was becoming the Monad.

Other Jewish writers, however, were much less accepting of foreign cultures and traditions. One of the greatest of all heroes in ancient Israelite stories was Enoch. In the Bible, "Enoch walked with God; and he was not, for God took him" (Gen. 5:24). He was, apparently, so much a favorite of God that God translated him directly to heaven without the necessary step of death (so says *1 Clement* 9.4). Beginning perhaps early in the third century BCE— that is, a relatively short time after the beginning of Greek rule—

Jewish writers began composing a series of books under Enoch's name in their native language. The purpose of these books was to turn one of the more offensive aspects of Greek poetry into the very cause of evil on earth. What was precious to the Greek poets became in the stories of the Enoch writers the reason for calamity on earth.

Greek epic and poetic literature, for all its beauty and power, contained a motif that offended nearly everyone unwilling to grant the authors their "poetic license": the stories contained shocking tales of immorality among the gods. Greek philosophers castigated and ridiculed their own poets for these impossible stories, countering that if the gods were gods at all, they could not be immoral; they could not break the very standards of ethics they required from humans. Plato banished such literature from his ideal state, forbidding even Homer to be read. Christians, in agreement with the philosophical tradition, time and again criticized Greek and Roman "paganism" for such stories, denying that such gods were gods at all; they could only be evil demons.

But Plato lived after Greek science had spiritualized the gods into the Monad. Earlier, that the gods should mate together and produce divine offspring was a standard story in all the cultures of the ancient world, as we have seen. It was even the standard story in Israel itself, though that fact is difficult to see in the Bible, since those who composed and edited the canonical texts lived in an era when such ideas had fallen out of favor. The scriptural writers and editors deleted from the traditional Israelite stories what had clearly been there in the beginning. For example, it is quite certain from indications that remain in the Bible, and especially from archaeology, that for most of its history, Israel had a God who had a wife and a divine family. That the gods had families like human families was not surprising, nor was it considered immoral (except when one or another of the gods had an adulterous affair). What offended ethical humans most were stories of the lustful gods mating with humans. In Greek tradition, this cross-species mating was the origin of the heroes, the offspring of a divine and human pairing, whose wars, violence, and sufferings fill the pages of Homer and Greek tragedy.

We must be careful not to credit anyone in the fourth century BCE, outside of a handful of Greek scientists and philosophers, with the insight that gods mating with humans was physically impossible. For the scientists and philosophers, of course, the Monad and the emanated, high spiritual servants had neither genitalia nor passions; they did not have bodies at all. For the rest — for the prescientific traditionalists — the old and "true" stories told that sexual unions and violence were what gods did normally; gods were forever mating with each other and killing off their disobedient mud-servants. But they did not normally mate with humans; they had their own divine partners and marital difficulties. The problem was viewed as one of keeping to one's proper species — in the words of the book of Jude, of keeping one's proper "domain" or "abode" (Jude 6). But since the Greek poets shared Hesiod's view that "gods and mortal men sprang from one source," the line between divine and human was easily crossed. Unlike the stories of Semitic cultures, in Greek stories gods and humans were so close that they could mate.

It was this aspect of Greek tradition — that of gods mating with humans — that the Jewish writers chose to turn on its head. They overturned its meaning from an explanation for why the heroes were so great into one that showed why they were so violent and why there was evil on the earth. They composed stories that took the theme of divinities mating with humans and made it the chief cause of human woes.

The *Book of Watchers*, one of the Enoch books from this period found as the first portion of the apocryphal book of *1 Enoch*, tells a story of two hundred angelic "Watchers" who decide to go to earth and mate with human females. In this story, briefly noted in Chapter 4, the Watchers teach the women all the skills that Prometheus (in the Greek tradition) provided to humans so that the race could survive: in hopes of gaining the women's favors, the Watchers reveal "the eternal secrets which are performed in heaven" (*1 Enoch* 9.6).

Instead of survival, however, the fallen angels spread all kinds of sin and violence on the earth. They bear a race of giants who are so rapacious and violent that they eat up first the produce and the animals and finally the people of the earth. As a result of their oppression, God decrees the flood to destroy the giants. The leader of the fallen angels, Azazel, is bound hand and foot and imprisoned in a pit in the desert, which is then covered with sharp and jagged rocks. In the Greek story, Prometheus was bound to a jagged rock. The writers of the Enoch narrative turn the story upside down: the culture hero Prometheus becomes the fallen angel who brings with his "secrets" overwhelming sin and violence.

It is hard not to see these stories as a commentary on the violence and rapaciousness that the Greek conquests had brought to the foreign lands that were occupied. The Enoch writers look forward to a time when God will destroy the oppressors and restore the land to prosperity.

RULERS AS HUMAN SAVIORS

The ancient world was not often at peace; forces of chaos seemed constantly to break in and overturn order. The old religious explanation was that chaos was a punishment of the gods for human unrighteousness; it was neither an independent agent nor random in its activity. It was sent for some higher purpose: *pathei mathos,* "one learns by suffering."

The Need for Deliverance from Suffering

On the level of human life, however, that theory seldom worked smoothly; chaos could be terrifying and seemingly indiscriminate. A whole nation could be destroyed for the wickedness of its rulers or that of a fragment of the population, overwhelming the great mass of innocent subjects. The Bible represents the destruction of Egypt at the Exodus of Israel as just such a form of punishment, as it does the destruction of Israel itself at the Exile. Likewise, Troy was destroyed for the adulterous affair of Paris, son of its king, with Helen, wife of Menelaos, Greek king of Sparta.

Whole families could be caught in seemingly endless cycles of suffering lasting generation after generation, fostered by the unrighteousness of some distant ancestor. So Agamemnon, ruler of the Greeks and victorious general in the Trojan war, was murdered by his wife, who was in turn murdered by their son, because of a curse on their line that had begun generations before. The Bible similarly cursed the unrighteous with punishment to the third and fourth generations, as well as whole nations that descended from the wrong patriarch: "'The elder shall serve the younger.' As it is written, 'I have loved Jacob, but I have hated Esau'" (Rom. 9:12–13).

People needed deliverance from suffering, and the world needed order. That was the duty of human kings. Hammurabi, ruler of the old Babylonian empire (ca. 1792–1750 BCE), represented himself in just that fashion: he claimed to have been appointed by the god Marduk before the world began, destined from before creation to bring order and the rule of law to "the black-headed people" of Mesopotamia. He was "the shepherd," the victorious military general who pacified the land and defended the rights of the poor against the abusive rich.[9] Similarly, the pharaohs of Egypt represented themselves as the guardians of right, sons of the sun god Re or of Amon. Akhenaton saw himself as the one who distributed divine knowledge and life itself from Atum, the only God to his people. After the time of Joshua, when God delivered the Israelites over to their enemies because of their sins, they would cry out for help; God would raise up a Judge who would defeat the foreigners and restore political freedom and proper worship. Cyrus, king of Persia, took on exactly this role for Israel during the Exile, and Second Isaiah called him "the messiah" as a result (Isa. 45:1).

Victorious kings who brought peace, prosperity, and the rule of law were seen as the saviors of their societies. Remarkable correspondences with Christian ideas may be seen in language used of the Roman emperors. Julius Caesar, Roman dictator who was assassinated in 44 BCE, is several times called "savior" (among other titles) in inscriptions. The city of Cartheia in Greece, for example, honors him in an inscription as follows: "The city of the Carthaeans honors Gaius Julius Caesar as god and absolute ruler and savior of the world." Caesar was literally deified, in that city and elsewhere, after his death. Pliny the Elder (23/4–79 CE), Roman politician and writer, preserves the reason in an account of the games celebrated in honor of Caesar's death: "[A] comet was seen for seven days in the northern region. . . . This comet, the people thought, indicated that Caesar's soul had been received among the immortal gods" (*Natural History* 2.94).

Augustus Caesar (63 BCE–14 CE), the nephew and adoptive heir of Julius Caesar and first Roman emperor, brought to a close a long period of civil war and inaugurated a new age of prosperity for the empire. He was therefore honored in even greater terms. Queen Dynamis of Phanagoria on the Bosporus dedicated an inscription to "the absolute ruler Caesar, son of god, Augustus, the ruler of all land and all sea and savior of them."[10] He was "son of god" because he was son of a god, the deified Julius Caesar. He was savior of the whole world because of the peaceful rule of law that he had instituted. His "salvation" clearly took the form of peace, economic prosperity, and civil order in a chaotic world; it was not the salvation of eternal souls. The entire frame of thought necessary for such a concept as salvation of souls is missing in the Roman sources.

Romans clearly had "saviors of the world" in their successful emperors, but what they meant by that phrase was far removed from what the Christian conception eventually came to be. Christians spoke of a "kingdom of God" that had nothing what-ever to do with "this world." It was a spiritual kingdom entirely divorced from the material and temporal concerns of earthly life. The Roman emperors were saviors only in and of this material world (as praiseworthy and necessary as that function was). Few, even among the Christians, censured them for succeeding at bringing peace and order to society; that was their divinely appointed function. Quite the same basic view had been current in various cultures from time immemorial. Kings were supposed to usher in peace and prosperity for their peoples; that is what the Sumerian and Babylonian kings, the pharaohs of Egypt, and the Greek tyrants had been claiming to do for millennia.

That was also what Saul and David and the long line of David's descendants were supposed to do for Israel, but theirs was not a level playing field. Because of the insurmountable obstacles facing a small and poor people surrounded by great and wealthy empires, the Israelite kings were more often vassals or conquered subjects than independent agents, required to balance alliances with and monetary payments to competing empires.

This is the very fact that made the River of God so rich: Israel had little or no time to exist on its own; it was forced time and again to assimilate or react to ideas and influences of its conquering overlords. Even when it experienced anything like political independence, it was beholden to the larger empires on its borders. It was this inexorable pressure of outside influences that forced the changes, the evolutionary steps in the "punctuated equilibrium" of Israel's religious development, and that gave opportunity for the rise of Christianity.

Israel's Disaster of the Exile and the Hope of National Restoration

According to the biblical tradition, Israel's relationship with God was governed by three covenants: the covenant with Abraham that promised the land of Israel and innumerable descendants (see Gen. 17:1–8); the covenant with David that promised that a descendant of David would always sit on the throne of Israel in Jerusalem, bringing peace and blessing to the people (see Ps. 132); and the covenant at Sinai that promised blessing for obedience to God's laws and punishment for unrighteousness (see Deut. 28). Fundamental to the view of the biblical authors was that

Israel was to worship Yahweh, its national God, exclusively. The first of the Ten Commandments reads: "I am the Lord your God, who brought you out of the land of Egypt, out of the house of slavery. You shall have no other gods before me" (Exod. 20:2–3). Yet it was only rarely (if ever) the case in the actual history of the nation that Israel worshiped Yahweh only.

The small number of faithful prophets warned again and again of judgment and disaster that would overtake the people because they worshiped not only Yahweh, but also all of the other gods of the Canaanite east. Yet what was any sane person to do? If one neglected the worship of the other gods, they would also, just as would Yahweh, strike one down. The ancients were not fools: sacred stories abounded with the harsh punishments of this or that god on humans who neglected or abrogated prescribed rites.

Yet, especially in retrospect, the fact that Israel was not focused on its national God alone but courted the favor of all the gods of Canaan came to be seen by the prophetic minority as betrayal of the covenants and sufficient reason for God to punish and even abandon his people. As the northern kingdom of Israel drifted closer and closer to the brink of disaster at the hands of Assyria in the eighth century, and then as the small southern kingdom of Judah defied the Neo-Babylonian empire in the early sixth century, the prophets painted future expectations in increasingly dark colors: they foresaw only disaster and divine wrath. Eventually the entire country was overrun, its temple destroyed, its material resources and skilled classes exported to Babylon. The prophetic voices were vindicated, but at the price of national disaster and the Exile.

Yet it was in the era of the Exile that hopes for national restoration were slowly kindled. Perhaps there would come a day when God would remember and reinstate the covenants, when the land would be restored to Israel and the people would again multiply on it. Perhaps a new descendant of David would reign again in Jerusalem and bring peace, and perhaps again the people would serve God in righteousness and enjoy his blessing. Prophets began to hazard the unthinkable: God would judge harshly those nations who had so maltreated Israel and restore his people to the inheritance of the covenants in peace and blessing; Israel would rule the nations that had for so many centuries ruled them. Not only would the promises to Abraham be renewed and finally fulfilled, not only would the Israelites enjoy the blessings of Sinai, but there would also one day be a righteous king, a son of David, a savior who would rule the nations and lead his people. This king would, like the Roman emperors, be not a savior of souls but a savior of the country.

The Israel of idealized retrospect would one day be a reality—only better than ever, far better than anyone had previously hoped: it would become the most powerful and important nation on earth, not just a small pawn pushed around between empires. Jerusalem would become the world's capital, not just a small and isolated mountain town far off the trade routes. Israel and Jerusalem would attain their proper status; they would have a new David, a king who would bring peace and prosperity to the nation and see to the punishment of their enemies.

THE END OF THE ORIGINAL GOOD WORLD

The world of Israelite history, including its hopes for national restoration, was still the good world of God's creation. What had gone wrong was connected to Israel's disobedience, not to the earth itself. The book of Genesis informs us that "God saw all that He had made, and behold, it was very good" (Gen. 1:31). Originally, the world everywhere was good (or at least serviceable).

In fact, before the advent of Zoroastrianism, the very idea that it might not be had not occurred to anyone; the subject never came up at all. Depending on the culture, the world arose of itself out of the primeval waters or was created by the gods, eventually to become the place for humans to serve the needs of the divine world. The world was simply a part of the overall Plan, the "where" in which things in the human sphere took place. Humans were on (or under) the earth, while the high gods were in their various locales: generally they were in heaven, but they could also be found in the sea and the underworld, with various underlings spread throughout the cosmos as stars and planets, sun and moon, desert storm and mountain spring.

That there should be something wrong with the physical world where both the gods and humans lived occurred to no one. That the world should need to be destroyed by fire and either annihilated altogether or replaced by a new and improved version would have brought howls of objection and disbelief. What would one do with the divinities whose very reasons for being were about to be destroyed? If heaven and earth were destroyed, what would become of Uranos and Ge, Father Heaven and Mother Earth? If the trees and streams were to be burned up, what would become of the dryads and nyads, and the myriad lesser divinities whose very lives and functions were identified with the various aspects of the physical world?

What could have been the problem in any case? What could possibly be wrong with dirt and water? There had been in the past conflicts among the gods, but all of those had been resolved in the mythic past: Marduk had defeated Tiamat; Zeus had defeated the Titans. In the aftermath, the world was at peace; the combats of the "combat myths" were over. If there were problems on earth, they were caused by humanity's failure to fulfill its proper function and follow the dictates of the gods. Humans, or so the theory went, were responsible for their own lives of blessing or cursing.

Creation Defiled: Zoroastrianism

Yet sometime in the second millennium BCE, a revelation was made to a priest and prophet, Zoroaster, that would enter the River of God nearly a thousand years later and become one of the foundations on which Christianity would be based. According to Zoroastrian doctrine, there was only one true God, who was opposed by a nearly equal and opposite Devil. In order to defeat evil, God created a good world that he knew would be attacked and defiled yet that would serve as a battleground between the forces of good and evil. Eventually, after the final battle during which the forces of evil would be destroyed, that good world would have to be destroyed and replaced by a new one because of the defilement it had suffered.

In reference to that event, the second epistle of Peter declares that "the heavens will be destroyed by burning, and the elements will melt with intense heat" (2 Pet. 3:12). The apostle Paul describes the reason: "[C]reation was subjected to futility, not willingly, but because of Him who subjected it, in hope that the creation itself also will be set free from its slavery to corruption" (Rom. 8:20–21). In Paul's understanding, God allowed the good creation to come under the control of the Devil and his forces in order that the Devil could be defeated; thereafter, creation itself would be renewed.

The view that the good creation of the world would be attacked and defiled by spiritual forces that would impel its destruction was a doctrine of Persian Zoroastrianism. The Persians ruled Mesopotamia and Israel for more than two hundred years, from 539 BCE to the conquests of Alexander in the 330s. Their viewpoint of a dualism between God and the Devil that necessitated an eschatology of cosmic proportions, not merely national restoration, slowly began to influence small groups of intellectuals among their Jewish subjects. These writers reacted against their overlords, both accepting and rejecting aspects of the new culture they faced.

The Zoroastrians worshiped God while tending the sacred fire (not because fire was God, but because the highest element was fire, akin to the substance of God). So Second Isaiah declares in God's name: "[A]ll of you who are kindlers of fire, lighters of firebrands, walk in the flame of your fire. . . . This is what you have at my hand: you shall lie down in torment" (Isa. 50:11, NRSV). The very idea of a fiery hell was Zoroastrian (and Greek); it shows up in Israelite texts only after the Exile. The prophet accepts the Zoroastrian idea of hell and then sends the Zoroastrians into it!

Later, another prophet of the same school accepts even more:

God declares through him, "I am about to create new heavens and a new earth" (Isa. 65:17). The larger meaning of the prophet is specific to Israel and focuses on national restoration; in the subsequent verse God declares, "I am about to create Jerusalem as a joy and its people as a delight" (Isa. 65:18). This is not a Zoroastrian battle between God and the Devil being discussed here. Yet Israel's world of thought has clearly been heavily influenced by that of the conquerors: the language is now that of cosmic eschatology. The very heavens that used to be the throne of God and the earth that was his footstool now, even in a mundane context of national restoration, need to be created anew.

Creation as Foreign to the Divine Nature: Greek Philosophy

More than two centuries of Persian rule in the Near East were ended by the conquests of Alexander the Great, which brought the advent of the Hellenistic empires that stretched from the borders of India to Egypt to the homeland of Greece itself. The minor nations of Palestine, Judah included, exchanged one set of overlords for another and again faced the challenge of adapting to the new ideas of a superior culture.

Greek scientists and philosophers had brought into juxtaposition two scientific propositions: the traditional understanding of the elements as earth, water, air, and fire, and their own discovery of the geocentric universe, with its huge, spherical earth surrounded by the enormous series of eight concentric spheres, the whole of which was surrounded by the infinite and immaterial Monad. The discoveries were made after millennia-long observations of the heavens that had been undertaken in Mesopotamia and Egypt as well as Greece. The Greeks had certainly profited from the observations of their predecessors. But they were the first, so far as one can tell, to develop a system of mathematics sophisticated enough to calculate the vast distances and circumferences that the geocentric universe required. (Imagine just balancing one's checkbook using Roman numerals, and the magnitude of the problem becomes clearer.) The level of science in Egypt and Mesopotamia, though admirable in many respects, was not yet sufficient to tackle the realities of the size of the physical universe.

Proof of the Greeks' remarkable advances in knowledge, and the theological developments that followed as a result, is readily seen in the concept of the gods of the various cultures of the River. The Mesopotamian gods were material beings with bodies, identified with the various physical aspects of the material world: An was heaven, Enlil was Lord Wind, Enki was freshwater, Tiamat was saltwater, and so on. In Egypt, Re was the sun, Amon was the wind, and Aten was the sun disk itself. In Israel, Yahweh was either a version of Baal, the storm god (but who came from the south), or later El, the father of the gods (who lived in a tent on the top of the cosmic mountain in the north). He could show his hand and back to Moses on the mountain, or ride in a chariot that was seen by Ezekiel.

Myths from Greece before that region's own scientific (and glacially slow) "revolution" show much the same thing. Greek art depicts gods who were human in form and about twice human size. The gods clearly had bodies made of some material substance, though that substance was not identical to that of mortals: the gods ate ambrosia and drank nectar, and when they bled, it was "ichor" and not blood that ran in their veins. Yet they were sufficiently close to humans to mate with them and bear offspring, the heroes who fill the pages of Greek literature.

By the sixth century BCE, two forces were effecting a fundamental change among Greek intellectuals: Orphism and related movements were changing the way human beings understood themselves, and science was changing the way the cosmos and then the divine nature itself were understood. Orphism, as we saw in Chapter 5, postulated that the body and soul were of two separate origins: the body of the earth and the soul of heaven. Not only were the two parts unlike in origin and character, they were opposite in destiny: the body belonged to the earth and was destined to remain where it had originated; the soul was a "child of starry heaven" and was destined to return to its original home in the divine sphere of spirit and fire.

Greek science, for its part, expanded — even exploded — the old view of the world as a small, three-story structure into a vast geocentric universe of near infinite size, unheard of and impossible in any of the preceding cultures of the River. These scientific discoveries had devastating effects on the old conceptions of the gods. Gods with bodies were not God at all; they were at best underlings of the real God, the one God above and beyond and containing all else — the infinite, immaterial, and unknowable Monad who dwelt beyond and contained the geocentric universe.

The effect of these discoveries was that those who understood their implications saw themselves as dwelling in a material world that was not in fact their home. The number of people who shared this view in the beginning was quite small (a few philosophers and their adherents), but the importance of these ideas for later Christianity was fundamental. By 30 CE, the approximate date of the culmination of the ministry of Jesus, by far the majority of people both in Israel and in the Roman empire in general still held to the old traditional views that humans were mud-creatures with air in them, destined for annihilation after death or a shadowy (non)existence in the underworld.

Jesus, much to the contrary, taught of the spiritual kingdom of God: he warned people to lay up their treasures in heaven (Matt. 6:20) and asked, "What does it profit to gain the world and lose one's soul?" (Mark 8:36). The apostle Paul expressed these ideas well in a discussion of those who had oriented their lives to their bodies and this world; he wrote that, in contradistinction to his opponents, "our citizenship is in heaven, from which also we eagerly wait for a Savior, the Lord Jesus Christ" (Phil. 3:20). The Greek word translated "citizenship" means "the country of which we are citizens." In other words, Christians, as born of the spirit (John 3:8), are like their Lord, "aliens and strangers" (1 Pet. 2:11), noncitizens and visitors in the body and in this world.

Creation as Foreign to God and Ruled by the Devil: Gnosticism

In the second century BCE, there began to develop among certain highly educated Jews the roots of what today is known as Gnosticism. The word "Gnosticism" derives from the Greek word *gnosis*, meaning "knowledge" (or, in this context, "enlightenment"). The "enlightenment" required by Gnosticism was that one realize that one's soul was a part of the divine nature, that it had fallen into a dark material cosmos ruled by the Devil, and that its proper destiny was to return to God and its divine home. Visible here quite easily is one form of a combination of Greco-Roman and Zoroastrian dualism: the soul is a spiritual entity that does not belong in this material world (from Greek philosophy), and the material world is ruled by the Devil and his false and deceptive religions (from Zoroastrianism). A form of that combination lies at the base of Christianity.

The legitimacy of the Jewish Law and the Jewish understanding of God in general came into question in the Hellenistic age — that is, in the third to second centuries BCE. When compared to Greek philosophy, the traditional Jewish view of God and religion was seen by many Jews as too lowly. The Lord seemed a mere tribal God of a small and inconsequential people who were forever being conquered. Some Jews, therefore, simply abandoned many of the long-held notions of Israelite tradition and began following Greek practices wholesale. Others, Jewish apologists of the educated upper classes, defended the traditional customs and texts, raising their status by filling their old traditions with new ideas drawn from the Greco-Roman world. They wrote accounts of the scriptures and Jewish traditions as though those documents and concepts were the highest form of Greek thought. Abraham, Isaac, Jacob, and especially Moses were really consummate Greek philosophers. Among both groups of Jews, there was felt a need for transformation — either the rewriting of Jewish traditions in the categories of Greek philosophy, or a conversion to Greek ways.

At the same time, however, others resisted the changes in religion advocated by the Hellenizing Jews. Conflicts between the groups became violent; attacks and reprisals became common; lives were lost on both sides. The Greek overlords sided with their partisans, of course, and sometime around 175 BCE persecution became a government policy (for reasons obscure to us today). The government began to try to stamp out the old religion and impose the Hellenized form of Judaism advocated by Jewish upper-class partisans.

As we saw earlier, this forced imposition of Greek culture provoked a rebellion under the Maccabees (named for Judas Maccabeus, the first of a line of brilliant military leaders) in 166 BCE that eventually overthrew Greek rule and instituted an independent state in Israel—independence that lasted nearly one hundred years. The family of Judas, known as the Hasmoneans (from the name of the town they came from) ruled as a dynasty throughout the period. The Hasmoneans, however, were themselves something of a compromise group between Greeks and Jewish conservatives. They did not keep to the rules of the strictest traditionalists, but eventually combined priesthood and kingship and lived in typical royal luxury that offended many. It was in protest to these supposed "illegitimate" rulers that the Qumran sectarians withdrew into the desert, isolating themselves from what they understood to be a defiled temple cult and leadership. The Qumran sectarians used in their writings not only their understanding of the Bible, but also a great number of ideas and doctrines drawn from Zoroastrianism. The new Jewish dynasty, for its part, began its own persecutions and imposed its form of Judaism on all of Israel and the surrounding peoples by military means. People were forced to accept circumcision, for example, or lose their lands; many were killed.

It was in this atmosphere of persecution by a Jewish government that claimed to espouse traditional Judaism that Gnosticism arose. The Gnostic authors were highly educated, strongly Hellenized Jews. They understood quite clearly that the Monad, the divinity of Greek philosophy, was far superior to any god with a body, any jealous tribal god filled with passions who fought wars. They were also influenced by Persian traditions about the Devil and his demonic forces of false religion. They composed texts that combined both sets of ideas and turned their new conceptions against their Hasmonean persecutors and Hasmonean allies, the Jewish apologists who defended the old traditions by recasting them as Greek philosophy. The Greek Monad could have no equal by definition: the Monad was the one and only source of all things and could have no real competitor. To incorporate the idea of the Zoroastrian Devil, then, the Gnostics had to demote the Devil significantly. Other Jews—those writing in the name of Enoch—had made the fallen angels the source of evil in the world in the story of the Watchers who mated with human women. Soon the leader of that angelic group was identified with the Devil.

In reaction against the Jewish government, the Jewish Gnostics made that fallen angel into the God of Israel himself, demonizing the religion of their persecutors, while reserving worship of the one true God, the Monad, for themselves. The effect on creation was devastating. The creator god was no longer good, but demonic, and creation itself was merely a kingdom to glorify its maker, foreign to both the true God and the elect who found themselves trapped in it. The goal and plan of the Monad was to recover those souls who were his and thereby recover what had been lost of the divine nature. The great problem that the elect faced was the deception of the dark powers headed by the one who had created and now ruled this world. The powers had created false religion, and especially the Law of Moses, to deceive humanity into believing that the Jewish God was the only and highest God. What the elect needed was information about what this world really was and who ruled it. They needed *gnosis,* "enlightenment," from a heavenly source; they needed God to send down a savior to lead them to the truth.

JEWISH MESSIAHS AND DELIVERERS

The Christian claim that Jesus was the Jewish Messiah and king of the Jews came under withering criticism from Jewish contemporaries: no messiah was supposed to be crucified. Traditionally, those few in Israel who were awaiting a royal messiah at all had a relatively clear idea of what this messiah should be, arising (as we saw earlier) out of hopes for national restoration: he should be a victorious king and military conqueror who would restore the fortunes of Israel, defeating any and all foreign oppressors and bringing peace and prosperity to the people. The office had been historically that of the acclaimed king, descendant of David, appointed as Son of God by the royal enthronement ceremony of anointing. Psalm 2, often seen as a part of the ceremony, declares the king both "the anointed" (= "messiah") and "the Son of God." Indeed, the very phrase "anointed to office" in Hebrew gives us the word "messiah."[11]

Two historical moments show that the expectation of a victorious king defeating the enemies of Israel was in some measure a qualification for this royal messiah. At the time of the Persian conquests, the victorious ruler, Cyrus, was called "the Lord's anointed" (= "messiah") by the prophet Second Isaiah (Isa. 45:1). Much later, at the very end of the history of ancient Israel, in the last great rebellion against Rome in 132–135 CE under Emperor Hadrian, the leader of the uprising, Simon Bar Cochbah, was declared to be the messiah by one of the leading rabbis of his day. It was not that he was a divine being from heaven, for he was a perfectly normal human. His great qualification was that he had defeated the Romans and reinstituted a restored Jewish kingdom. A reflection of this idea may be seen in the Gospel of John: we are told that after Jesus fed the five thousand, those in the crowd "were intending to take him by force and make him king" (John 6:15).

Scholars have pointed out the obvious: that over the nearly fourteen-hundred-year presence of Israel as a national entity in Palestine, the vast majority of Jews were not looking for a heavenly messiah at all. They were merely living their lives in relation to the covenant between the Lord and the people of Israel (some closer and some farther away from its religious system). The same thing could be said for any number of nations all around the ancient Near East: neither were they looking for some or another type of savior. Greeks, Mesopotamians, Romans, Egyptians, and nearly everyone else were simply living out their short lives under the watchful gaze of their gods, according to the contract between the divine and human spheres. They were not waiting for "salvation" of their souls; in fact, as discussed earlier, the term "soul" would have meant almost nothing to them. The vast majority of people in the entire Mediterranean world, Jews included, had no belief in immortal souls. Recall that neither the Torah nor the Deuteronomistic history — the fundamental contract of Judaism — ever mentions eternal life or the punishments of hell; everything is a "this life" proposition.

Three offices were said to be anointed positions in Israel: the high priest, the king, and the prophets. For example, the high priest is often called the anointed, beginning with Aaron and his sons (Exod. 29:29); David and his royal descendants are so called as well (Ps. 18:50); and the prophets as a whole are called "anointed ones" of the Lord (Ps. 105:15). In historical order, Moses the prophet took pride of place, followed by Aaron the high priest (both in the thirteenth century BCE). Israel did not anoint a king for hundreds of years: the first was Saul, the second David, and finally Solomon, from approximately 1020 to 930 BCE. After that, the nation was divided into the northern and southern kingdoms; Israel was a united kingdom, according to the biblical writers, for only ninety years or so. In 721 the north was defeated and its useful classes were exiled by the Assyrian empire; the south suffered a similar fate in 586 at the hands of the Neo-Babylonian empire.

Throughout that period, from David to the Exile of the southern kingdom, the three offices of prophet, priest, and king operated legitimately together, simultaneously. The king ruled the country, the priests ran the religious cult, and the prophets provided divine counsel and direction. The expectation was that these offices would *always* function together. They were normal offices in all countries: Greeks, Mesopotamians, Egyptians—all had rulers, priests, and prophets, the latter often functioning as oracles at world-famous sites (such as the Apollo oracle at Delphi, in Greek tradition the very center of the earth).

As Israel suffered national disaster after national disaster, it lost and then regained, lost again, regained, and then finally lost entirely these essential offices. For the majority of the country, the northern kingdom, the offices were lost forever quite early, first under Assyrian rule and then under continual, though changing, foreign occupation. For the small southern kingdom, the offices of king and priest were lost at the Exile, with the loss of sovereignty and the destruction of the temple. The prophets, however, continued to function for a time. Especially during the dark era after the Exile in the 500s and later, when Israel under Persian rule had no native king or political sovereignty, some prophetic visions expanded to look toward a bright future of someday: God would again turn the fortunes of the nation and bring an era of blessedness.

The Zoroastrian overlords had brought eschatology, the doctrine of a future age of restoration, when the cosmic forces of evil would be destroyed in a great battle won by a savior at the head of the forces of righteousness. Israel had its own hopes for national restoration, and combined with Persian influence, the hopes of the prophets expanded the rule of the future Israel beyond its own borders to include the surrounding nations: Israel and its future king-messiah would rule their world. But unlike the later Christian understanding, he would not be alone. The vision of the Jewish prophets was not that of the Greek philosophers; the vision was not spiritual as opposed to material. There would still be a future and central Jerusalem with its temple, in which a high priest would be needed to offer and oversee sacrifices; the holy land of the revived kingdom of David would need a ruler; and a prophet would continue to dispense the divine will. Among the three offices, the king would not even be supreme.

Two significant moments survive in the Bible that fostered the expectations of the different messiahs we read of in the literature of the Essenes and in the New Testament itself. The first is found in the book of Deuteronomy, which was first composed after the defeat of the northern kingdom and then reedited rather extensively after the Exile of the southern kingdom; the second is found in the prophecies of Haggai and Zechariah.

Deuteronomy contains a famous prediction by Moses that God would someday raise up a prophet like himself again to lead the people: "The Lord your God will raise up for you a prophet like me from among you, from your countrymen; you shall listen to him" (Deut. 18:15). In this story, at the time Moses speaks, he is the only prophet; the context requires the reader to understand that the text is referring to the prophets, one by one, whom God would raise up in each following generation to direct the people in God's will. Yet eventually, after the long series of national disasters, the office of prophet died out. Ezekiel watched the glory of God leave the temple and then the city of Jerusalem (Ezek. 9:3; 10:18–19; 11:23). By the time of the Maccabean revolution (166–160 BCE), no prophets remained. During their valiant efforts at restoration of the "defiled" temple, rebuilding the fallen altar and cleansing the temple, they did what they thought best, "until a prophet should arise to tell them what to do" (*1 Maccabees* 4:46). But neither the hope of a future restoration nor remembrance of the prophecy died out: when John the Baptist and then Jesus began their remarkable ministries, people wondered (the New Testament tells us) whether or not first John, and then Jesus, was "the prophet" (John 1:21; 7:40). Expectation was still alive that the prophecy of Moses would one day be fulfilled in some special and divinely sent individual.

Nearly fifty years after the Exile of the south in 586, a new glimmer of hope arose in Judah. After Cyrus, the Persian leader, conquered Babylon in 539, he allowed the exiled Jews to return to Jerusalem and rebuild their temple (Ezra 1:1–4). He sent Zerubbabel (a Babylonian Jew and descendant of David) as Persian representative and governor, along with Joshua as high priest, to begin the work of restoration (Hag. 1:1, 14). The work began promptly but soon fell off, until it all but ceased. Economic conditions were harsh, and there was opposition from neighboring governors.

Sometime early in the reign of Darius I of Persia (522–486), the prophets Haggai and Zechariah began admonishing their contemporaries, stirring up the leaders and people to return to the work of rebuilding. The harsh economic conditions were, in their vision, punishments because the people had left off their proper work: God himself had sent the drought as punishment; the leaders and the people must return to their divinely appointed task of rebuilding the house of the Lord (Hag. 1:11; 2:17). Their energies spurred the construction on, and soon Darius himself supported them out of the royal Persian coffers and warned opponents not to hinder the work (Ezra 6:6–12). By 516, the temple was completed: a high priest was again offering sacrifices and a new descendant of David was in power in Jerusalem. The two prophets envisioned the dawning of a new era.

As Haggai declares the high hopes for Zerubbabel, the Lord instructs him to

> [s]peak to Zerubbabel governor of Judah, saying, "I am going to shake the heavens and the earth. I will overthrow the thrones of kingdoms and destroy the power of the kingdoms of the nations. . . . On that day," declares the Lord of hosts, "I will take you, Zerubbabel, son of Shealtiel, my servant," declares the Lord, "and I will make you like a signet ring, for I have chosen you," declares the Lord of hosts. (Hag. 2:21–23)

Zechariah, for his part, foresaw a dual reign of ruler and priest. He had a vision of two olive trees that supplied oil to the seven-branched golden lampstand of the Lord. The angel who interpreted the vision explained that "these are the two anointed ones who stand by the Lord of the whole earth" (Zech. 4:14), referring to Zerubbabel the ruler and Joshua the high priest. In this important vision, there are two anointed ones, two "messiahs."

Unfortunately, nothing came of the high hopes of these two prophets. Both Joshua and Zerubbabel disappeared from history, except that Zerubbabel was included in the genealogy of Jesus (Matt. 1:12–13). The nations were not overthrown, nor were the powers of the kingdoms destroyed. Zerubbabel, the chosen signet ring, apparently simply died when his hour came. The Persians ruled, apparently unhindered, until the time of Alexander, two centuries later. But the prophecies about the two messiahs—the king and the priest—and the promise of a prophet like Moses lived on in the River of God, in the minds and hopes of the people: some day, in the eyes of faith, they would be fulfilled.

There were at least two other important "messianic" figures, saviors of an even higher status in the tradition. Prophet, priest, and king were human beings, chosen, anointed, commissioned, but nevertheless human. Yet the cosmic world of Israel was occupied by higher forces: God had agents in the archangels; and the highest archangel of all, Michael, was the special champion of Israel in the divine realm. The Persians had a well-developed system of divine agents, both good and evil, who participated unseen in the war between God and the Devil. In at least one famous passage of the Bible, Michael the archangel is prophesied to serve as the eschatological divine champion. One day, it is said, the competing divine forces will engage in a final battle:

> At that time Michael, the great prince, the protector of your people, will arise. There shall be a time of anguish, such as never occurred since nations first came into existence. But at that time your people shall be delivered, everyone who is found written in the book. (Dan. 12:1)

Then, the text continues, shall come the resurrection and the last judgment, exactly the program of the Zoroastrian inheritance, but in Daniel expressed in Jewish terms.

Still another divine figure that came to figure greatly in the Christian understanding of Jesus had even older roots in the cosmic world of the land of Israel and its neighbors. The great competitor of Yahweh in many texts of the Bible was Baal the storm god, son and agent of El, the Ancient One and high god of Canaan. In one of the cycles of stories surrounding Baal, he battles Yamm, the sea, representing the forces of chaos; and after his victory, he is presented with a kingdom. Scholars have noted that this sacred story stands behind the powerful imagery of Daniel's vision of the Lord and his agent:

> I kept looking in the night visions, and behold, with the clouds of heaven one like a son of man was coming, and he came up to the Ancient of Days and was presented before Him. And to him was given dominion, glory and a kingdom, that all the peoples, nations and men of every language might serve him. His dominion is an everlasting dominion which will not pass away; and his kingdom is one which will not be destroyed. (Dan. 7:13–14)

Here elements of the eschatology of Persia and the sacred stories of Canaan are combined by the Jewish prophet to foretell the conclusion of the final battle, when God's heavenly agent, the "one like a son of man," would finally institute a permanent kingdom of righteousness. The phrase "one like a son of man" is not a title here in this text, but a description of his appearance: the phrase, meaning "one who looks human," arises from the fact that nearly all upper-world gods in early antiquity were in some version of human form. In Daniel's vision, the Ancient One is seated on a throne, with white hair and white robes (Dan. 7:9); both the high God and his agent have human-like bodies.

These prophecies and traditions of a prophet, a priest, and a Davidic king, and the eschatological hope attached to them, lived on under Persian, and then Greek, and then Hasmonean, and finally Roman rule. Added to them were visions of an angelic champion and old traditions of the divine agent of the high god, "one like a son of man." The channels by which they were passed on, the groups who valued them, are nearly invisible to us today and extremely difficult to trace; too few clues survive. We find mere mentions of such hopes in the intertestamental Jewish literature that was composed in general after the Greek conquests and on into the first Christian century.

Especially intriguing is the literature of the Essenes, found among the Dead Sea Scrolls. There all three of the anointed office-holders are mentioned as eschatological figures, but with little consistency. In one text, the prophet, the priestly messiah, and the royal messiah are all mentioned as separate individuals. The community is admonished to continue living righteously and according to its traditions, "until the prophet comes, and the messiahs of Aaron and Israel" (1QS [*Rule of the Community*] 9:11). The messiah of Aaron is the priestly messiah, since Aaron was the first high priest, while the messiah of Israel is the royal messiah.

In other Dead Sea texts, appearance of the messiahs of Aaron and Israel are foreseen, while the prophet goes unmentioned (4Q *Florilegium* [4Q174] 1.11). In still other texts the messiahs of Aaron and Israel appear to be conflated into one figure, the "messiah of Aaron and Israel," again without mention of the prophet. The members are to continue their lives according to tradition: "These shall escape in the age of the visitation; but those that remain shall be delivered up to the sword when there comes the messiah of Aaron and Israel" (CD [*Damascus Document*] 19.10–11). Note that the messiah is again a military figure victorious in the last battle.

THE NECESSITY OF A SAVIOR

By the time of Jesus, there were two sides to the dilemma of human life, stemming from two venerable Indo-European cultures as they influenced the Semitic world of Palestine: the Devil of Persian Zoroastrianism, and the material body as foreign to the spiritual soul of Greek philosophy. Greek philosophers understood well this latter side: the problems faced by the soul incarnated in a body and the material world. The idea of a savior of the world, however, would still have meant only the successful ruler who brought peace and prosperity to the nation. "Savior of one's soul" would have meant nothing, for very good reason: there was no such job description in Greek philosophy. Each individual was personally responsible; no outside "saviors" need apply. The goal of philosophy was that the soul would be pure in relationship to the enticements of the body and the material world. At death, if successful, it would leave the material body behind and ascend to its heavenly home. But there were no outside "saviors" to help one; there were only teachers—"coaches," so to speak—who taught and encouraged one to proper behavior. If one failed, there was no salvation from punishment well deserved.

There was no Devil in the Greek world either, deceiving people with false religion, blinding them to "the truth." As was the case in many other cultures, there was no false religion, as long as the religion in question was ancient. The function of the Devil, to cause unmerited evil, was in Greece occupied by the Fates, as we saw in Chapter 4. Although horribly destructive of the innocent, these Fates were not "evil" in a moral sense. They might get a person killed early and for no just reason, but they were not moral forces that caused one to be sent to hell. Fate was the standard Greek answer to the question as to why the good die young and life is so harsh and unjust. It is not unlike the answer given in the central chapters of the book of Job in the Old Testament. Job the human sufferer, as we find out at the end, really had no grounds to complain about his innocent losses; his suffering was part of God's unknowable Plan.

Yet the case of the book of Job is quite instructive. Sometime after the Exile and the subsequent Persian conquest of the Near East (ca. 539 BCE), a second author added what are now the opening two chapters of the book. In these chapters, the sufferings of Job are attributed to the Devil, an evil being that the second author had learned about from his Persian overlords. He drew on a new explanation for the suffering of the righteous provided by Zoroastrianism: the more one was just, the more one was persecuted unjustly. At least among a few Jewish intellectuals, this gallows-humor reason for the suffering in the world made sense.

Instead of the righteous being blessed, the righteous were persecuted, while the servants of the Devil were successful.

In both Greek philosophy and Persian conception, the righteous would suffer here on earth at the hands of unjust persecutors, but they would eventually be vindicated in a judgment after
death, and the wicked would eventually be punished. Such ideas
began gaining ground among intellectual Jews as well. One
Jewish text among several from late in the first century BCE that
take this stance tells the story of a typical righteous man who is
persecuted to death by wicked opponents. Yet, we are told, there
will be a judgment after death, "when the righteous will stand with
great confidence in the presence of those who have oppressed
them," for "the righteous live forever" (*Wisdom of Solomon* 5:1, 15).
There is mention of the Devil, but his advent is seen only as the
cause of death: "Through the Devil's envy death entered the
world" (*Wisdom of Solomon* 2:24). But the Devil, in the view of
other authors, could cause much more harm.

In fact, the Devil was the reason that a savior from the divine
world became necessary at all. In the original Zoroastrian revelation, the Devil was an eternal and elemental power who created
false religion to deceive the whole human race. The gods of the
nations were demonic powers. Nevertheless, humans were required,
as responsible adults, to make moral choices offered to them by
God or the Devil: righteous thoughts, words, and deeds gained
them heaven; the opposite earned the punishments of hell.
Zoroastrianism had postulated two primeval but opposite principles, good and evil, and a final cosmic battle in which the forces of
good, headed by a champion, the eschatological savior, would at
the end of the age defeat the Devil, the demons, and his human followers. Here was the first savior of the world, a cosmic warrior
who would battle on the side of God against the forces of the Devil
and defeat them.

Gnostic writers were the first to combine the dualism of
Zoroastrianism with the Monad of Greek philosophy, producing a
comprehensive religious worldview that was a direct precursor of

Christianity. The real God was immaterial and infinite, dwelling outside the geocentric cosmos in a world of light. The elect were souls incarnated in bodies; their bodies were of the earth while their souls were ultimately derived from the Monad. Their destiny was to leave the material world behind and return to their spiritual home. The material cosmos was ruled by an arrogant usurper destined for destruction. To keep humanity deceived into worshiping him, he created false and demonic religions. He used fleshly and worldly temptations as rewards for his "righteous." The elect who would not follow him he persecuted.[12]

This was a world that needed a savior of a kind wholly different from kings who defeated national enemies and brought peace or material prosperity, different even from messiahs who defeated eschatological enemies and permanently restored the nation of Israel. The problems that humans faced were twofold. First, they were incarnated in fleshly bodies that tempted them to worldly pleasures and passions. They were blind because they followed after pleasures; they were blind in their sins. Second, people lived in a world of religious deception: they were deceived by the Devil into thinking that following rules that resulted in rewards of pleasures and wealth and human honors were what human life was about. They were deceived into thinking that this world was all there was and that the gods with bodies of this world were the real gods. They were led to think that temples and animal sacrifices, firstfruits of the fields, and money were somehow important and effective in gaining divine favor. Not only were they blind; they were blinded by deception. They needed the truth; they needed enlightenment. They were in the darkness of the dark forces; they needed light from above. In Christian terms, they needed "the light of the world" (John 9:5).

JESUS AS SAVIOR OF THE WORLD

In stark contrast to the traditional view of a kingly messiah who would restore Israel's fortunes (or an eschatological high priest or a prophet like Moses), a quite small group among the Jews began to claim what seemed a contradiction in terms: that a certain crucified Galilean was the Messiah of all Israel and the Savior of the whole world. Victorious ruler of Judah and crucified Galilean were opposites that represented an incompatible impossibility. The traditional view of who the messiah was supposed to be and the realities of who Jesus actually was were very much at odds.

In a conversation between Justin Martyr, a Christian philosopher, and Trypho, a Jew, that took place about 135 CE, Trypho disdained Justin's claims about Jesus and declared that "this so-called Christ of yours was dishonorable and inglorious, so much so that the last curse contained in the law of God fell on him, for he was crucified" (*Dialogue with Trypho* 32). Tertullian, one of the great writers of the early church, also disputed (ca. 200 CE) with Jews about the Christian claim that Jesus is the Christ: "To this moment they affirm that their Christ is not come, because he is not come in majesty" (*Answer to the Jews* 14). The fundamental disagreement was that the Jewish messiah was to "come in majesty" to rule the world, while the Christian Christ had been crucified: the messiah was not supposed to lose but win, and he was *certainly* not supposed to get himself crucified.

The basic problem was that the two sides were only partially in the same conversation. They were using many of the same terms and the same Bible, often even the same biblical texts, but for very different reasons and to conflicting ends. The Jewish "ruler of the world" and the Christian "Savior of the world" were unconnected, even contradictory, concepts.

The ruler of the world for Jews was, of course, the God of Genesis, the God of the Old Testament. But the title "ruler of the world" implied something about the world itself that was fundamentally not Christian. God forbid, of course, that any Christian should claim in any ultimate sense that God the Father or Jesus was not ruler of the world. Both God and Jesus were worthy of the title, the Father as the Monad, source of All, and the Son as agent in the making of the world, as "firstborn of all creation" (Col. 1:15).

Yet the "world" could be understood in two fundamentally opposing ways. In the viewpoint of the early monistic cultures, which most of the Old Testament reflected, it was simply chaos/water that had either become on its own or been formed by one or another creator deity into a benign "place" for human and divine habitation. It was merely the "stage" on which the human and divine drama took place, inert and almost imperceptible. But, on the other hand, it could also be an inimical "system," alive with contrary forces, a "kingdom of darkness."

Jesus and the early Christians, as opposed to many modern religionists, were in this latter category. In the temptation narratives of the Gospels, for example, Jesus is impelled into the wilderness by the Spirit of God to be tested by the Devil. During the three tests, "the Devil took him to a very high mountain and showed him all the kingdoms of the world and their glory; and he said to him, 'All these things I will give you, if you fall down and worship me'" (Matt. 4:8–9). Jesus, of course refuses to worship anyone but the Father and passes the test, but it is clear that the Devil owns the world and can give it to whomever he wishes. In the Gospel of John, the Devil is three times called "the ruler of the [or *this*] world" (John 12:31; 14:30; 16:11). Paul once calls him "the god of this world" (2 Cor. 4:4). Understood against this dualistic background, the "ruler of the world" was the Devil.

Jesus was very definitely dualistic in his worldview, as Chapter 5 suggested. Fundamental to his entire religious understanding were the two opposing pairs of soul and body, and God and the Devil. As we saw in the previous chapter, a saying in the Gospel of Mark stands as a key to his basic viewpoint: "What will it profit one to gain the whole world, and lose one's soul?" (Mark 8:36).

The "world" to which "soul" is opposed consists of two separate entities: the "world" of the body and the "world" of the Devil. Both worlds are intended in the passage from Mark just quoted, for Jesus had just said to Peter, "Get behind me, Satan!" (Mark 8:33). Both views of the world appear in Jesus' most famous parable as well, the Parable of the Sower. As Chapter 5 reminded us, the

Sower of that parable sows seed on four types of ground. Three types fail to bear crops: the first because the Devil takes away the seed; the second because of persecution; the third because of the worries of the world and the lure of riches (Mark 4:14–20). The types of ground — that is, the hearers of Jesus' teaching — are faced with two major obstacles, one internal and one external. The internal is the natural desire to have a good life in this world, a desire that often draws one away from following the gospel. The external is "the world" as a spiritual system run by the Devil, opposing anyone wishing to follow Jesus.

Faced with these obstacles, human beings needed help from outside. It was no longer a case of being obedient to the Law while living in a good "place," the world created by the God of Genesis. The world was, in reality, not such a good place anyway: life was short and difficult, full of diseases and hardships. But now people had souls that they could lose and did not know their danger; in addition, they were living in the enemy's camp. They were trapped.

That is the point of the scriptural story about tying up the strong man cited in Chapter 4: "No one can enter a strong man's house and plunder his property without first tying up the strong man; then indeed the house can be plundered" (Mark 3:27). The "strong man" is the Devil; his "house" is the world system he rules. Jesus came as the Savior, as the Devil's opponent from outside his "world," to plunder his house; he came to rescue his people. Those who came to have eyes to see, as in the story of the Samaritan woman at the well, could say, "This is truly the Savior of the world" (John 4:42).

7

OVERTURNING THE WORLD:
THE RIVER OF GOD IN THE
TWENTY-FIRST CENTURY

We have been following the River of God, the totality of the interaction between God and human culture in the ancient Near East, from its early appearance at the dawn of writing to the time of Jesus and beyond. At each major confluence of cultures, when one civilization conquered and succeeded another, there were significant changes in religious conceptions. For Israel, as a small nation often at the mercy of the world around it, there were many minor exchanges of ideas, as there were for any ancient culture—exchanges due to treaties and official international interactions, storytelling along trade routes, intermarriage, and migrations small and large. There were "major confluences" as well: the series of national disasters, as Israel was conquered time and again by one or another great empire. At each point it was influenced from outside; it was forced to change and adapt or die out. To Israel's credit, it adapted; it evolved and survived as the child of new parents. It accepted new ideas into its older traditions and produced hybrid forms, Israelite versions of the Egyptian or Mesopotamian or Persian or Greek originals. At each stage some things were gained, some lost; but the result was something new, never before seen, constructed out of what was old by the genius of new inspiration fostered by the pressure of new circumstances. In individual humans, the flow of time and experience, the process of growing older and "suffering" (as the Greeks would have expressed it), changes one inexorably. The process is visible in religious culture as well: Israel also suffered and changed.

But Israel was not a unity: it had been divided early in its history into a northern kingdom known as "Israel" and a smaller southern kingdom known as "Judah." The northern kingdom had its own distinctive versions of proper religious thought and practice from the tenth century BCE to the Roman era—versions different from those found in Jerusalem. The north had its own temples and centers of worship, which competed with the Jerusalem temple and its claim to be the one and only legitimate temple of the Lord. Early on, the south criticized the north for worship of the "golden calves" set up by Jeroboam in the cities of Bethel and Dan to prevent pilgrimages to Jerusalem (1 Kings 12:28; 2 Kings 10:29). Later it was criticized for its worship of Baal and Asherah and all the host of heaven.

But one needs to stand back from the polemical condemnations and ask what those in the northern kingdom of Israel thought that they themselves were doing. The nation as a whole was certainly not plotting evil against the divine world; that would have been suicide. They were, however, trying to survive, as futile as that was, given their geographical location as a crossroads among empires. They were forced to be open to the religious traditions of their environment and chose to meld freely their Israelite traditions with those of other peoples of Canaan and the surrounding empires (2 Kings 17:15–16).

There was a great deal of antipathy between north and south that is hardly visible to us. The northern kingdom of Israel was itself divided by geography into two districts, Samaria and Galilee, neither of which were positively disposed to Jerusalem. Samaria, named after its capital city, was made up of the central highlands of Palestine—that area known as the "West Bank" today—and constituted much of the territory of Israel. The Samaritans throughout their history were very much at odds with Jerusalem. Samaria was conquered by Sargon II of Assyria in 721 BCE. Both the biblical story and Assyrian accounts report the deportation of important segments of Samaritan society and the settling of foreigners in the land after the conquest (2 Kings 17:23–24). Farther to the north was Galilee, much of which, like Samaria, was not even "Jewish"; as we saw in Chapter 5, the prophet Isaiah called it "Galilee of the Gentiles" (Isa. 9:1). It was conquered by Assyria even earlier than Samaria, in 732 BCE, by one of Sargon's predecessors, Tiglath-Pileser III, and became an Assyrian province.

By the second century BCE, the Jewish population of Galilee was a small minority surrounded and threatened by Gentile groups. During the Maccabean revolt against Greek rule (166–160 BCE), a report was received in Judea that the Jews of Galilee were in mortal danger from their non-Jewish neighbors. Simon, one of the Maccabean brothers, led a military rescue expedition against the Galilean Gentiles:

> Simon went to Galilee and fought many battles against the Gentiles, and the Gentiles were crushed before him. . . . Then he took the Jews of Galilee . . . with their wives and children and all they possessed and led them to Judea with great rejoicing. (*1 Maccabees* 5:21–23)

If we are to believe this text, Galilee was abandoned and left to the Gentiles; the Jews were repatriated to Judea. But the claim that all the Jews of Galilee were removed to Judah by Simon is simply not true. Later history shows quite clearly that Jews remained in Galilee long after Simon. Simon removed "the Jews of Galilee" to Judea, yet Jews certainly remained behind. How is one to understand this contradiction?

The answer lies in the long history of antipathy between north and south. The very word "Jew" comes from the name of the tribe of Judah. Simon took back to Judea those who had appealed to the south for deliverance, who felt threatened in Galilee and saw their natural home and place of safety in Judea. The reference must be to the portion of Jews among the larger community of Israelites of Galilee. These alone were recognized as "genuine Jews" by Simon and the Jerusalem contingent. Simon took the Jews who agreed with Jerusalem to Judea and left behind those who did not. The remaining Jews were those who did not feel threatened by their Gentile neighbors and had not appealed to Jerusalem for deliverance from oppression. They were not being oppressed and were at relative peace in their religious environment. Simon did not recognize them as his kind of Jews, so he left them in the world where they were comfortable, in "Galilee of the Gentiles."

JESUS AND THE "NEW WINE" OF THE GOSPEL

Galilee was the home of Jesus. He lived in the part of Israel that for most of eight hundred years had been occupied and ruled by foreign powers. It was the region most open to "major confluences," the ideas brought to and forced upon it by invading empires that won and lost Palestine in their battles with one another. Galilee was the region of Israel that was most distant, in more than one sense, from the influences and practices of the Jerusalem temple culture. Jews still lived in Galilee, keeping their traditions in their own way, as they had from the beginning of the nation; thus Galilee was certainly part of the traditional greater Israel. Yet in another sense, both Jerusalem and Galilee saw each other as faraway lands almost foreign to each other.

According to 2 Chronicles, when Hezekiah, king of Judah from 715 to 687 BCE, began to reform his own people's idolatrous practices, he sent an ambassador north to Samaria and Galilee to invite people of those regions to celebrate the Passover at Jerusalem. The northerners, however, "laughed them to scorn and mocked them. Only a few humbled themselves . . . and came to Jerusalem" (2 Chron. 30:10–11). The north had its own temples and festivals to the Lord; "only a few" agreed with Jerusalem. Hezekiah's attempt at inclusion and reconciliation was rare in the extreme. For Jerusalem, Galilee was out of sight and out of mind: after the Exile, it is not even mentioned in the biblical literature written in Judah.

Yet Galilee was a crossroads of the religious inspirations of the greatest cultures of antiquity. It was not important culturally or politically in its own right, but it was on the route to somewhere else for everyone in the region. Anyone going anywhere across Palestine went through Galilee, with its abundant water, flora, and fauna. Jerusalem, on the other hand, was relatively isolated by geography. It was in the arid mountains off the trade routes, too far south and east and certainly too high up; the caravans went around it in the valleys, where there was water and life.

In this context, one may begin to understand the disjunction between Jesus and much of the Jerusalem religion of his day. What we read in the Gospels is a long series of conflicts between Jesus and the Judean authorities. His view of real relationship to God was in direct opposition to that of the Judean authorities. The differences were not merely matters of practice; they were of fundamental importance and went to the very heart of what it meant for humans to know and relate properly to God. Jesus was a Jew, but he viewed the world as had no Jew before him.

As a result, the early disciples were painfully slow to understand Jesus, and they never came to agreement on who or what he was. "Agreement," such as it was, had to wait for Constantine and the era of the creeds starting in 325, when people were forced to sign doctrinal statements that "defined" who Jesus was or suffer exile. The early disciples followed Jesus not because of doctrines but because he held out to them a promise and hope that they had rarely (if ever) encountered.

The River of God contains simultaneously what is new and what is very old. Because people are slow to change, at any one moment what is old in the River predominates. The "scribes" had been from the time of Ezra the teachers and interpreters of the religion of Judaism. The Gospel of Mark describes the message of Jesus as a "new teaching with authority," "not as the scribes"

(Mark 1:22, 27). From the outset, Jesus contradicted not only the scribes, but even Moses himself: several times in the Sermon on the Mount in Matthew and the Sermon on the Plain in Luke, he either "upgrades" or contradicts Moses. For Jesus' opponents, Moses was the unassailable authority, the giver of the Law. But Jesus lived in an entirely different thought-world from that of Moses, heir to the ideas of several empires that had ruled Palestine since Moses. Moses' enemies were Egyptians and Canaanites; he knew nothing of the dualistic ideas so important to Jesus. Jesus' enemies were not human beings at all, but worldly desires and the temptations of the Devil.

The earliest hearers of Jesus expected a victorious military messiah, if they expected any such figure at all. In a revealing passage in the Gospel of John, Jesus uses the enigmatic self-designation "the Son of Man" and tells his listeners that he will be "lifted up," a euphemism for crucifixion (12:23, 32). The people respond, "We have heard out of the Law that the Christ is to remain forever; and how can you say, 'The Son of Man must be lifted up'? Who is this Son of Man?" (John 12:34). Clearly, the people had expected an earthly and victorious Christ who would remain alive forever, yet Jesus was much closer to the opposite. For him, the poor were blessed; the persecuted and reviled were to rejoice. The rich and powerful, on the other hand, were in eternal danger: "Go and sell all you possess and give to the poor, and you will have treasure in heaven; and come, follow me" (Mark 10:21). Jesus' goals were not land, riches, and long earthly life, but heaven, spiritual blessing, and eternal life. He was reversing the values of millennia; he was overturning the world.

THE RIVER OF GOD AND THE SCANDAL OF THE CROSS

Jesus stood at the beginning of the largest religious tradition the world has ever known. He lived at a crossroads of ideas, and his life was the catalyst for new and eventually overwhelming change in religious conception. As had happened many times before, the course and content of the River was altered and expanded; because of his input, the River was again changed for all later religious development. The Greco-Roman religions were forced to respond to the harsh and persuasive critique of Christians; eventually they were defeated, gradually dying out. Judaism was also forced to respond not only to the Christians, but also to the destruction of their temple and state. Judaism would never again be the same. Islam much later drew on the ideas of the River, many of which, by the time that tributary was added, had been developed by the Christians.

Likewise, Christianity itself continued to change and develop as it reacted to and debated with not only its environment, but also competing understandings of Jesus among Christians themselves. Christians had to learn, for example, to overcome the criticism from Jews such as Trypho that Jesus could not have been the Christ because he had been crucified. If there were crucifixions to be done, surely the Messiah would be on the other side—as the judge and not the victim. Christians also had to learn how to explain the fact of the crucifixion to themselves. Paul describes the problem succinctly: "[W]e preach Christ crucified, to Jews a stumbling block and to Gentiles foolishness" (1 Cor. 1:23). According to Paul's statement, the Jews could not accept as messiah anyone who had been crucified, and the Greeks (a cipher for everyone else) knew that such gallows-birds were low-class criminals. Honorable individuals were executed by beheading; the unworthy were first tortured, and then crucified or thrown to the beasts or burned alive. Only fools would follow someone who had been crucified.

The crucifixion was a major problem indeed. One story in the Gospel of Luke illustrates this well. As the risen Jesus walked unrecognized with two disciples on the road to Emmaus, they began discussing Jesus. The disciples tell him, "We had hoped that he was the one to redeem Israel" (Luke 24:21). Their point was that everything with Jesus seemed to them to have been going well until his arrest. He had been teaching and performing miracles that authenticated him in the eyes of his followers, raising their hopes that he would turn out to be the expected kingly messiah. And then came the fatal impossibility: he was crucified, and their hopes were dashed. In each of the Gospels, when Jesus was arrested, the disciples abandoned him. Cowardice may have been a factor, but contradicted expectations and dashed hopes were certainly the main issue. The disciples had been looking to Jesus to be a victorious king, the one who would rescue Israel from foreign domination and bring the blessing of the future age to the land. And then he was crucified.

Christians used two opposing strategies to deal with the crucifixion. Some simply denied it. Jesus was God from heaven who had come to save humanity, and God could not be crucified; therefore he only "seemed" to suffer and die on the cross. This view was one of the earliest heresies, and was quite common in the early church. It is known today as Docetism, from the Greek word *dokein*, "to appear, to seem." Other Christians, on the other hand, did exactly what the Gospel of Mark says Jesus told them to do: they took up their crosses and followed him (Mark 8:34). Docetism was a direct affront to this latter group. If Jesus had not really died on the cross, then what was the point of being a martyr? Why should one be crucified for One who had given his life only "seemingly"? The faithfulness of the martyrs contradicted the Docetists rather convincingly—Christians were dying as martyrs because they were following their Leader—and that was the beginning of the doctrine's demise: Docetism was eventually defeated.

It was finally the Greek heroic tradition that helped Christians understand the cross. Greek heroes, sons of the gods, had from earliest times died for their peoples, tragically in the midst of life, but according to the plan and will of the divine world. The elite among them, such as Herakles and Asklepios (among others), rose again from the dead and ascended into heaven, becoming divine advocates for their worshipers. This was clearly the underlying model for the Christian crucifixion and resurrection story. Nothing like it had existed in the stories of the old Semitic cultures, including the

Old Testament. By adding the dimension of the Devil and his dark world to the story of the heroes, Christians understood the life of Jesus as that of a righteous one sent from God who had been killed by the forces of evil for the sake of those whom he had come to save. He then rose from the dead and ascended to heaven to become their ever-present help in time of need.

Here was a way to deal with the issues underlying the argument between Trypho the Jew and Justin Martyr the Christian philosopher. Trypho claimed that Jesus could not fill the role of messiah because Jesus had been crucified, violating the traditional expectation that the Messiah was to appear in glory. The Christian counterclaim was simple and entirely new, but perfectly understandable in the River of God. Jesus was both: he was both crucified and conqueror, lowest and highest, servant of all and ruler of all. Jesus encompassed all that was good in the savior traditions of the cultures in which he lived. Christians added and melded the two conflicting savior traditions together: they believed that Jesus was destined to appear twice, first as the hero who died to save his people, and second as the victorious kingly messiah expected by Trypho.

At his first appearance, Jesus was who he actually had been, a divinely sent leader and savior who had bravely suffered a humiliating crucifixion for the sake of his followers. But at his second appearance, he would be the heavenly Son of Man, riding the clouds of heaven, who would defeat the forces of evil everywhere. If Herakles and Asklepios were sons of gods and examples of Greek heroes, and the Son of Man and the kingly messiah were Sons of God and examples of Jewish heroes, then Christians applied both types to Jesus. But there was an important distinction for Christians between Jesus and the heroes both Greek and Jewish: for Christians, Jesus was the one and only real Son of God, the one and only Messiah, who was the best of all heroes of whatever culture.

Yet Christians still faced the problem of being "new," the problem with which this book began. Their solution was again an old one, shared not only by Greeks and Jews, but by every culture of antiquity. The fundamental theology the ancient world over was that everything was in "the Plan": everything was in the divine decrees, the tablets of destiny, the astral configurations. For the Jews everything was in the Law, the Scriptures, and it was to these that the earliest Christians, Jews themselves, looked for justification and legitimacy. If a religion was new, then it was suspect; everyone, including these early Jewish Christians, agreed to that. But the logic of the River made the Christian defense almost easy and nearly irrefutable. Since Jesus and his understanding of the human relationship to God had arisen from the River of God, its roots and ancestry were in the River. They could be traced without difficulty to ancient and venerable traditions.

Christians readily found many texts that supported their "Way" (as they called their religion) in the Old Testament, and they applied the texts to Jesus. Most familiar for his first appearance was the Suffering Servant of Isaiah 53, who would die in innocence and humiliation because of the sins of others. At his second appearance, he would come as the Son of Man of Daniel 7, fulfilling the traditional expectations held by those who looked forward to a judge and ruler of the future world.

MAKING UP TRUE STORIES

Religious traditions are products of their antecedent traditions, the pressures of their environment, and the inspiration of their founders and adherents. Christianity was no exception. Creative individuals have forever "made sense" out of contradictions and difficulties presented by new circumstances. Ancient world religion was less a matter of creeds, a list of propositions to which one had to assent, than it was about sacred stories. Ancient peoples had no way of knowing for sure what the gods had done before time or how their heroes had acted at critical moments centuries before. They had been brought up on stories that expressed the religious truths of their cultures. They then retold those stories with new episodes or in quite new versions to take account of different ideas as their cultures changed.

The stories in general tell of the proper place of human beings in the world. They help one understand and accept the human condition, and they answer the hard questions: Why do people have to suffer during life and then die? Why is there so little equality and justice? What is the meaning of life? In general, the answers are based on "the Plan": God (or the gods) knows and understands; life is not random or meaningless.

Here is the reason why there is Truth in things that are false, why obviously false religious claims can nevertheless be "true," because they bring order to what is otherwise chaos; they "make sense" out of what makes no sense. A religious tradition is deeply true for its adherents; the cosmos it envisions is therefore also true, whether it is or not. The three-story cosmos of the early cultures of the River of God had to be replaced. The gods no longer sat on thrones on the top of the sky a few thousand feet up. Yet old and false stories of human-shaped gods who lived a short distance away said something important: the gods understand us because they are like us; they are near, so they can hear and watch over us.

The three-story universe gradually gave way to the geocentric cosmos. Its old, small gods were superseded and replaced by the Monad, the one God, the spiritual and infinite source of all. The process was a slow one that took centuries, and it was still going on at the time of the rise of Christianity. Early Christians were still products of the old cultures; few were scientists or philosophers.

The very need to find ancient justification for innovation in religion made "progress," or any change at all, nearly impossible. Although those who invented new *technology* were praiseworthy — Virgil placed among the blessed dead those who discovered ideas or invented ways to improve human life (*Aeneid* 6.663) — Christian "invention" in the field of religion was still being censured by pagans nearly four hundred years after Christ, though Christians were finally in the majority. The pagan philosopher Sallustius, for example, was still defending the old traditions of sacrifice in the face of Christian abandonment of those old rites for their new ideas of a God who did not eat dead animals (*On the Gods* 16).

What was old died hard, and many Jewish Christians still lived in the old universe. Some still held to the God with a body who sat on a throne and was someday to restore their fortunes—that is, their prosperity and bank accounts—now, however, through the agency of Jesus. Nor has time erased such ideas in the intervening centuries: many Christians today still hold similar doctrines of the restoration of an earthly Israel or the hope that if they are obedient, God will make them rich. The River of God seldom discards anything.

Eventually, however, the church came to accept and incorporate the geocentric cosmos into its doctrinal understanding for deeply held religious reasons. The geocentric universe was surrounded and overseen by God. The stars on their paths obeyed God perfectly; in fact, one could see in creation the invisible attributes of God: his greatness, wisdom, power, and especially justice (Rom. 1:21). At the center of it all was the stationary sphere of the earth, created by God for humans. One could see easily that God had in fact created the whole universe for humans, who were at the very center of God's care and attention.

And then, after more than a thousand years of complacent ignorance, science changed again. Nicholas Copernicus discovered that the earth revolved around the sun, not the other way around; Galileo discovered that Jupiter had moons. Other discoveries abounded, producing the heliocentric universe, which in turn called into question not only the cosmology of the church, but also the religious truths that the geocentric universe had supported. Further science has produced a view of the earth as a nearly infinitesimal and unimportant part of a universe so vast that its size is unknown. Religion in general has not yet assimilated the implications of these and many other scientific discoveries.

FAITH VERSUS BELIEFS

The cultural and scientific crises that brought about changes in the River of God in the ancient Near East also brought about crises of faith. People were exposed to new ideas that had been absent from or contradicted their older religious traditions. They were forced to make hard choices: our "supreme god" has been defeated and humiliated; do we continue to believe in our old doctrines, or do we accept the doctrines (and gods) of our conquerors? Religious conceptions, faced with such necessity, had to evolve or be left behind to die out. New ideas brought by conquering empires were challenges to old systems of belief that could not be ignored.

Beliefs are the claims people make about God or the gods: God is (or the gods are) omnipotent, omniscient, or the like. All such doctrinal formulations of the ancient world, secure and cogent as they were at the time they were formulated, came under fatal attack as the River flowed on. The beliefs of polytheism, for example, were challenged by various types of monotheism. As we saw in Chapter 2, all of the cultures in the ancient Near East were at one time polytheistic; and eventually they all accepted one or another version of monotheism. The belief systems of the polytheists died out; Marduk, the old god of Babylon, is unknown today; Baal survives only as a name for the Devil; Zeus and Herakles are no more. One must contemplate the relationship of worshiper to deity: If there are no longer worshipers of Marduk, and he is therefore no longer named, in what way does he, or did he, exist at all?

The overturning of beliefs by cultural change, whether in the ancient world or our own, undermines the faith invested in them. Faith is the ability to place trust in the God understood according to one's beliefs. Faith is given to everyone by God; beliefs, on the other hand, are given by one's culture and century.[1] All peoples have faith; only those of a particular culture at a specific time have their unique set of beliefs. Every human society known to us has faith; there has been none without religion as far back as recorded history takes us. Yet no two societies have the same beliefs. Further, no single society in different eras, regardless of its claims to the contrary, has the same beliefs over time. Beliefs inevitably evolve to incorporate new ideas forced upon them by external stimuli.

THE DIVERSITY OF EARLY CHRISTIAN BELIEFS

Many modern groups claim to be the one true Christian church because of their faithfulness to early tradition. Yet these claims are all marred by the fact that there was no *single* early tradition. Rather, there were many groups with wildly contradictory viewpoints, stemming from this or that portion of the inheritance of the River. In addition, the traditions of the early Christians did not remain the same over time (just as those of their ancestors had not): they were adjusted and upgraded over and over to incorporate new ideas forced on them by controversies with Jews, pagans, and each other, by better science and new philosophy. Today, modern groups create their own never-before-seen "systematic theologies" of the early church to suit their modern needs and then claim that their reconstruction mirrors the way the early church actually was; they also are products of the River and are acting exactly as did their predecessors. They are making up new "true stories" that are based on new "true histories" that help them understand their now modern world.

No one today is an early Christian or agrees uniformly with the first generations of the church, though one often hears the conviction that if we could get back to the early church, everything would be fine. But that conviction is an impossibility based on false presuppositions: the first generations of Christians did not agree among themselves; there was no single "early church" to go back to. The diversity of opinions about God and Jesus in antiquity far exceeded anything we find in the church today.

Nearly all Christians now subscribe to the creeds. Yet there were no creeds for the first three hundred years of the church. On one extreme, some groups of Jewish Christians thought that Jesus was the son of Joseph and Mary, who had grown up to become the only man righteous enough to fulfill the Law; he was therefore chosen to be the Messiah because of his obedience. On another extreme, certain groups (mostly Gentile) thought of Jesus as God himself, walking the earth in human guise. In between were several important yet quite different conceptions, all justified by this or that tradition inherited from the River. The creeds of the fourth and fifth centuries defined the Trinity and the divine-human nature of Christ. No such doctrines existed among the early generations of the church. Not even the terminology of the creeds yet existed. The word "Trinity," for example, is first found near the end of the second century; and Tertullian, writing around 200, tells us that most Christians of his day were modalists: they thought that the Father had simply descended to earth disguised as the man Jesus and then returned to heaven to be the Spirit.

THE UNKNOWABLE GOD

One of the effects of ancient scientific observation on theology was the realization that God is beyond human comprehension. As Greek philosopher-scientists began to understand how enormous the universe is, their ideas of how great God is expanded correspondingly. Ancients had long praised their gods for their surpassing greatness and wisdom, explaining human suffering by reference to God's inscrutable Plan. There had always been things that one did not, or could not, know about the gods. Some knowledge, however, was always possible: gods had bodies, looked like us, acted and felt like we do. That was why the gods were angry or jealous or passionate in other ways; so were we.

The One that the philosopher-scientists had discovered, however—the infinite and immaterial God of the vast universe—did not have, *could* not have, a body at all, and was therefore not like humans. The One was so big, so eternal, so other, that it could properly be described only in negative terms, by what it was not. As we saw in Chapter 2, God was immaterial, infinite, immeasurable, undying, unchangeable, while we were all the opposites. Yet these few philosopher-scientists had also redefined what humans beings were. They had deduced that people were not merely clay pots with air in them; humans were not simply lost to the earth after death. We had a point of contact, a fundamental unity with the one

God: the purest part of the soul, the mind or spirit, had originated in the One and was made of the same spiritual substance.

The God and Father of Jesus was the One, not the god-with-a-body of the Canaanites; in addition, human beings were, for Jesus, eternal souls incarnate in perishable bodies. These theological developments, a new stage in the Plan of God, helped Christians understand themselves as "new wine" that required a "new wine-skin." Given the ancient bias against anything new in religion, Christian claims to legitimacy at first depended on their assertion that they had superseded Israel in God's Plan. That was (and still is) clearly offensive in the extreme to the Israel of tradition.

Yet Christianity in reality did not need to be legitimized by any-one; it was wholly able to stand on its own. It was not in reality a sect of Judaism, though it drew on much that was Jewish; nor was it a new type of Greek philosophy, though it drew heavily on Hellenistic thought. It was viewed as one or the other in antiq-uity—as a Jewish sect or a new philosophy—and is still thought to be one or the other today. In fact, though, it was *both*, mixed together at the same time, with much else in addition: it included elements that were not only Jewish and Greek, but also Canaan-ite, Egyptian, Mesopotamian, Assyrian, Persian, and Roman, along with others less visible today. It grew out of the River and inherited all that the River contained.

Christians were slow to realize that fact, but eventually they understood that the Christian revelation was sufficient unto itself, just as the religious traditions of Israel or Greece or Rome or Egypt stood on their own. The raw materials out of which Christianity arose had existed from time immemorial. What made it unique was the new inspiration, the new revelation, the new turn in the River of God. Jesus drew on the traditions of the River, but what he added to them changed its course forever.

To many observers in the early church, it seemed that knowl-edge of God among humans had been changing, evolving, growing. God could not change by definition, but humans certainly did so daily. In individual life, a person grew from childhood to adulthood, from ignorance to wisdom. Culture, science, and technology had certainly changed and grown over time as well; and to any wise observer, so had human knowledge of God. The world of polytheism was being superseded; "idols" were being called into question.

Accordingly, Christians developed the idea of the gradual unfolding of the revelation of God: many things about God and the Plan had lain hidden in the past because of human inability to understand. The problem lay not with God, of course, but with the imperfections of humans. God gave out only a little information at a time because the race, given its stage of development, could handle only so much. It had in some way to "grow up" to be able to understand and receive further revelation; when it did, then more revelation was given. That is the apostle Paul's understanding of Israel and his own spiritual journey as a Jew formerly strictly observant of the Law and now free from the Law as a Christian. The Law represented a period of "child training" for humanity; faith in Christ was the stage in life of coming to maturity (Gal. 4:1–10). Jesus had inaugurated a new era in the Plan of God.

THE RIVER OF GOD IN THE TWENTY-FIRST CENTURY

Each of the cultures we have surveyed believed itself to be a bearer of the torch of truth, the knowledge of the true God. Each believed that its own conception of God was the divine reality, that Marduk or Re or Zeus was in fact how God actually was. But the River did not stop with any of them; it could not be stopped. It flowed through and beyond Mesopotamia, Egypt, Persia, Israel, and Greece, and then passed through and beyond even later cultures. These societies all produced sophisticated theologies that claimed their God supreme, with answers for nearly every question and rebuttals for nearly every objection.

Yet each ancient theology, viewed from later stages of the River, turned out to be inadequate: Enlil was replaced by Marduk, who was in turn replaced by Ashur. Eventually, all the gods of the ancients were either replaced (and forgotten) or upgraded to become something much greater, more in accord with new knowledge and circumstance. One wise observer, the Greek philosopher Heraclitus, saw the obvious foolishness of such partisan claims and declared, "That which is wise alone is one; it is unwilling and willing to be called by the name of Zeus" (frag. 32 Diels). In other words, whatever God actually *was*, names and theologies such as those of Zeus and Marduk and Re and all others were clearly inadequate; the real God was far too big to be described so neatly.

Viewed from the present, every ancient theology contained obvious flaws because of the limitations of ancient knowledge in general: the world is not a mere six or eight thousand years old; diseases are caused not by demons but by microbes and viruses; the real universe is neither the three-story nor the geocentric cosmos. From the inside, however, these systems worked wonderfully well in serving the needs of their adherents. They created order out of chaos; they gave individuals a place to stand in the overall divine Plan. Yet, in time, each theology was replaced as culture changed. Gods of empires defeated and absorbed gods of conquered nations, and then in turn were themselves replaced or upgraded. The River dictated that nothing could remain the same and survive. The lesson was that no single culture had full knowledge of God; subsequent history would teach that human beings still do not know God as God is.

Christians did not understand Jesus. They followed him, at times to their deaths, but they knew him only in part, darkly, as an enigma, to paraphrase Paul's words (1 Cor. 13:12). They interpreted him against the background of their own religious conceptions and produced a breathtaking variety of different and contradictory denominations, each with its own Christ, its own Christology, far more diverse than anything common today. Nearly three hundred years after Jesus' time, a viewpoint was put together under Emperor Constantine that got enough support to become official orthodoxy; but no such orthodoxy existed in the beginning.

Heresy, of course, was simply a perfectly workable and defensible viewpoint that did not get enough votes in the councils to carry the day. Any number of viewpoints held by James, the Lord's own brother, or Thomas, or John, or many others of the original disciples were either rejected outright or accepted only in part. In fact, the whole question of the viewpoints of the early disciples makes little sense in the doctrinal controversies of the fourth and fifth centuries—controversies that defined orthodoxy for all subsequent generations of Christians. The disciples were not in the same conversation. The fundamental early-church issue of faithfulness to the Lord and Leader meant little to the councils in the fourth and later centuries. The early church was faced with persecution and the possibility of death for confession of Christian faith. The later church was concerned with how doctrines should be defined. Persecution for confession of Christian faith was at an end; now this or that slight nuance of doctrine became paramount.

Jesus, in Matthew, declared that "no one knows the Father except the Son" (Matt. 11:27) and that (in the language of the Gospel of John) no one "has seen the Father except the one who is from God" (John 6:46). The point was that God, the infinite One, is ultimately unknowable and can be known in part only as God reaches out and reveals. For Christians, that reaching out was the point of the advent of Christ, yet Christians did not agree on who or what Christ was, or on what he said.

Divine inspiration of prophets and creative religious thinkers did not stop in antiquity. Time and again in the history of the church someone or another, heretic or saint, Christian or not, has been the bearer of a new word from God that has brought change in direction and reformulation of old ideas. New circumstances and new science bring new revelation and corresponding religious understanding. What is old is challenged and must respond. What we know of God today is again being challenged and forced to respond. That has forever been the divine Plan. That is the process of the River of God.

NOTES

CHAPTER 1

1. As do, for example, Justin Martyr (*First Apology* 66.4 and *Dialogue with Trypho* 70.1) and Tertullian (*Prescription Against Heresies* 40).

2. On diversity in early Christianity, see Walter Bauer, *Orthodoxy and Heresy in Earliest Christianity*, ed. Robert Kraft and Gerhard Krodel; trans. the Philadelphia Seminar on Christian Origins (Philadelphia: Fortress Press, 1971); Helmut Koester, *"GNOMAI DIAPHORAI*: The Origin and Nature of Diversification in the History of Early Christianity," in James M. Robinson and Helmut Koester, *Trajectories through Early Christianity* (Philadelphia: Fortress Press, 1971), 114–157; Birger Pearson, "Unity and Diversity in the Early Church as a Social Phenomenon," in *idem, The Emergence of the Christian Religion: Essays on Early Christianity* (Harrisburg, PA: Trinity Press International), 169–185; and Gregory J. Riley, *One Jesus, Many Christs* (San Francisco: HarperSanFrancisco, 1997).

3. "The Mosaic cosmology . . . indicates that the world is not yet ten thousand years old but is much less than this. . ." (Origen, *Contra Celsum* 1.19). The *Epistle of Barnabas* (15.4) claims that the entire length of time from creation to the eschatological end of the world would be six thousand years.

4. See N. Eldredge and S. J. Gould, "Punctuated Equilibria: An Alternative to Phyletic Gradualism," in *Models in Paleobiology*, ed. T. J. M. Schopf (San Francisco: Freeman, Cooper, 1972), 82–115; R. K. Gnuse, "Punctuated Equilibria as an Evolutionary Model for the Social Sciences and Biblical Studies," in *idem, No Other Gods: Emergent Monotheism in Israel* (Sheffield: Sheffield Academic Press, 1997), 321–345.

5. Jeffrey S. Siker, *Disinheriting the Jews: Abraham in Early Christian Controversy* (Louisville, KY: Westminster/John Knox Press, 1991).

6. Socrates describes this "divine sign" in Plato, *Apology* 40a–b.

7. J. N. D. Kelly, *Early Christian Creeds*, 3rd edition (New York: Longman, 1972).

8. Larry Hurtado, *One God, One Lord: Early Christian Devotion and Ancient Jewish Monotheism* (Philadelphia: Fortress Press, 1988).

CHAPTER 2

1. Arthur O. Lovejoy, *The Great Chain of Being* (Cambridge, MA: Harvard, 1936).

2. V. Nikiprowetzky, "Ethical Monotheism," in *Daedalus* 104 (1975): 73. Thorkild Jacobsen, *The Treasures of Darkness: A History of Mesopotamian Religion* (New Haven: Yale Univ. Press, 1976), 176ff.

3. H. W. F. Saggs, *The Greatness That Was Babylon* (New York: The New American Library, 1962), 352.

4. Morton Smith, "The Common Theology of the Ancient Near East," in *Journal of Biblical Literature* 71 (1952): 139–140.

5. Denis Baly, "The Geography of Monotheism," in *Translating and Understanding the Old Testament: Essays in Honor of Herbert Gordon May*, ed. H. Frank and W. Reed (Nashville: Abingdon Press, 1970), 266.

6. M. R. Wright, *Cosmology in Antiquity* (London and New York: Routledge, 1995), 114–116.

7. Bishop Demetrios Trakatellis, *The Transcendent God of Eugnostos*, trans. Charles Sarelis (Brookline, MA: Holy Cross Orthodox Press, 1991).

CHAPTER 3

1. William F. Albright, *From the Stone Age to Christianity: Monotheism and the Historical Process*, 2nd edition (Baltimore: Johns Hopkins Press, 1957), 247.

2. Siegfried Morenz, *Egyptian Religion*, trans. Ann E. Keep (Ithaca, NY: Cornell University Press, 1973), 142–246.

3. William V. Harris, *Ancient Literacy* (Cambridge, MA: Harvard University Press, 1989), 22–23.

4. J. A. Emerton, "The Origin of the Son Man Imagery," in *Journal of Theological Studies* 9 (1958): 225–242.

5. Timothy D. Barnes, *Constantine and Eusebius* (Cambridge, MA: Harvard University Press, 1981), 194.

6. Robert C. Gregg and Dennis E. Groh, *Early Arianism: A View of Salvation* (Philadelphia: Fortress Press, 1981), 53–55.

7. Cited in Jaroslav Pelikan, *The Christian Tradition: A History of the Development of Doctrine. Vol. 1, The Emergence of the Catholic Tradition (100–600)* (Chicago and London: University of Chicago Press, 1971), 103.

8. Gerhard May, *Creatio ex Nihilo: The Doctrine of "Creation Out of Nothing" in Early Christian Thought,* trans. A. S. Worrall (Edinburgh: T and T Clark, 1994), 76.

9. Barnes, *Constantine and Eusebius,* 208–212.

10. Graydon F. Snyder, *Ante Pacem: Archaeological Evidence of Church Life before Constantine* (Macon, GA: Mercer University Press, 1985), 13–26.

11. J. N. D. Kelly, *Early Christian Creeds,* 3rd edition (New York: Longman, 1972), 152.

CHAPTER 4

1. Thorkild Jacobsen, *The Treasures of Darkness: A History of Mesopotamian Religion* (New Haven: Yale Univ. Press, 1976), 164–191.

2. Michael David Coogan, ed. and trans., *Stories from Ancient Canaan* (Louisville: Westminster Press, 1978), 75–115.

3. Frank Moore Cross, *Canaanite Myth and Hebrew Epic: Essays in the History of the Religion of Israel* (Cambridge, MA: Harvard University Press, 1973); Mark S. Smith, *The Early History of God: Yahweh and the Other Deities in Ancient Israel* (San Francisco: Harper and Row, 1990).

4. Jon D. Levinson, *Creation and the Persistence of Evil: The Jewish Drama of Divine Omnipotence* (Princeton: Princeton University Press, 1988), xxiii.

5. Gherardo Gnoli, "Zoroastrianism," in *Religions of Antiquity,* ed. Robert M. Selzer (New York: Macmillan Publishers, 1987), 131; Mary Boyce, *Zoroastrians: Their Religious Beliefs and Practices* (London and New York: Routledge and Kegan Paul, 1979), 20.

6. Mary Boyce, *Textual Sources for the Study of Zoroastrianism* (Chicago: University of Chicago Press, 1990), 46.

7. Neil Forsyth, *The Old Enemy: Satan and the Combat Myth* (Princeton: Princeton University Press, 1987); Jeffrey Burton Russell, *The Devil: Perceptions of Evil from Antiquity to Primitive Christianity* (Ithaca and London: Cornell University Press, 1977).

8. Norman Cohn, *Cosmos, Chaos and the World to Come: The Ancient Roots of Apocalyptic Faith* (New Haven and London: Yale University Press, 1993).

9. Karen Rudolph Joines, "The Serpent in Genesis 3," *ZAW* 87 (1975): 1–11.

10. T. Jacobsen, *The Treasures of Darkness,* 13.

11. H. W. F. Saggs, *The Greatness That Was Babylon* (New York: The New American Library, 1962), 291.

12. Jacobsen, *The Treasures of Darkness,* 13.

13. Saggs, *The Greatness That Was Babylon*, 300.

14. Bernhard Lang, *Monotheism and the Prophetic Minority: An Essay in Biblical History and Sociology* (Sheffield: Almond Press, 1983).

15. R. H. Charles, *A Critical and Exegetical Commentary on the Revelation of St. John* (Edinburgh: T and T Clark, 1920), 1.364–368; W. Bousset, *The Antichrist Legend: A Chapter in Christian and Jewish Folklore* (London: Hutchinson, 1896).

CHAPTER 5

1. *Ancient Near Eastern Texts Relating to the Old Testament*, 3rd edition, ed. James B. Pritchard (Princeton: Princeton University Press, 1969), 503.

2. *Ancient Near Eastern Texts*, 94–95.

3. Translated by G. J. Riley from the Latin text in Herbert Musurillo, *The Acts of the Christian Martyrs* (Oxford: Clarendon Press, 1972), 168–174.

4. *Ancient Near Eastern Texts*, 72–99 (Gilgamesh), and 101–103 (Adapa).

5. *Odyssey* 11.475–476

6. Miriam Lichtheim, *Ancient Egyptian Literature* (Berkeley and Los Angeles: University of California Press, 1976), 1.101.

7. Stephen Quirke, *Ancient Egyptian Religion* (London: British Museum Press, 1992), 162.

8. Werner Jaeger, *The Theology of the Early Greek Philosophers* (Oxford: Oxford University Press, 1947), 73.

9. Larry J. Alderink, *Creation and Salvation in Ancient Orphism* (Chico, CA: Scholars Press, 1981), 55–85.

10. W. K. C. Guthrie, *Orpheus and Greek Religion*, revised edition (New York: W. W. Norton, 1966), 173.

11. Jacques Le Goff, *The Birth of Purgatory*, trans. Arthur Goldhammer (Chicago: University of Chicago Press, 1984).

12. Richmond Lattimore, *Themes in Greek and Latin Epitaphs* (Urbana: University of Illinois Press, 1962), 260–263.

CHAPTER 6

1. Mirko D. Grmeck, *Diseases in the Ancient World*, trans. M. Muellner and L. Muellner (Baltimore and London: Johns Hopkins, 1991), 99–109.

2. Graydon F. Snyder, *Ante Pacem: Archaeological Evidence of Church Life before Constantine* (Macon, GA: Mercer University Press, 1985), 125.

3. Grmeck, *Diseases in the Ancient World*, 111.

4. Hector Avalos, *Illness and Health Care in the Ancient Near East: The Role of the Temple in Greece, Mesopotamia, and Israel* (Atlanta: Scholars Press, 1995).

5. Morton Smith, *Palestinian Parties and Politics that Shaped the Old Testament* (London: SCM Press, 1987), 48.

6. Harold W. Attridge and Robert A. Oden, Jr., *Philo of Byblos The Phoenecian History: Introduction, Critical Text, Translation, Notes* (Washington, D. C.: The Catholic Biblical Association of America, 1981).

7. Thorkild Jacobsen, *The Sumerian King List* (Chicago: University of Chicago Press, 1939).

8. Emma J. Edelstein and Ludwig Edelstein, *Asklepius: Collection and Interpretation of the Testimonies* (Baltimore: Johns Hopkins, 1945).

9. *Ancient Near Eastern Texts Relating to the Old Testament*, 3rd edition, ed. James B. Pritchard (Princeton: Princeton University Press, 1969), 163–180.

10. Inscriptions in Lily Ross Taylor, *The Divinity of the Roman Emperor* (Middletown, CN: American Philological Association, 1931), 267–270.

11. James H. Charlesworth, ed., *The Messiah: Developments in Earliest Judaism and Christianity* (Minneapolis: Fortress Press, 1992).

12. On Gnosticism in general, see Kurt Rudolph, *Gnosis: The Nature and History of Gnosticism*, trans. by R. McL. Wilson (San Francisco: Harper and Row, 1987).

CHAPTER 7

1. Wilfred Cantwell Smith, *Faith and Belief* (Princeton, NJ: Princeton University Press, 1979), 166.

INDEX